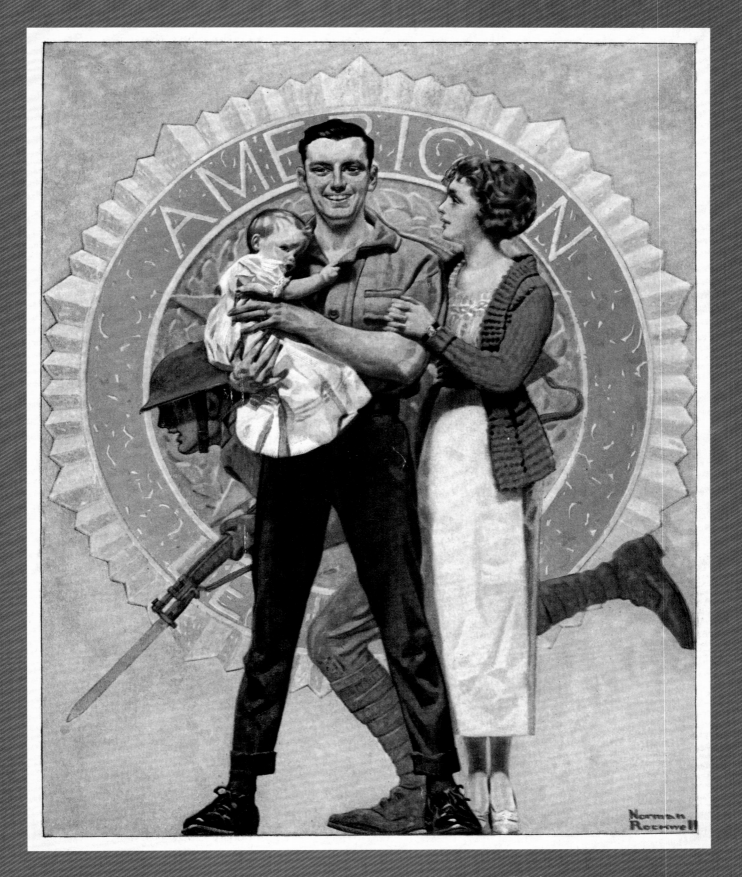

Norman Rockwell's
TREASURY FOR FATHERS

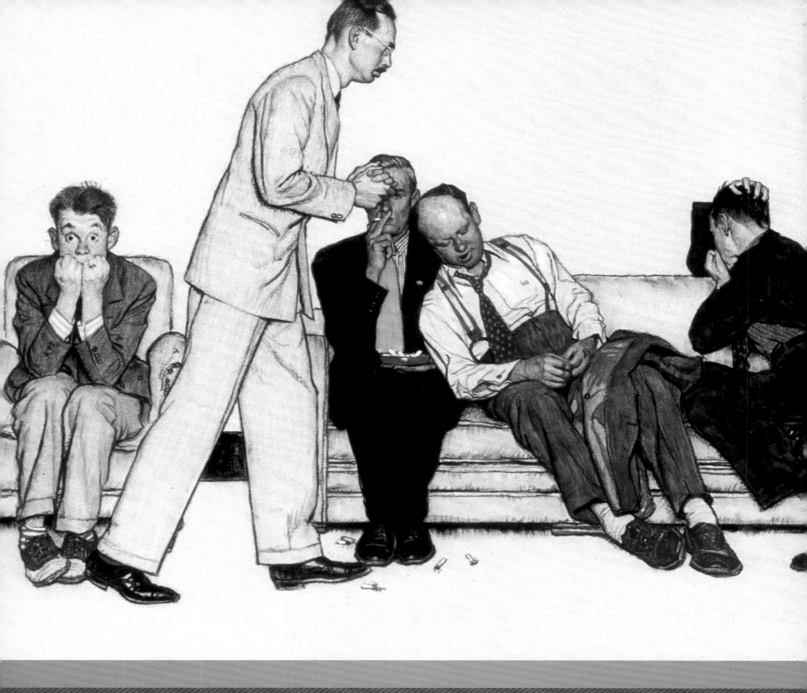

ABRAMS, NEW YORK

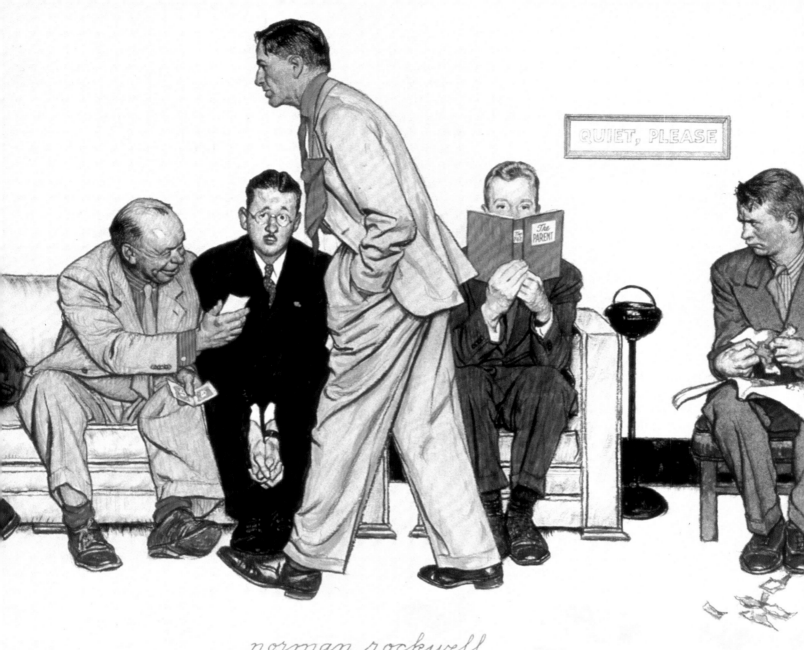

QUIET, PLEASE

The PARENT

norman rockwell

Norman Rockwell's
Treasury for Fathers

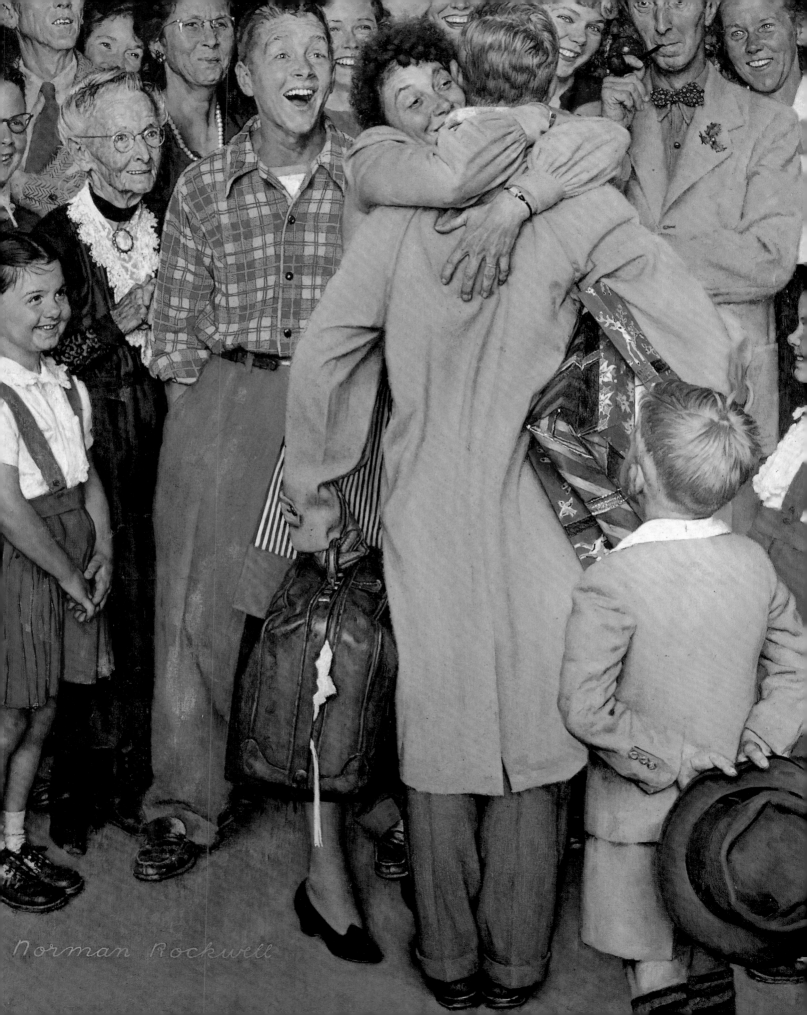

Table of Contents

* *

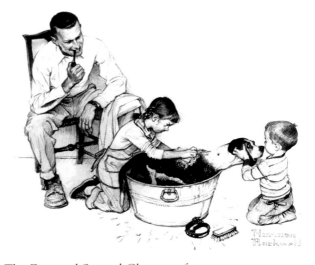

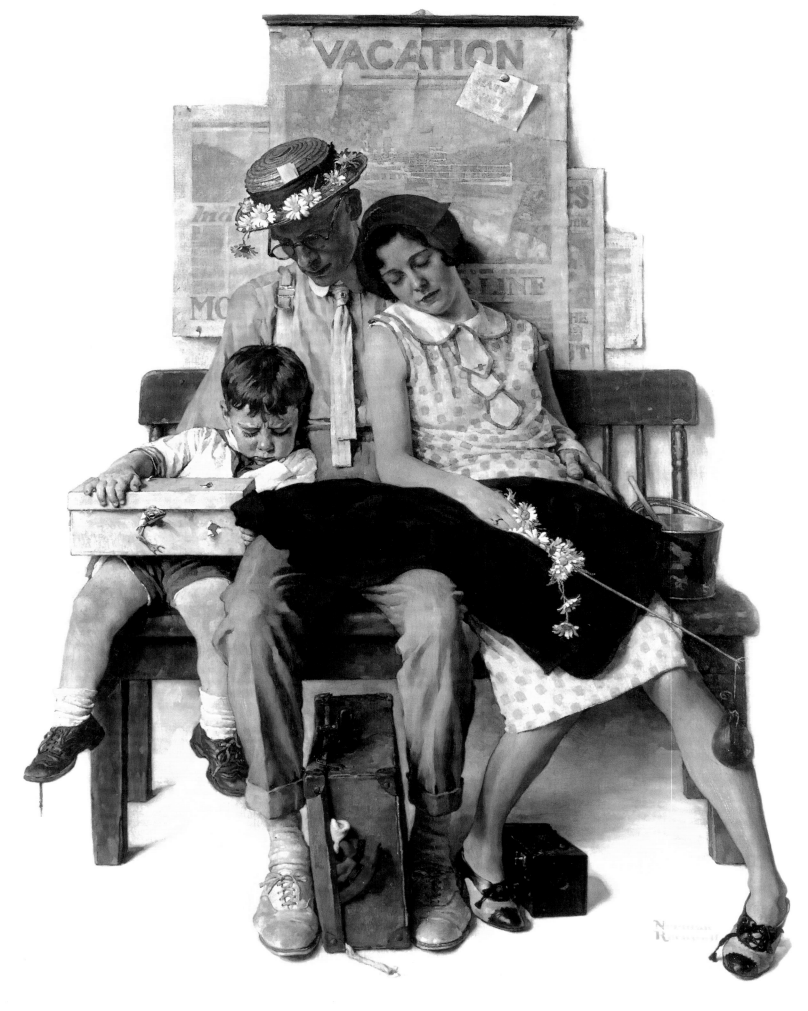

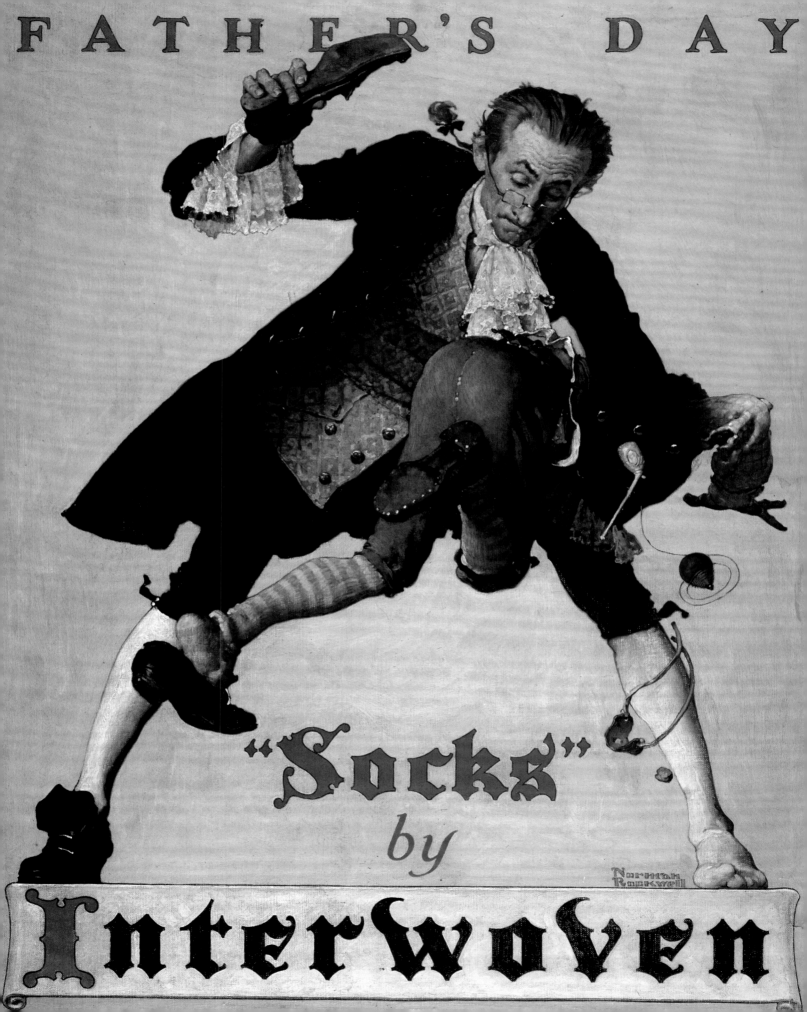

History of Father's Day

ON JULY 5, 1908, a West Virginia church sponsored the nation's first event explicitly in honor of fathers, a Sunday sermon in memory of the 362 men who had died in the previous December's explosions at the Fairmont Coal Company mines in Monongah, but it was a one-time commemoration and not an annual holiday. The next year, a Spokane, Washington, woman named Sonora Smart Dodd, one of six children raised by a widower, tried to establish an official equivalent to Mother's Day for male parents. She went to local churches, the YMCA, shopkeepers and government officials to drum up support for her idea, and she was successful: Washington State celebrated the nation's first statewide Father's Day on July 19, 1910.

Slowly, the holiday spread. In 1916, President Wilson honored the day by using telegraph signals to unfurl a flag in Spokane when he pressed a button in Washington, D.C. In 1924, President Calvin Coolidge urged state governments to observe Father's Day. However, many men continued to disdain the day. As one historian writes, they "scoffed at the holiday's sentimental attempts to domesticate manliness with flowers and gift-giving, or they derided the proliferation of such holidays as a commercial gimmick to sell more products—often paid for by the father himself."

During the 1920s and 1930s, a movement arose to scrap Mother's Day and Father's Day altogether in favor of a single holiday, Parents' Day. Every year on Mother's Day, pro–Parents' Day groups rallied in New York City's Central Park—a public reminder, said Parents' Day activist and radio performer Robert Spere, "that both parents should be loved and respected together." Paradoxically, however, the Depression derailed this effort to combine and de-commercialize the holidays. Struggling retailers and advertisers redoubled their efforts to make Father's Day a "second Christmas" for men, promoting goods such as neckties, hats, socks, pipes and tobacco, golf clubs and other sporting goods, and greeting cards. When World War II began, advertisers began to argue that celebrating Father's Day was a way to honor American troops and support the war effort. By the end of the war, Father's Day may not have been a federal holiday, but it was a national institution.

In 1972, in the middle of a hard-fought presidential reelection campaign, Richard Nixon signed a proclamation making Father's Day a federal holiday at last.

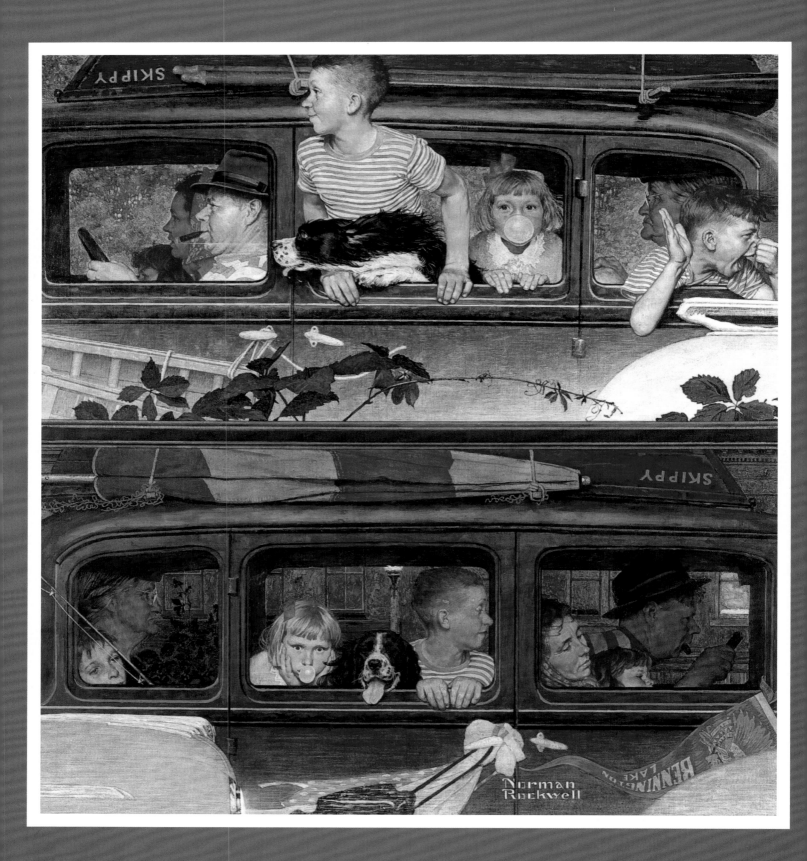

Part One

★ ⌁⌁⌁ *★*

Dear Old Dad

*

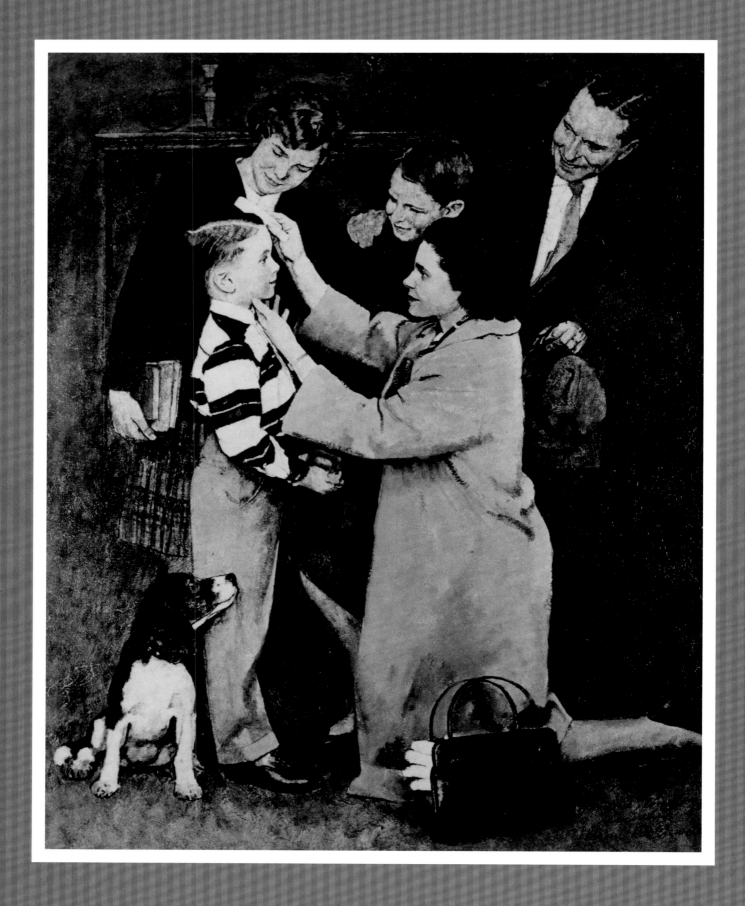

DADDIES

EDGAR GUEST

I WOULD RATHER BE the daddy
Of a romping, roguish crew,
Of a bright-eyed chubby laddie
And a little girl or two,
Than the monarch of a nation
In his high and lofty seat
Taking empty adoration
From the subjects at his feet.

I would rather own their kisses
As at night to me they run,
Than to be the king who misses
All the simpler forms of fun.
When his dreary day is ending
He is dismally alone,
But when my sun is descending
There are joys for me to own.

He may ride to horns and drumming;
I must walk a quiet street,
But when once they see me coming
Then on joyous, flying feet
They come racing to me madly
And I catch them with a swing
And I say it proudly, gladly,
That I'm happier than a king.

You may talk of lofty places,
You may boast of pomp and power,
Men may turn their eager faces
To the glory of an hour,
But give me the humble station
With its joys that long survive,
For the daddies of the nation
Are the happiest men alive.

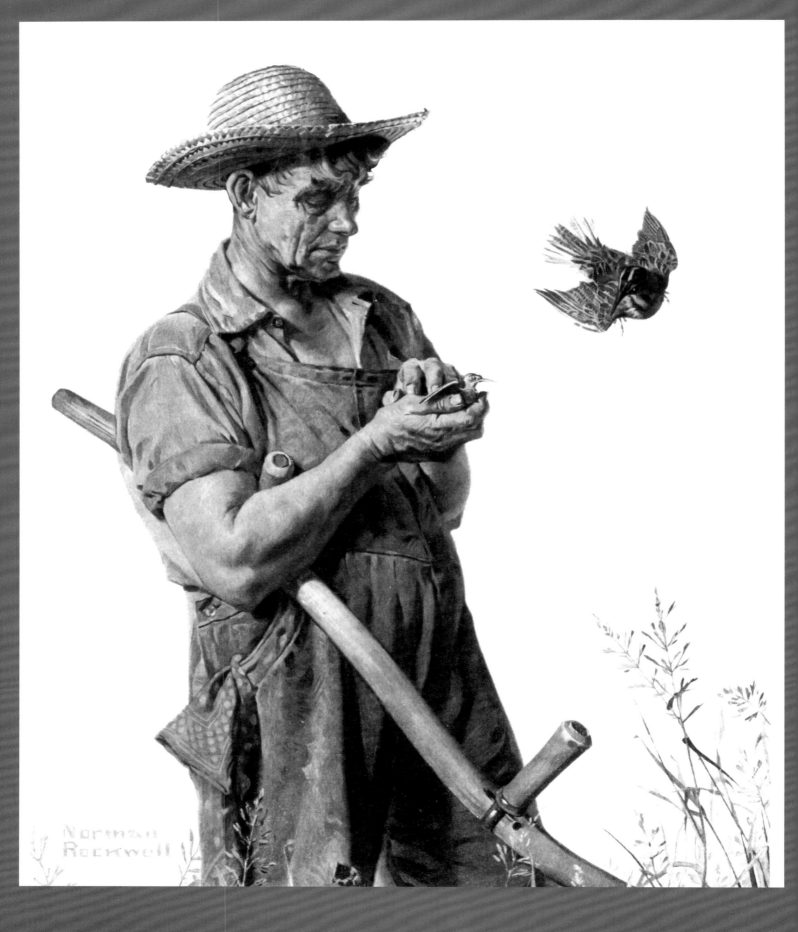

High from the Earth I Heard a Bird

Emily Dickinson

High from the earth I heard a bird;
He trod upon the trees
As he esteemed them trifles,
And then he spied a breeze,
And situated softly
Upon a pile of wind
Which in a perturbation
Nature had left behind.
A joyous-going fellow
I gathered from his talk,
Which both of benediction
And badinage partook,
Without apparent burden,
I learned, in leafy wood
He was the faithful father
Of a dependent brood;
And this untoward transport
His remedy for care,—
A contrast to our respites.
How different we are!

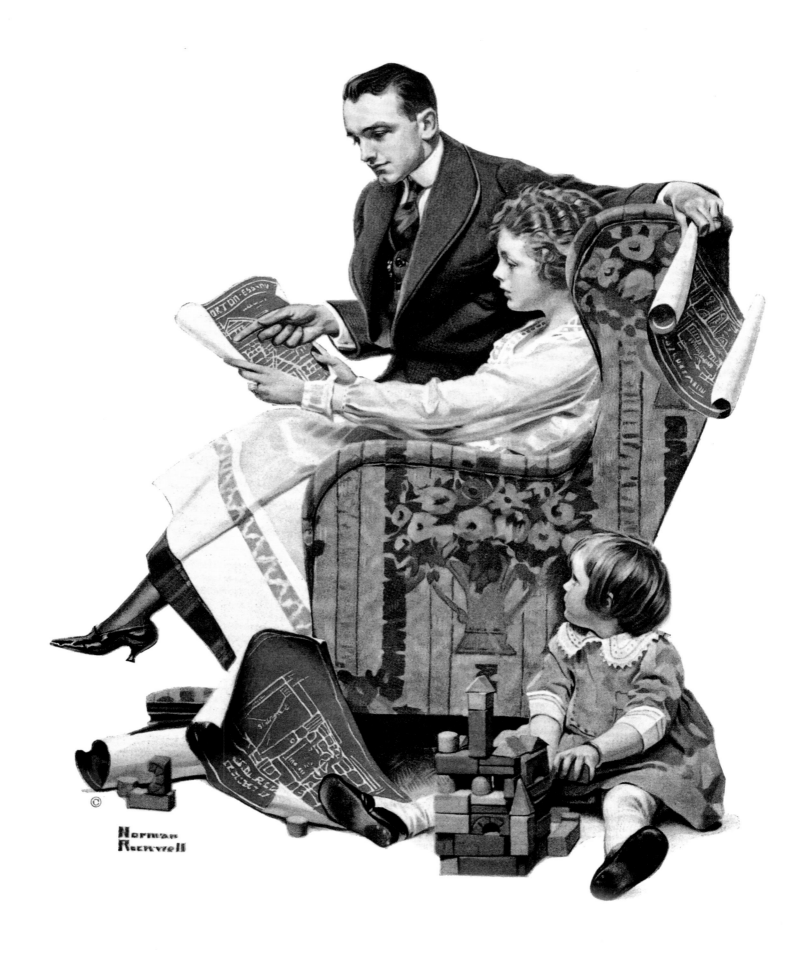

TO HER FATHER WITH SOME VERSES

ANNE BRADSTREET

⁕

MOST TRULY HONOURED, and as truly dear,
If worth in me or ought I do appear,
Who can of right better demand the same
Than may your worthy self from whom it came?
The principal might yield a greater sum,
Yet handled ill, amounts but to this crumb;
My stock's so small I know not how to pay,
My bond remains in force unto this day;
Yet for part payment take this simple mite,
Where nothing's to be had, kings loose their right.
Such is my debt I may not say forgive,
But as I can, I'll pay it while I live;
Such is my bond, none can discharge but I,
Yet paying is not paid until I die.

ONLY A DAD

EDGAR GUEST

ONLY A DAD with a tired face,
Coming home from the daily race,
Bringing little of gold or fame
To show how well he has played the game;
But glad in his heart that his own rejoice
To see him come and to hear his voice.

Only a dad with a brood of four,
One of ten million men or more
Plodding along in the daily strife,
Bearing the whips and the scorns of life,
With never a whimper of pain or hate,
For the sake of those who at home await.

Only a dad, neither rich nor proud,
Merely one of the surging crowd,
Toiling, striving from day to day,
Facing whatever may come his way,
Silent whenever the harsh condemn,
And bearing it all for the love of them.

Only a dad but he gives his all,
To smooth the way for his children small,
Doing with courage stern and grim
The deeds that his father did for him.
This is the line that for him I pen:
Only a dad, but the best of men.

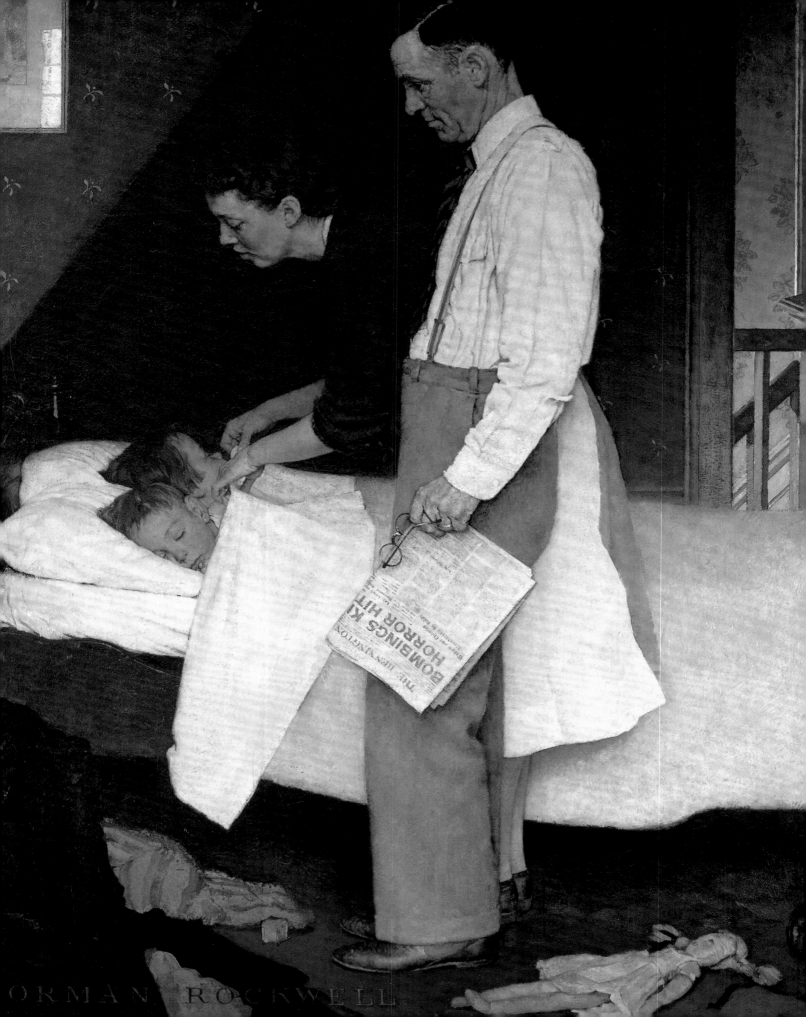

THOSE WINTER SUNDAYS

ROBERT HAYDEN

SUNDAYS TOO my father got up early
and put his clothes on in the blueblack cold,
then with cracked hands that ached
from labor in the weekday weather made
banked fires blaze. No one ever thanked him.

I'd wake and hear the cold splintering, breaking.
When the rooms were warm, he'd call,
and slowly I would rise and dress,
fearing the chronic angers of that house,

Speaking indifferently to him,
who had driven out the cold
and polished my good shoes as well.
What did I know, what did I know
of love's austere and lonely offices?

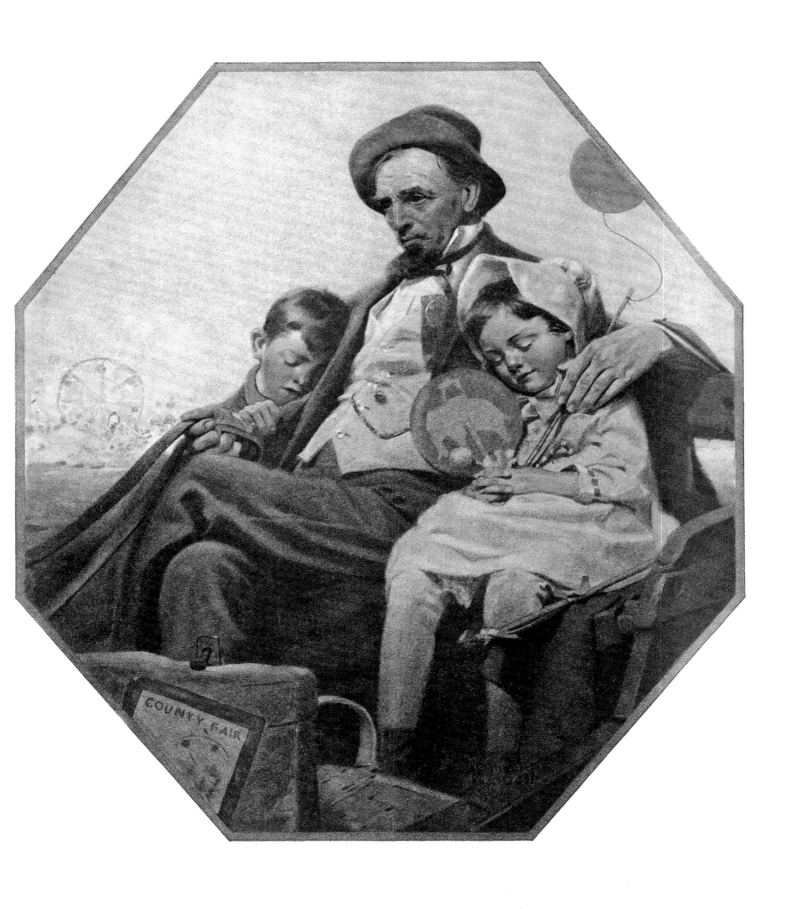

WHEN PA COMES HOME

EDGAR GUEST

—∞∞∞—

WHEN PA COMES HOME, I'm at the door,
An' then he grabs me off the floor
An' throws me up an' catches me
When I come down, an' then, says he:
"Well, how'd you get along to-day?
An' were you good, an' did you play,
An' keep right out of mamma's way?
An' how'd you get that awful bump
Above your eye? My, what a lump!
An' who spilled jelly on your shirt?
An' where'd you ever find the dirt
That's on your hands? And my! Oh, my!
I guess those eyes have had a cry,
They look so red. What was it, pray?
What has been happening here to-day?"

An' then he drops his coat an' hat
Upon a chair, an' says: "What's that?
Who knocked that engine on its back
An' stepped upon that piece of track?"
An' then he takes me on his knee
An' says: "What's this that now I see?
Whatever can the matter be?
Who strewed those toys upon the floor,
An' left those things behind the door?
Who upset all those parlor chairs

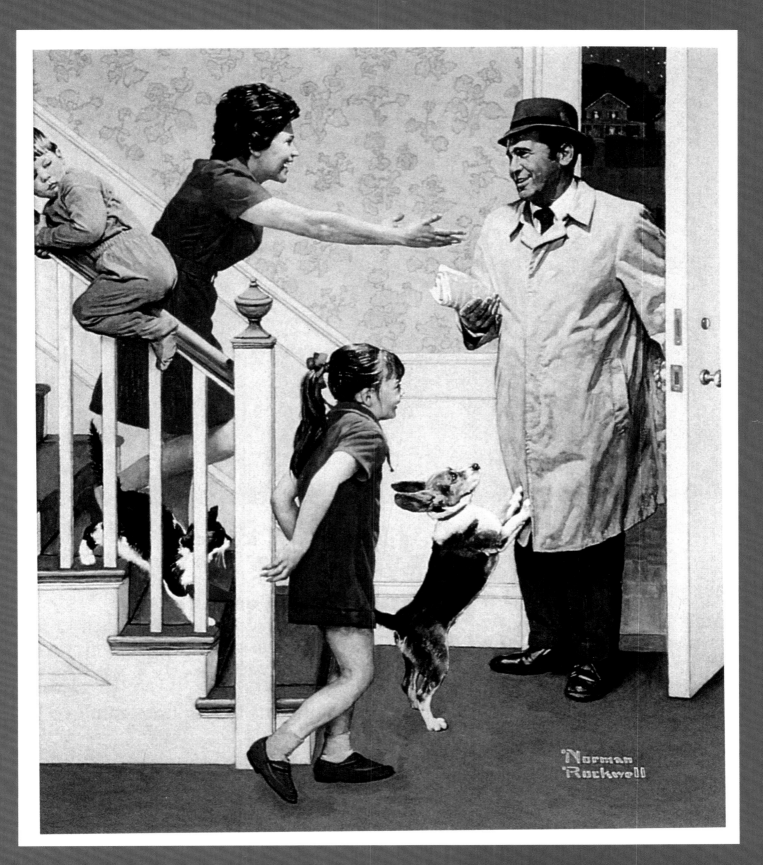

An' threw those blocks upon the stairs?
I guess a cyclone called to-day
While I was workin' far away.
Who was it worried mamma so?
It can't be anyone I know."

An' then I laugh an' say: "It's me!
Me did most ever'thing you see.
Me got this bump the time me tripped.
An' here is where the jelly slipped
Right off my bread upon my shirt,
An' when me tumbled down it hurt.
That's how me got all over dirt.
Me threw those building blocks downstairs,
An' me upset the parlor chairs,
Coz when you're playin' train you've got
To move things 'round an awful lot."
An' then my Pa he kisses me
An' bounces me upon his knee
An' says: "Well, well, my little lad,
What glorious fun you must have had!"

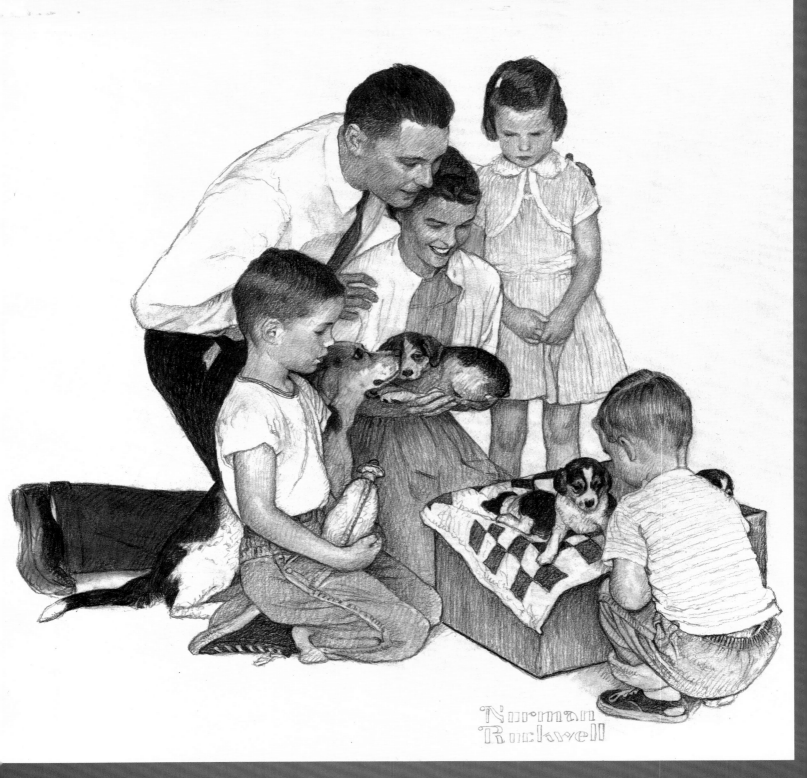

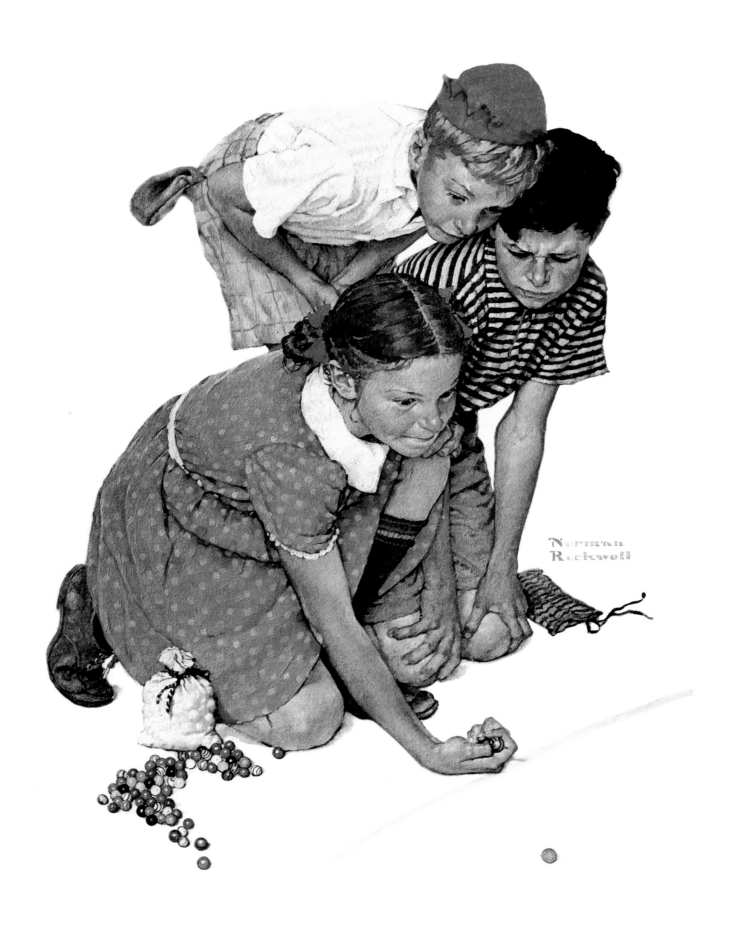

FATHER

ELLA WHEELER WILCOX

HE NEVER MADE a fortune, or a noise
In the world where men are seeking after fame;
But he had a healthy brood of girls and boys
Who loved the very ground on which he trod.
They thought him just little short of God;
Oh you should have heard the way they said his name—
"Father."

There seemed to be a loving little prayer
In their voices, even when they called him "Dad."
Though the man was never heard of anywhere,
As a hero, yet somehow understood
He was doing well his part and making good;
And you knew it, by the way his children had
Of saying "Father."

He gave them neither eminence nor wealth,
But he gave them blood untainted with a vice,
And opulence of undiluted health.
He was honest, and unpurchable and kind;
He was clean in heart, and body, and in mind.
So he made them heirs to riches without price—
This father.

He never preached or scolded; and the rod—
Well, he used it as a turning pole in play.
But he showed the tender sympathy of God.
To his children in their troubles, and their joys.
He was always chum and comrade with his boys,
And his daughters—oh, you ought to hear them say
"Father."

Now I think of all achievements 'tis the least
To perpetuate the species; it is done
By the insect and the serpent, and the beast.
But the man who keeps his body, and his thought,
Worth bestowing on an offspring love-begot,
Then the highest earthly glory he was won,
When in pride a grown-up daughter or a son
Says "That's Father."

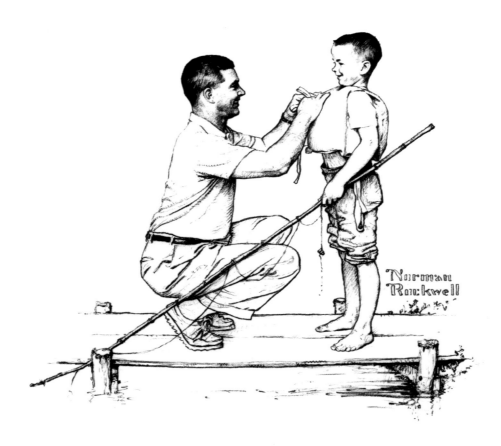

My Father is Extremely Tall

A., E., and M. Keary

MY FATHER is extremely tall
When he stands upright like a wall—
But I am very short and small.
Yet I am growing, so they say,
A little taller every day—
It's not enough to notice it,
Except when dresses will not fit,
And Nurse says, "Let it down a bit."

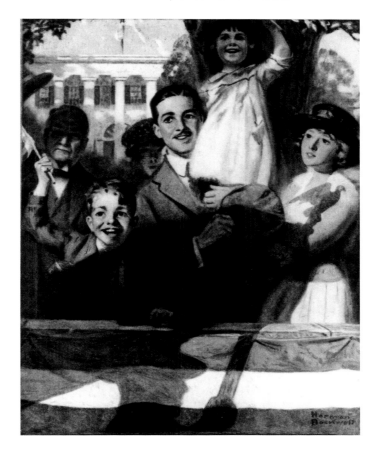

MY FATHER'S HATS

MARK IRWIN

SUNDAY MORNINGS I would reach
high into his dark closet while standing
on a chair and tiptoeing reach
higher, touching, sometimes fumbling
the soft crowns and imagine
I was in a forest, wind hymning
through pines, where the musky scent
of rain clinging to damp earth was
his scent I loved, lingering on
bands, leather, and on the inner silk
crowns where I would smell his
hair and almost think I was being
held, or climbing a tree, touching
the yellow fruit, leaves whose scent
was that of clove in the godsome
air, as now, thinking of his fabulous
sleep, I stand on this canyon floor
and watch light slowly close
on water I can't be sure is there.

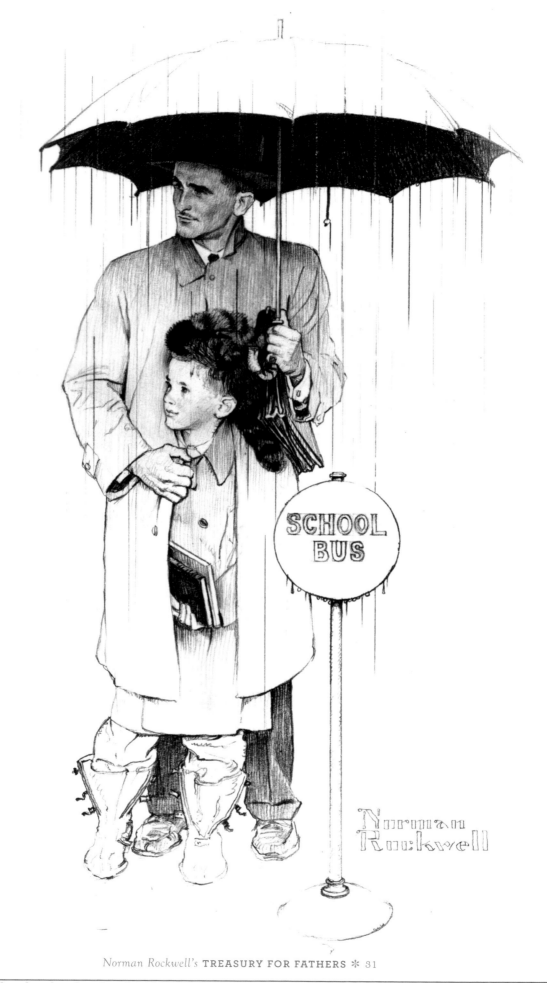

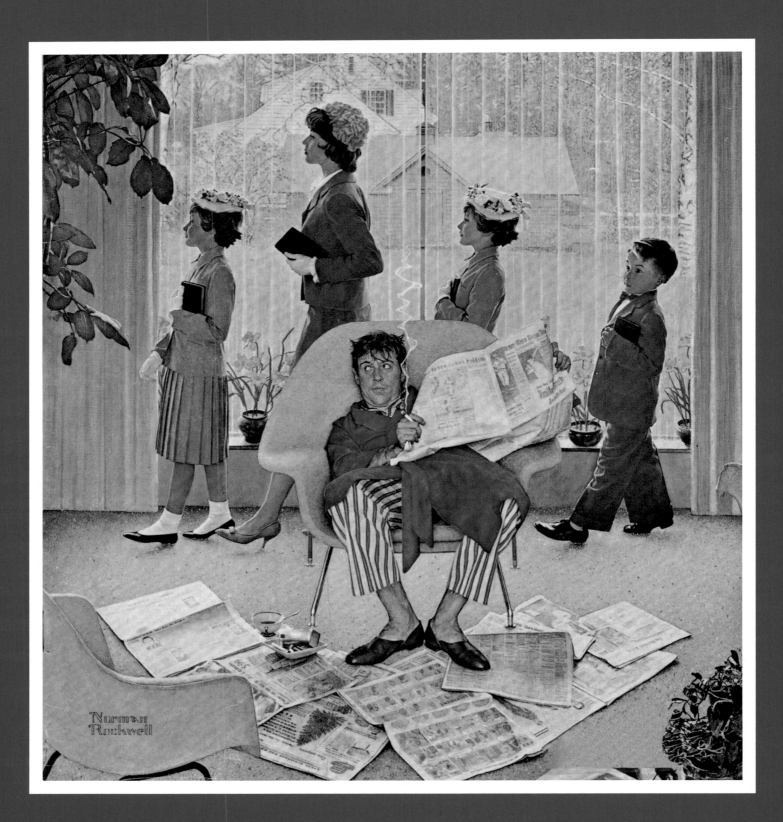

Part Two

THE OLD MAN

*

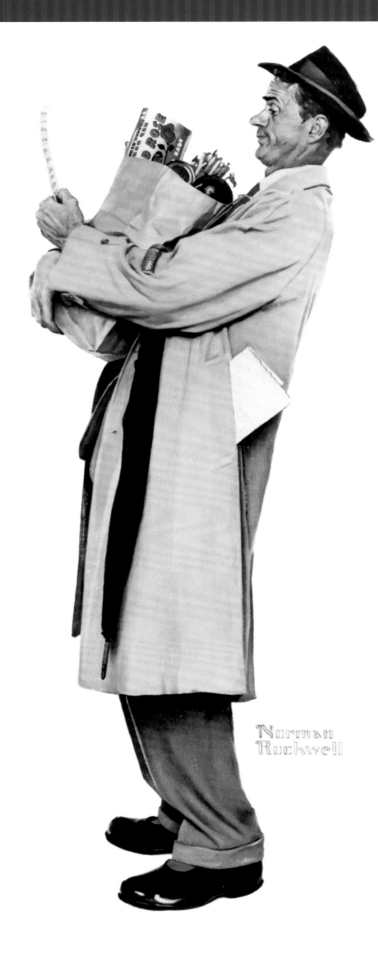

SOLILOQUY IN CIRCLES

OGDEN NASH

BEING a father
Is quite a bother.

You are as free as air
With time to spare,

You're a fiscal rocket
With change in your pocket,

And then one morn
A child is born.

Your life has been runcible,
Irresponsible,

Like an arrow or javelin
You've been constantly travelin'.

But mostly, I daresay,
Without a *chaise percée*,

To which by comparison
Nothing's embarison.

But all children matures,
Maybe even yours.

You improve them mentally
And straighten them dentally.

They grow tall as a lancer
And ask questions you can't answer,

And supply you with data
About how everybody else wears lipstick sooner and stays up later,

And if they are popular,
The phone they monopular.

They scorn the dominion
Of their parent's opinion,

They're no longer corralable
Once they find that you're fallible

But after you've raised them and educated them and gowned them,
They just take their little fingers and wrap you around them.

Being a father is quite a bother,
But I like it, rather.

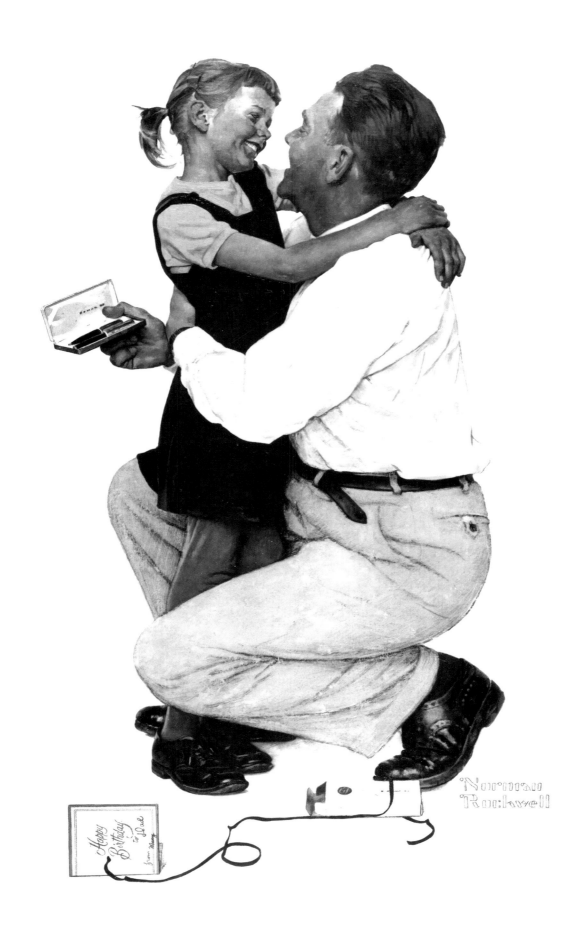

FATHER

EDGAR GUEST

MY FATHER KNOWS the proper way
The nation should be run;
He tells us children every day
Just what should now be done.
He knows the way to fix the trusts,
He has a simple plan;
But if the furnace needs repairs,
We have to hire a man.

My father, in a day or two
Could land big thieves in jail;
There's nothing that he cannot do,
He knows no word like "fail."
"Our confidence" he would restore,
Of that there is no doubt;
But if there is a chair to mend,
We have to send it out.

All public questions that arise,
He settles on the spot;
He waits not till the tumult dies,
But grabs it while it's hot.
In matters of finance he can
Tell Congress what to do;
But, O, he finds it hard to meet
His bills as they fall due.

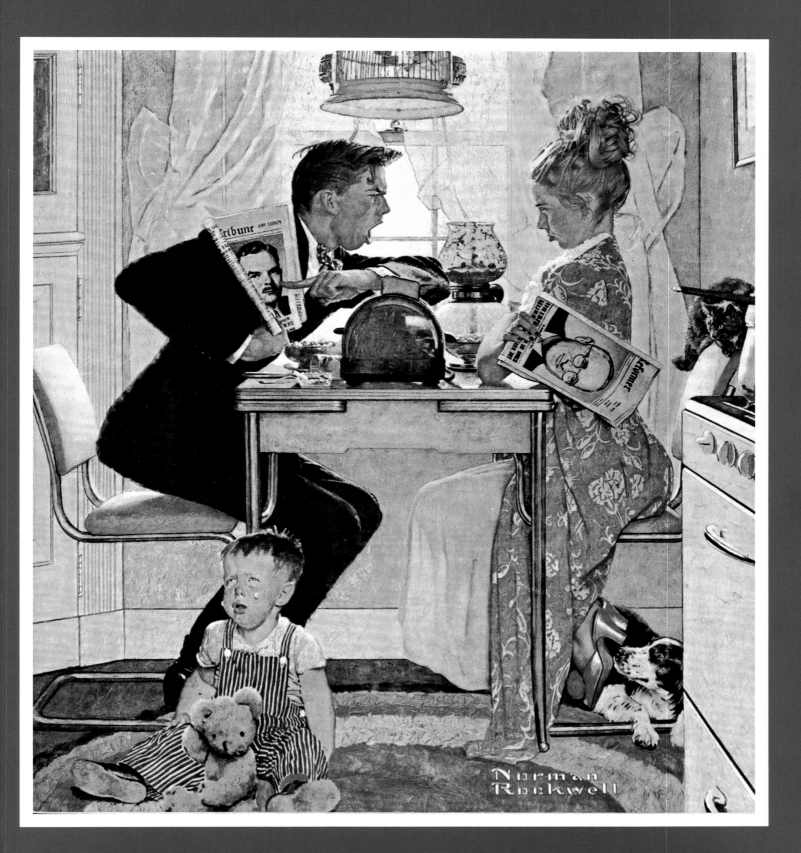

It almost makes him sick to read
The things law-makers say;
Why, father's just the man they need,
He never goes astray.
All wars he'd very quickly end,
As fast as I can write it;
But when a neighbor starts a fuss,
'Tis mother has to fight it.

In conversation father can
Do many wondrous things;
He's built upon a wiser plan
Than presidents or kings.
He knows the ins and outs of each
And every deep transaction;
We look to him for theories,
But look to ma for action.

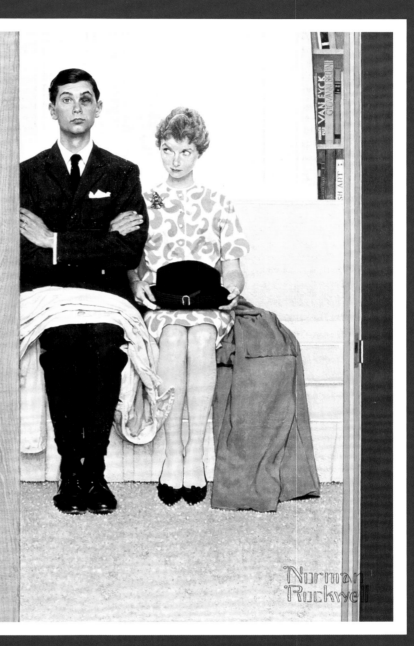

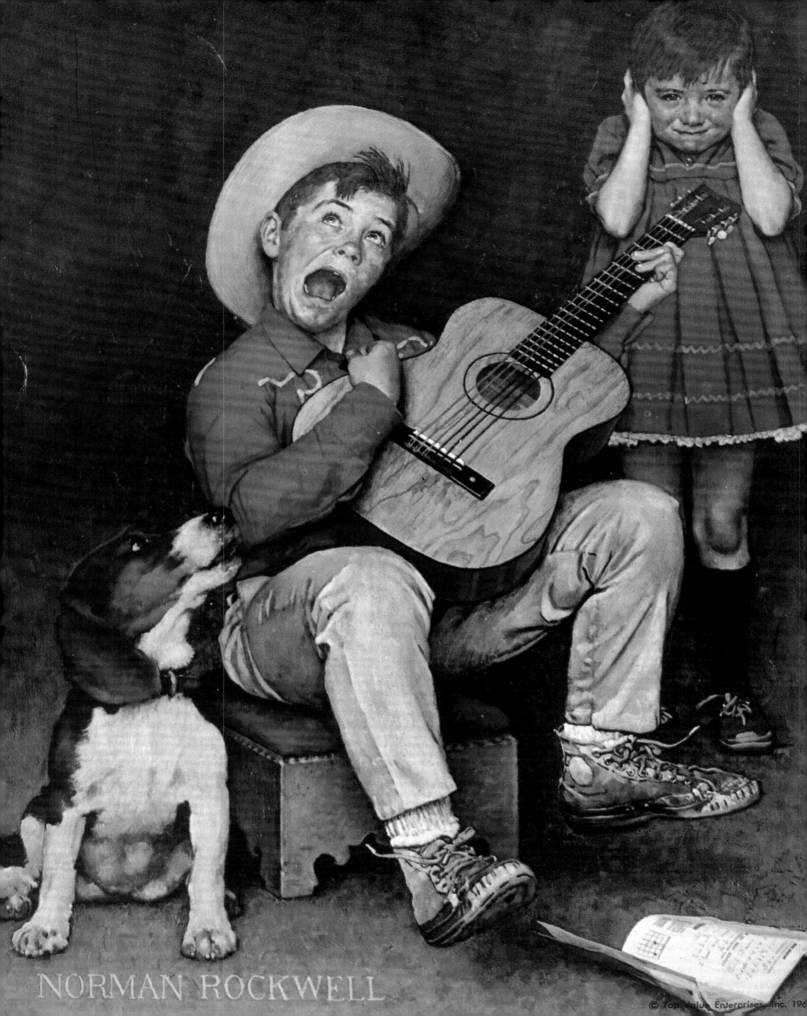

NORMAN ROCKWELL

OH WRITE ME A SONG OF MY FATHER

WRITTEN AND COMPOSED BY C. HENRY

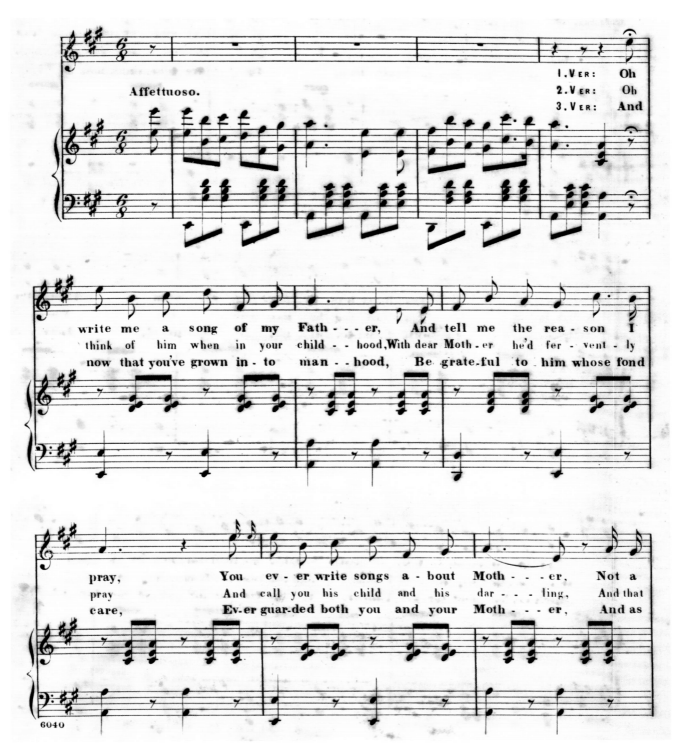

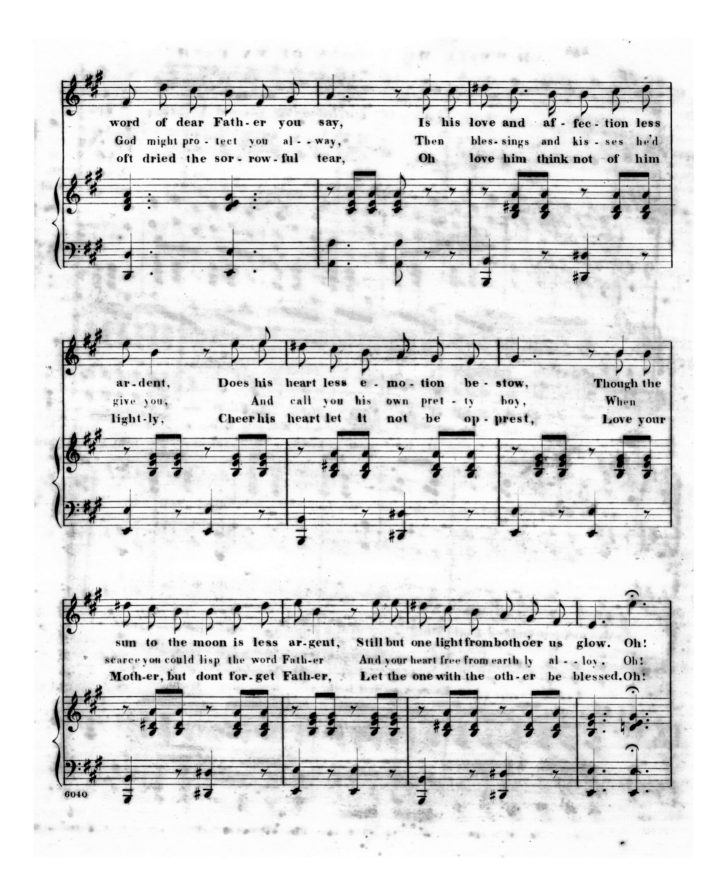

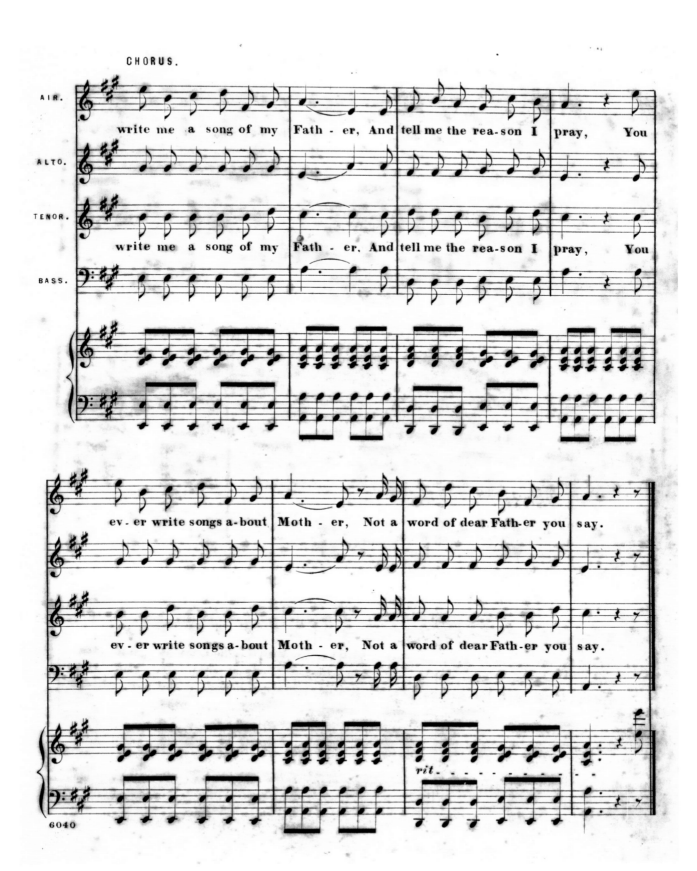

WHEN FATHER PLAYED BASEBALL

EDGAR GUEST

THE SMELL OF ARNICA is strong,
And mother's time is spent
In rubbing father's arms and back
With burning liniment.
The house is like a druggist's shop;
Strong odors fill the hall,
And day and night we hear him groan,
Since father played baseball.

He's forty past, but he declared
That he was young as ever;
And in his youth, he said, he was
A baseball player clever.
So when the business men arranged
A game, they came to call
On dad and asked him if he thought
That he could play baseball.

"I haven't played in fifteen years,"
Said father, "but I know
That I can stop the grounders hot,
And I can make the throw.
I used to play a corking game;
The curves, I know them all;
And you can count on me, you bet,
To join your game of ball."

On Saturday the game was played,
And all of us were there;
Dad borrowed an old uniform,
That Casey used to wear.
He paid three dollars for a glove,
Wore spikes to save a fall

He had the make-up on all right,
When father played baseball.

At second base they stationed him;
A liner came his way;
Dad tried to stop it with his knee,
And missed a double play.
He threw into the bleachers twice,
He let a pop fly fall;
Oh, we were all ashamed of him,
When father played baseball.

He tried to run, but tripped and fell,
He tried to take a throw;
It put three fingers out of joint,
And father let it go.
He stopped a grounder with his face;
Was spiked, nor was that all;
It looked to us like suicide,
When father played baseball.

At last he limped away, and now
He suffers in disgrace;
His arms are bathed in liniment;
Court plaster hides his face.
He says his back is breaking, and
His legs won't move at all;
It made a wreck of father when
He tried to play baseball.

The smell of arnica abounds;
He hobbles with a cane;
A row of blisters mar his hands;
He is in constant pain.
But lame and weak as father is,
He swears he'll lick us all
If we dare even speak about
The day he played baseball.

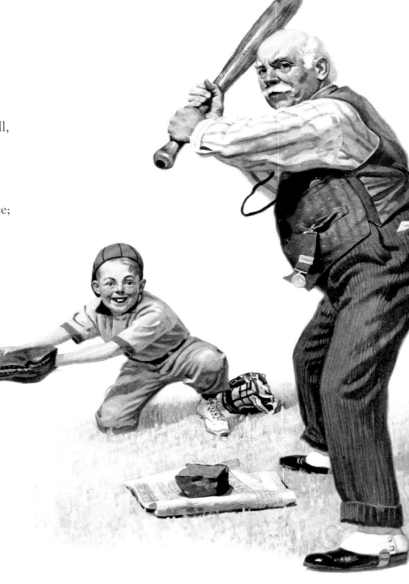

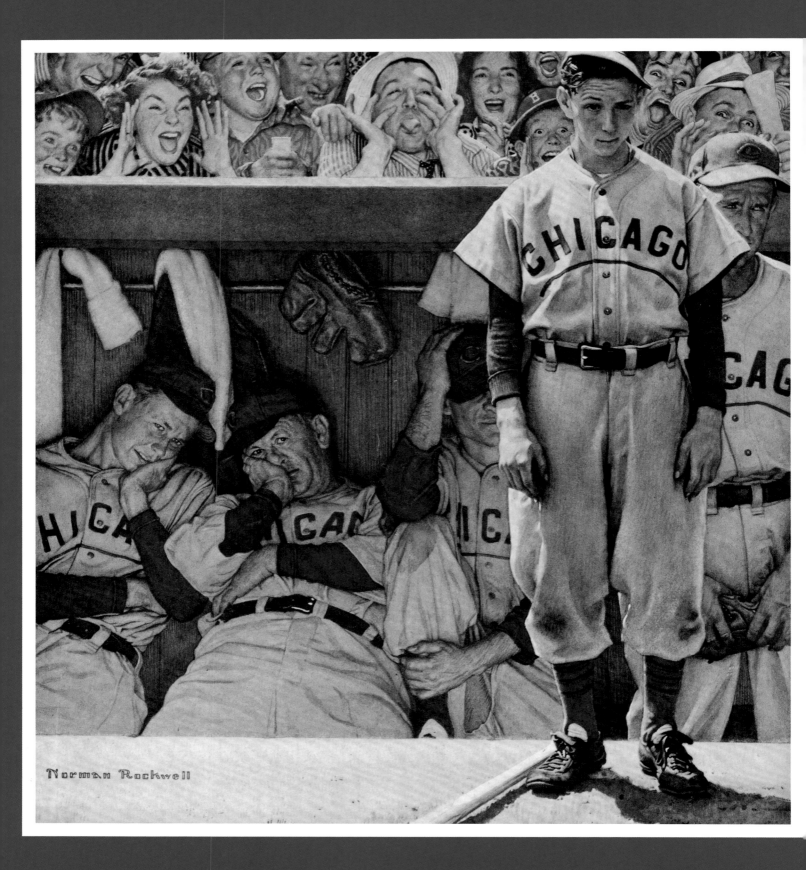

TAKE ME OUT TO THE BALL GAME

WORDS BY JACK NORWORTH AND MUSIC BY ALBERT VON TILZER

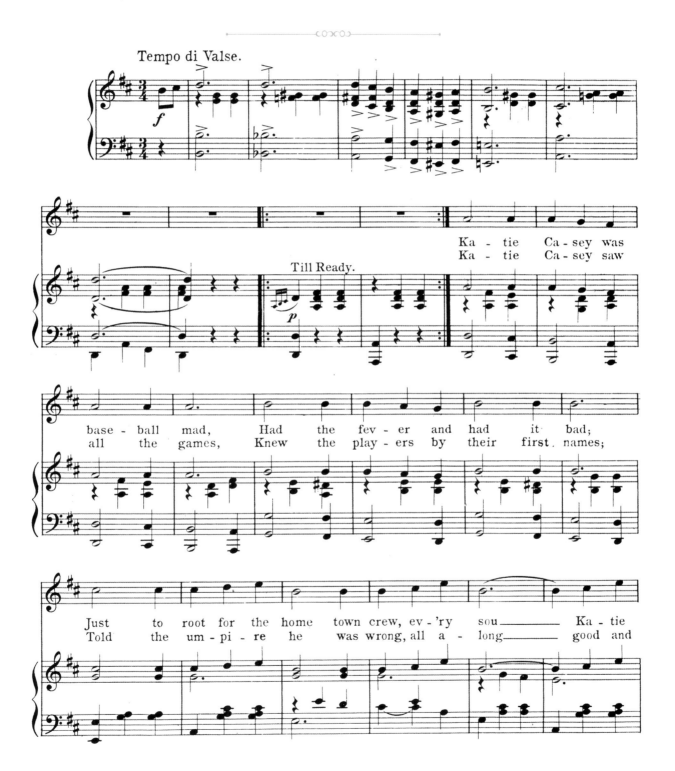

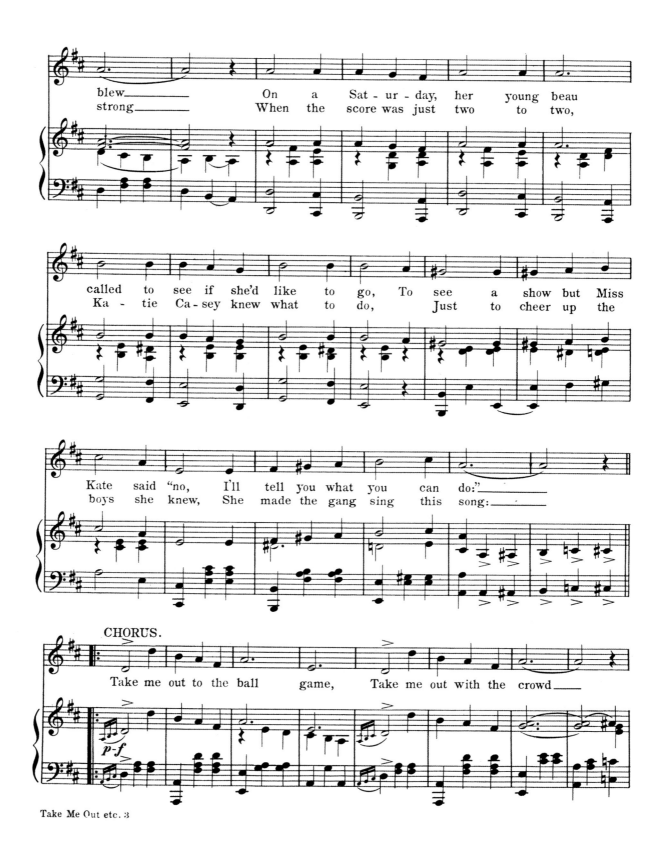

blew_____ On a Sat - ur - day, her young beau

strong_____ When the score was just two to two,

called to see if she'd like to go, To see a show but Miss

Ka - tie Ca - sey knew what to do, Just to cheer up the

Kate said "no, I'll tell you what you can do:"_____

boys she knew, She made the gang sing this song:_____

CHORUS.

Take me out to the ball game, Take me out with the crowd_____

p-f

Take Me Out etc. 3

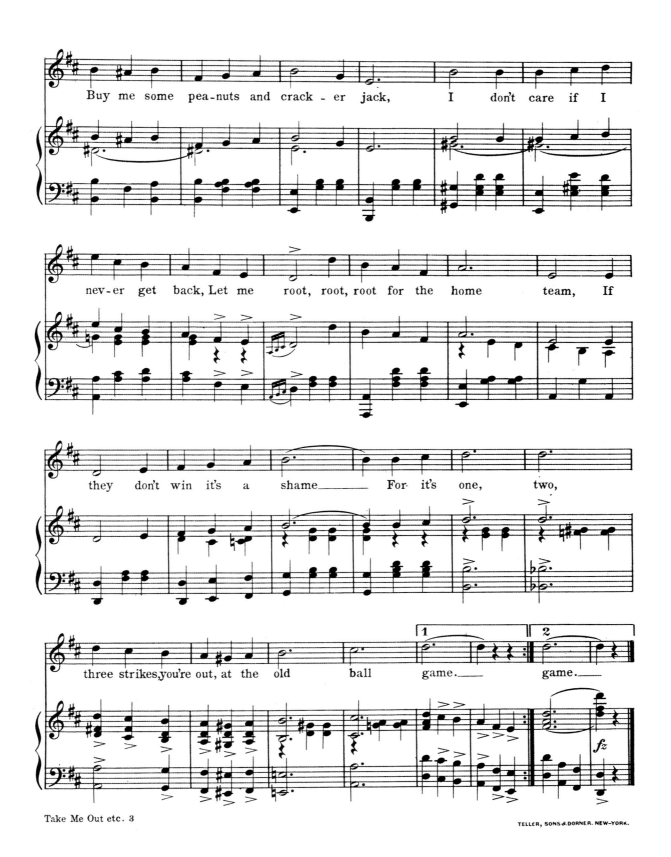

Take Me Out etc. 3

TELLER, SONS & DORNER. NEW-YORK.

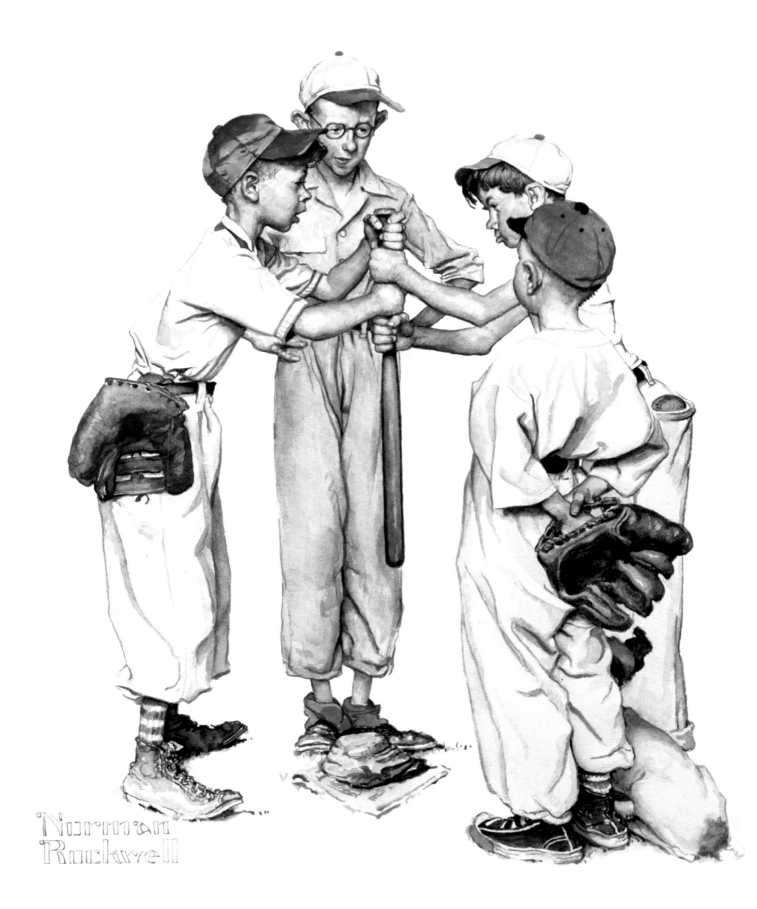

Commonly Used Baseball Terms and Phrases

ACE: A team's best starting pitcher

ALLEY: The section of the outfield between the outfielders (also known as the "gap")

AROUND THE HORN: A double play that goes from third base to second to first

BACKDOOR SLIDER: A pitch that appears to be out of the strike zone but then breaks back over the plate

BAG: A base

BALTIMORE CHOP: A ground ball that hits in front of home plate (or off of it) and then makes a large hop over an infielder's head

BANDBOX: A small ballpark that favors hitters

BANG-BANG PLAY: A play in which the base-runner hits the bag a split second before the ball arrives or vice versa

BASKET CATCH: When a fielder catches a ball with his glove near belt level

BRONX CHEER: When the crowd boos

BRUSHBACK: A pitch that nearly hits a batter

BUSH: An amateur play or behavior

BUSH LEAGUE: A league of amateurs

CAN OF CORN: An easy catch by a fielder

CAUGHT LOOKING: When a batter is called out on strikes

CELLAR: Last place (also known as the "basement")

CHEESE OR GOOD CHEESE: Either term refers to a good fastball

CHIN MUSIC: A pitch that is high and inside

CIRCUS CATCH: An outstanding catch by a fielder

CLOSER: The relief pitcher who finishes the game

CUTTER: A cut fastball with a late break to it

CYCLE: When a batter hits a single, double, triple, and home run in the same game

DINGER: A home run

DISH: Home plate

FIREMAN: A team's closer or late-inning relief pitcher

FUNGO: A ball hit to a fielder during practice, usually by a coach using a "fungo bat," which is longer and thinner than a normal bat

GAP: See "alley." A ball hit here is a "gapper"

GOPHER BALL: A pitch hit for a homerun, as in "go for"

HEAT: A good fastball (also known as a "heater")

HIGH AND TIGHT: Referring to a pitch that's up in the strike zone and inside on a hitter (also known as "up and in")

HILL: Pitcher's mound

HOMER: A home run. Other terms include a blast, dinger, dong, four-bagger, four-base knock, moon shot, tape-measure blast, and tater

HOT CORNER: Third base

IN THE HOLE: The batter after the on-deck hitter

JAM: When a hitter gets a pitch near his hands, he is "jammed," or when a pitcher gets himself in trouble, he is in a "jam"

LEATHER: Refers to how well a player plays defensively or handles the glove, e.g., "He flashed some leather on that play"

MEATBALL: An easy pitch to hit, usually right down the middle of the plate

MENDOZA LINE: A batting average of around .200

MOON SHOT: A very long, high home run

NAIL DOWN: As in to "nail down a victory," refers to a relief pitcher finishing off the game

ON THE SCREWS: When a batter hits the ball hard (also known as "on the button")

PAINTING THE BLACK: When a pitcher throws the ball over the edge of the plate

PEA: A ball traveling at high speed, whether it's either batted or thrown

PEPPER: Pepper is a common pregame exercise where one player bunts brisk grounders and line drives to a group of fielders who are standing about twenty feet away. The fielders try to throw it back as quickly as possible. The batter hits the return throw. (Some ballparks ban pepper games because wild pitches might land in the stands and injure spectators)

PICK: A good defensive play by an infielder on a ground ball (also known as a "pick-off")

PICKLE: A run-down

PUNCHOUT: A strikeout

RHUBARB: A fight or scuffle

RIBBIE: Another way of saying RBI (also known as a "rib-eye")

ROPE: A hard line drive hit by a batter (also known as a "frozen rope")

RUBBER GAME: The deciding game of a series

RUN-DOWN: When a base runner gets caught between bases by the fielders

RUTHIAN: With great power

SEEING-EYE SINGLE: A soft ground ball that finds its way between infielders for a base hit

SET-UP MAN: A relief pitcher who usually enters the game in the seventh or eighth inning

SHOESTRING CATCH: A running catch made just above the top of a fielder's shoe

SOUTHPAW: A left-handed pitcher

SWEET SPOT: The part of the bat just a few inches from the barrel

TABLE SETTER: A batter, often the leadoff or number 2 hitter, whose job is to get on base for other hitters to drive him in

TAPE-MEASURE BLAST: An extremely long home run

TATER: A home run

TEXAS LEAGUER: A bloop hit that drops between an infielder and outfielder

TOOLS OF IGNORANCE: Catcher's equipment

TOUCH 'EM ALL: Hit a home run (or, touch all the bases)

TWIN KILLING: A double play

UNCLE CHARLIE: A curve ball

UTILITY PLAYER: A player who can play multiple positions

WHEELHOUSE: A hitter's power zone, usually a pitch waist-high and over the heart of the plate

WHEELS: A ballplayer's legs

WHIFF: To strike out

YAKKER: A curve ball

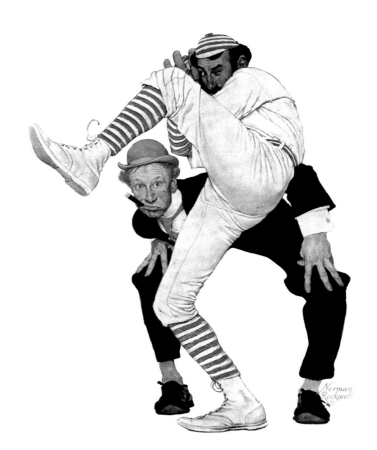

SCORING A BASEBALL GAME

DEFENSIVE PLAYERS BY THE NUMBERS

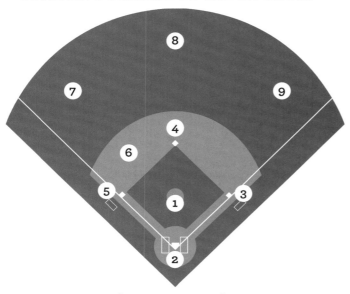

1. Pitcher
2. Catcher
3. 1st Base
4. 2nd Base
5. 3rd Base

6. Shortstop
7. Left Field
8. Center Field
9. Right Field

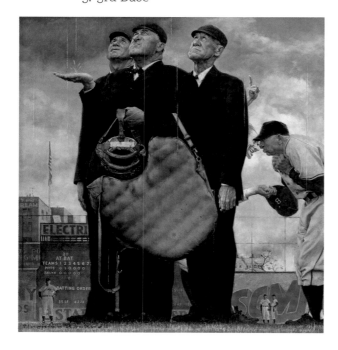

SYMBOLS FOR PLAY

Single	S or −
Double	D or =
Triple	T or ≡
Home run	HR or ≡
Walk	BB
Strikeout	K
Called out on Strikes	Я
Balk	BK
Fielder's choice	FC
Hit by pitch	HP
Wild pitch	WP
Passed ball	PB
Stolen base	SB
Double play	DP
Error	E
Sacrifice fly	SF
Intentional walk	IBB
Foul fly	F
Force out	FO
Line drive	L
Bunt	B
Unassisted	U

① 1ST INNING

1. Singled, advanced on next batter's walk, took 3rd on fielder's choice, scored on no. 4 batter's double

2. Walked, later forced out, shortstop to 2nd base

3. Reached on fielder's choice, advanced to 3rd on next batter's double, scored on no. 5 batter's single

4. Doubled, scored on no. 5 batter's single

5. Singled, advanced to 2nd on next batter's single, stole 3rd base, thrown out on grounder, shortstop to catcher

6. Singled, stole 2nd base

7. Reached 1st on fielder's choice

8. Popped out to 2nd base

② 2ND INNING

9. Leadoff with double

1. Flied out to center field

2. Popped out to shortstop

3. Struck out swinging

TEAM BATTING ORDER	1	2
1. Center Fielder	3 2 ④ —	8
2. Shortstop	6-4 BB	6
3. 1st Baseman	3 ⑤ FC	K
4. 3rd Baseman	⑤ =	
5. Right Fielder	BB 2 6-2	
6. Left Fielder	SB —	
7. Designated Hitter	FC	
8. 2nd Baseman	4	/
9. Catcher		=
TOTALS R / H	3 / 4	0 / 1

Different fans have different methods of keeping a scorecard, and many use their own notations, but here's a simple method:

If the hitter grounds out to shortstop, for example, write in "6-3," which shows the shortstop threw him out at first base. If the hitter flies out to left field, write a "7."

If the batter gets a hit, write in the hit according to which base he reached. Each corner of the box represents a base, with the lower-right corner being first.

If he singles, put a "–" in the lower right. If he doubles, write a "=" in the upper right, and so on. For a walk, use "BB" in the lower right. As the runner advances, mark the appropriate symbol in the appropriate corner.

If a runner scores, put a circle at the bottom of the box; inside the circle put the symbol of the play and/or the player that drove him in. For example, if the number 5 hitter drives in two runs with a single, mark his single in the bottom right of his box and mark a circle with the number "5" in it in the boxes of the runners who score (some people like to use uniform numbers here, so you can tell who did what, even after lineup changes).

At the end of each inning, total the hits and runs for that inning only. At the end of the game you'll be able to add the innings total to get the game score.

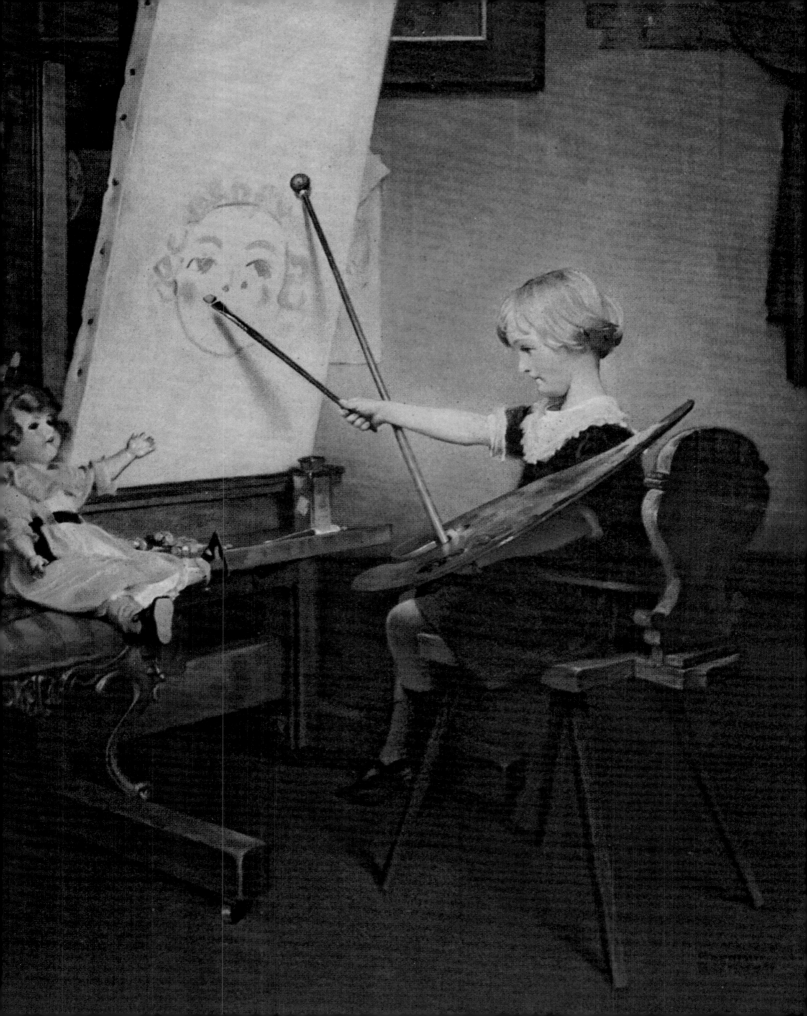

Part Three

★ ————— ⌒⌒⌒ ————— ★

FATHERS AND DAUGHTERS

✳

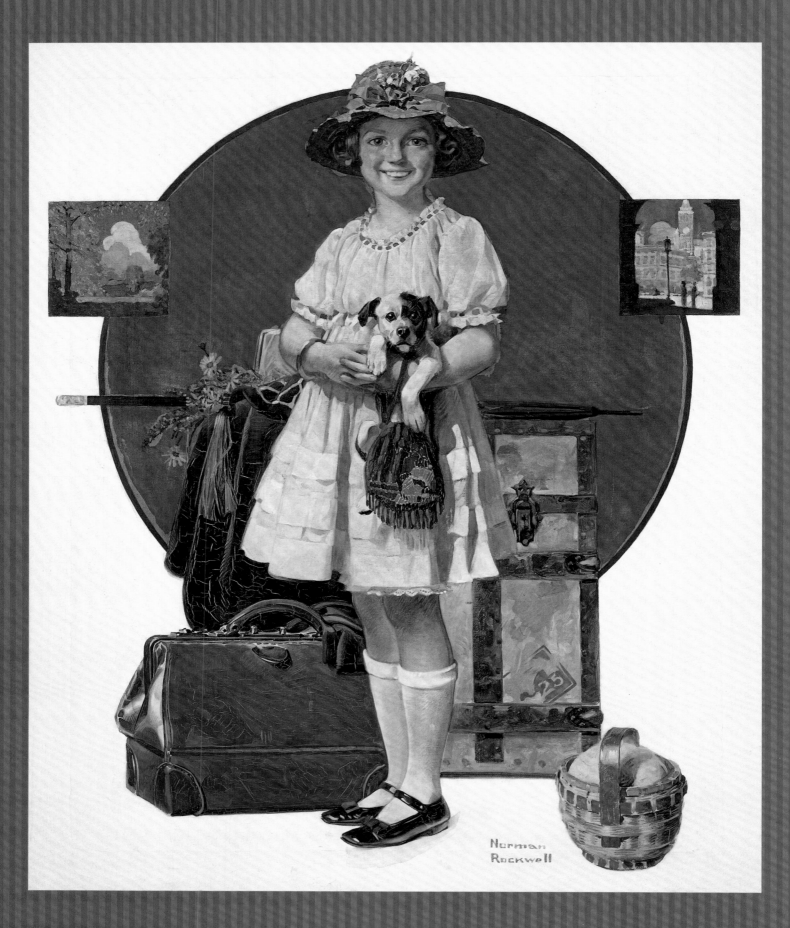

To an Old Father

EURIPIDES

TO AN OLD FATHER, nothing is more sweet
Than a daughter.
Boys are more spirited, but their ways
Are not so tender.

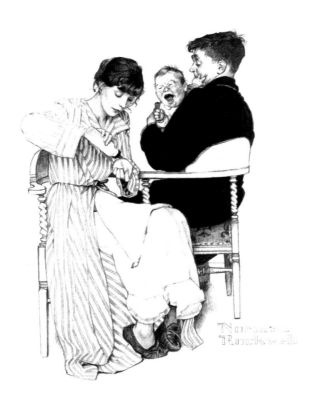

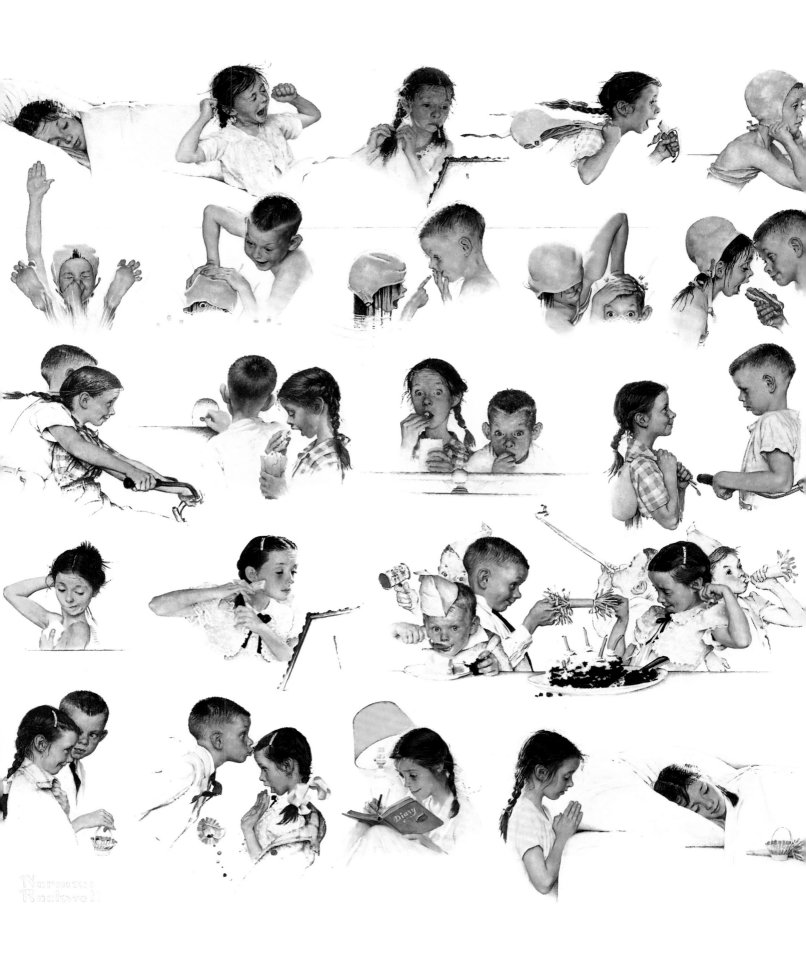

A Prayer for My Daughter

William Butler Yeats

ONCE MORE THE STORM is howling, and half hid
Under this cradle-hood and coverlid
My child sleeps on. There is no obstacle
But Gregory's wood and one bare hill
Whereby the haystack- and roof-leveling wind,
Bred on the Atlantic, can be stayed;
And for an hour I have walked and prayed
Because of the great gloom that is in my mind.

I have walked and prayed for this young child an hour
And heard the sea-wind scream upon the tower,
And under the arches of the bridge, and scream
In the elms above the flooded stream;
Imagining in excited reverie
That the future years had come,
Dancing to a frenzied drum,
Out of the murderous innocence of the sea.

May she be granted beauty and yet not
Beauty to make a stranger's eye distraught,
Or hers before a looking-glass, for such,
Being made beautiful overmuch,
Consider beauty a sufficient end,
Lose natural kindness and maybe
The heart-revealing intimacy
That chooses right, and never find a friend.

Helen being chosen found life flat and dull
And later had much trouble from a fool,
While that great Queen, that rose out of the spray,
Being fatherless could have her way
Yet chose a bandy-legged smith for man.
It's certain that fine women eat
A crazy salad with their meat
Whereby the Horn of plenty is undone.

In courtesy I'd have her chiefly learned;
Hearts are not had as a gift but hearts are earned
By those that are not entirely beautiful;
Yet many, that have played the fool
For beauty's very self, has charm made wise.
And many a poor man that has roved,
Loved and thought himself beloved,
From a glad kindness cannot take his eyes.

May she become a flourishing hidden tree
That all her thoughts may like the linnet be,
And have no business but dispensing round
Their magnanimities of sound,
Nor but in merriment begin a chase,
Nor but in merriment a quarrel.
O may she live like some green laurel
Rooted in one dear perpetual place.

My mind, because the minds that I have loved,
The sort of beauty that I have approved,
Prosper but little, has dried up of late,
Yet knows that to be choked with hate
May well be of all evil chances chief.
If there's no hatred in a mind
Assault and battery of the wind
Can never tear the linnet from the leaf.

An intellectual hatred is the worst,
So let her think opinions are accursed.
Have I not seen the loveliest woman born
Out of the mouth of plenty's horn,
Because of her opinionated mind
Barter that horn and every good
By quiet natures understood
For an old bellows full of angry wind?

Considering that, all hatred driven hence,
The soul recovers radical innocence
And learns at last that it is self-delighting,
Self-appeasing, self-affrighting,
And that its own sweet will is Heaven's will;
She can, though every face should scowl
And every windy quarter howl
Or every bellows burst, be happy still.

And may her bridegroom bring her to a house
Where all's accustomed, ceremonious;
For arrogance and hatred are the wares
Peddled in the thoroughfares.
How but in custom and in ceremony
Are innocence and beauty born?
Ceremony's a name for the rich horn,
And custom for the spreading laurel tree.

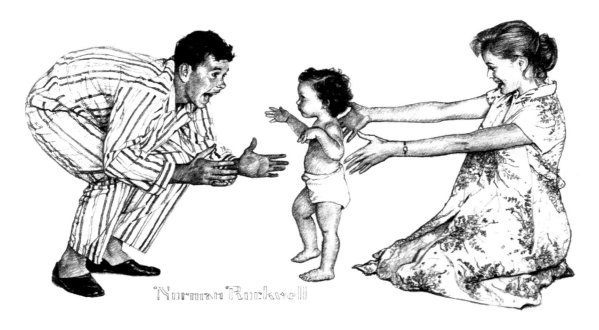

THE CHILDREN'S HOUR

HENRY WADSWORTH LONGFELLOW

BETWEEN THE DARK and the daylight,
When the night is beginning to lower,
Comes a pause in the day's occupations,
That is known as the Children's Hour.

I hear in the chamber above me
The patter of little feet,
The sound of a door that is opened,
And voices soft and sweet.

From my study I see in the lamplight,
Descending the broad hall stair,
Grave Alice, and laughing Allegra,
And Edith with golden hair.

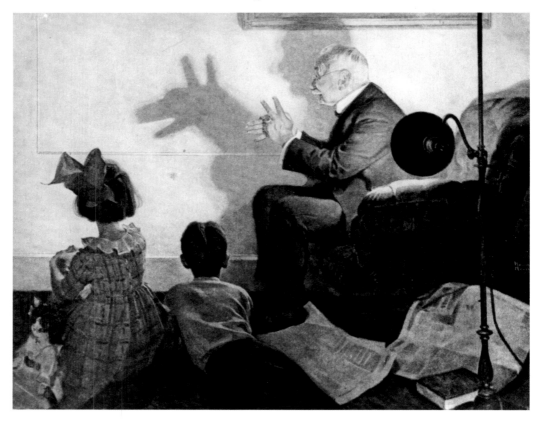

A whisper, and then a silence:
Yet I know by their merry eyes
They are plotting and planning together
To take me by surprise.

A sudden rush from the stairway,
A sudden raid from the hall!
By three doors left unguarded
They enter my castle wall!

They climb up into my turret
O'er the arms and back of my chair;
If I try to escape, they surround me;
They seem to be everywhere.

They almost devour me with kisses,
Their arms about me entwine,
Till I think of the Bishop of Bingen
In his Mouse-Tower on the Rhine!

Do you think, O blue-eyed banditti,
Because you have scaled the wall,
Such an old mustache as I am
Is not a match for you all!

I have you fast in my fortress,
And will not let you depart,
But put you down into the dungeon
In the round-tower of my heart.

And there will I keep you forever,
Yes, forever and a day,
Till the walls shall crumble to ruin,
And moulder in dust away!

FUN TOGETHER

MAKING HAND SHADOWS

―――――― ∞∞ ――――――

THROUGHOUT THE CENTURIES, fathers have entertained their children at bedtime with hand shadows. Here are instructions for some classic images that are fun and easy to create. All you need are two hands, a strong light source (a lamp or flashlight is perfect), and a white or light-colored wall to serve as a screen.

1. Place a lamp or strong flashlight several feet from the wall.

2. Set a chair close to the light source, between it and the wall. Position the chair so that when you're sitting in it, you can easily move your hands and arms in front of the light. The closer you sit to the wall, the smaller your hand shadows will be.

3. Turn out all but your one light, and begin!

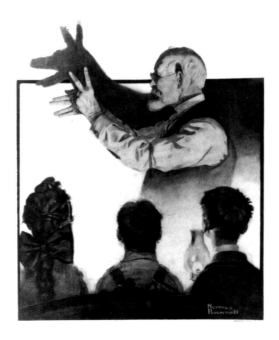

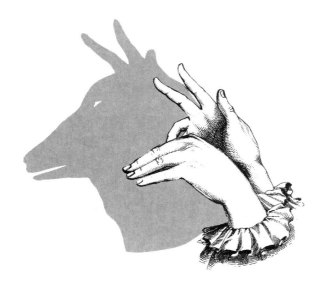

THE DEER

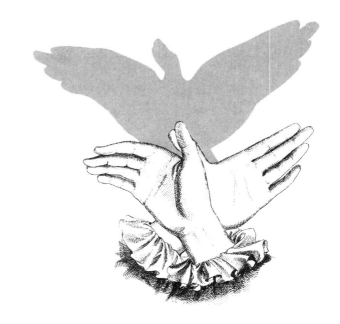

BIRDS

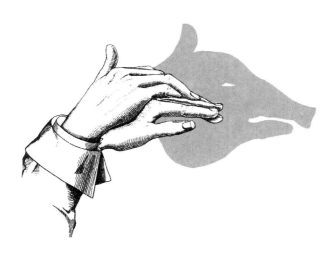

THE PIG

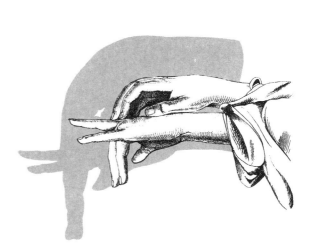

THE ELEPHANT

THE PRINCESS: SWEET AND LOW

ALFRED, LORD TENNYSON

SWEET AND LOW, sweet and low,
Wind of the western sea,
Low, low, breathe and blow,
Wind of the western sea!
Over the rolling waters go,
Come from the dying moon, and blow,
Blow him again to me;
While my little one, while my pretty one, sleeps.

Sleep and rest, sleep and rest,
Father will come to thee soon;
Rest, rest, on mother's breast,
Father will come to thee soon;
Father will come to his babe in the nest,
Silver sails all out of the west
Under the silver moon:
Sleep, my little one, sleep, my pretty one, sleep.

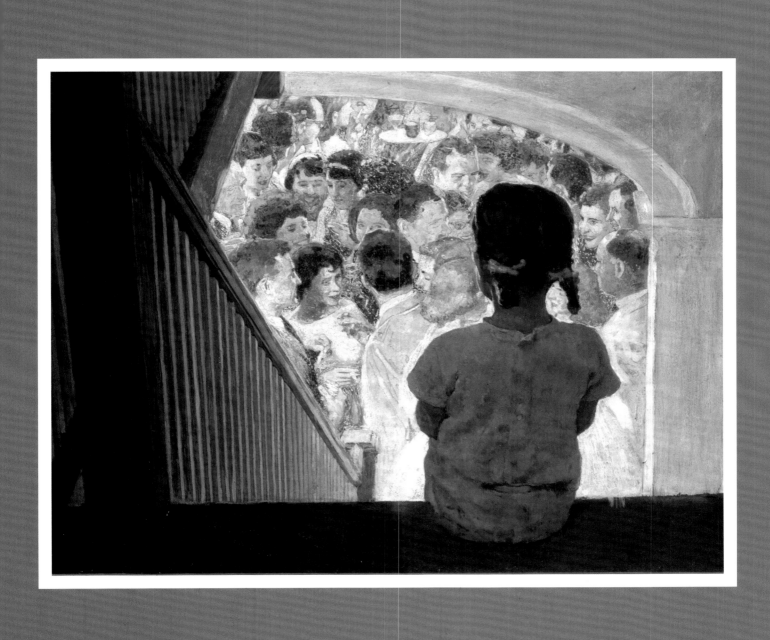

ON THE BEACH AT NIGHT

WALT WHITMAN

ON THE BEACH at night,
Stands a child with her father,
Watching the east, the autumn sky.

Up through the darkness,
While ravening clouds, the burial clouds, in black masses spreading,
Lower sullen and fast athwart and down the sky,
Amid a transparent clear belt of ether yet left in the east,
Ascends large and calm the lord-star Jupiter,
And nigh at hand, only a very little above,
Swim the delicate sisters the Pleiades.

From the beach the child holding the hand of her father,
Those burial-clouds that lower victorious soon to devour all,
Watching, silently weeps.

Weep not, child,
Weep not, my darling,
With these kisses let me remove your tears,
The ravening clouds shall not long be victorious,
They shall not long possess the sky, they devour the stars only in apparition,
Jupiter shall emerge, be patient, watch again another night, the Pleiades shall emerge,
They are immortal, all those stars both silvery and golden shall shine out again,
The great stars and the little ones shall shine out again, they endure,
The vast immortal suns and the long-enduring pensive moons shall again shine.

Then dearest child mournest thou only for Jupiter?
Considerest thou alone the burial of the stars?

Something there is,
(With my lips soothing thee, adding I whisper,
I give thee the first suggestion, the problem and indirection,)
Something there is more immortal even than the stars,
(Many the burials, many the days and nights, passing away,)
Something that shall endure longer even than lustrous Jupiter
Longer than sun or any revolving satellite,
Or the radiant sisters the Pleiades.

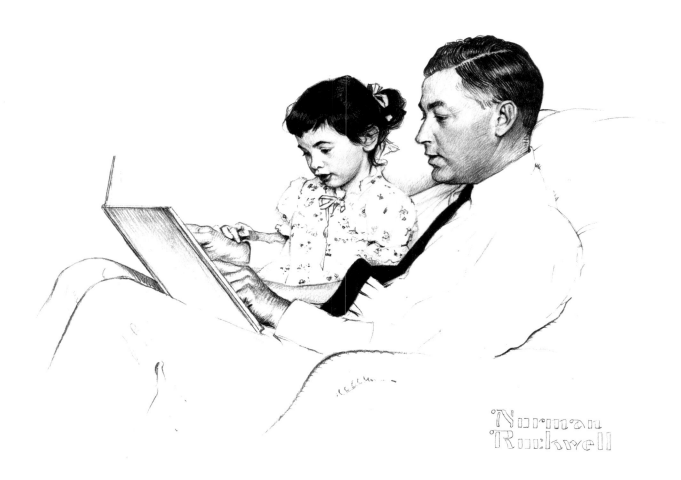

FUN TOGETHER

STARGAZING WITH BINOCULARS

———⟷———

DID YOU KNOW you can see a galaxy 2½ million light-years away with your unaided eyes? Craters on the Moon with binoculars? On any clear night, countless wonders await you. To begin, simply look up and ask, "What's that?" When you do, you're taking the first step toward a lifetime of cosmic exploration and enjoyment. But what, exactly, comes next? What advice would help beginners the most? Here are some pointers to help fathers looking to encourage their children past the most common pitfalls and onto the likeliest route to success.

1. LEARN THE SKY WITH THE UNAIDED EYE.

Astronomy is an outdoor nature hobby. Buy or download a monthly naked-eye star chart and go out into the night! Look up and identify the starry names and patterns overhead. Even if you live in a densely populated, light-polluted area, there's more to see up there than you might imagine. Even if you go no further, the ability to locate Polaris and Saturn will provide pleasure, and perhaps a sense of place in the cosmos, for the rest of your life.

2. VISIT YOUR PUBLIC LIBRARY.

Astronomy is a learning hobby. Its joys come from intellectual discovery and knowledge of the cryptic night sky. But you have to make these discoveries, and gain this knowledge, by yourself. In other words, you need to become self-taught. The public library is the beginner's most important astronomical tool. Comb the astronomy shelf for books about the basic knowledge you need to know, and for guidebooks to what you can see out there in the wide universe. Read about those stars and constellations you're finding with the naked eye, and about how the stars change through the night and the seasons.

3. TRY A PAIR OF BINOCULARS.

Binoculars make an ideal "first telescope" for several reasons. They show you a wide field of view, making it easy to find your way around. Binoculars show a view that's right-side up and straight in front of you, making it easy to see where you're pointing. Ordinary 7- to 10-power binoculars improve on the naked-eye view about as much as a good amateur telescope improves on the binoculars—for much less than half the price.

4. DIVE INTO MAPS AND GUIDEBOOKS.

A sailor of the seas needs top-notch charts, and so does a sailor of the skies. Fine maps bring the fascination of hunting out faint secrets in hidden sky realms. Many guidebooks describe what's to be hunted and the nature of the objects you find. Moreover, the skills you'll develop using binoculars to locate these things are exactly the skills you'll need to put a telescope to good use.

Plan indoors what you'll do outdoors. Spread out your charts and guides on a big table, find things that ought to be in range of your equipment, and figure out how you'll get there. Plan your expeditions before heading out into the nightly wilderness.

A neat star-chart trick is to make a wire ring the size of your binoculars' or finderscope's field of view. Slide it from point to point on the chart, and you'll see the star patterns that will appear in your view as you navigate the sky.

5. KEEP AN ASTRONOMY DIARY.

Keeping a record concentrates the mind—even if it's just jotting down a simple observation, such as "November 7th—out with the 10 x 50 binoculars—clear windy night—NGC 457 in Cassiopeia a faint glow next to two brighter stars." Get a spiral-bound notebook and keep it with the rest of your observing gear. Looking back on your early experiences and sightings will give deeper meaning to your activities in the years to come.

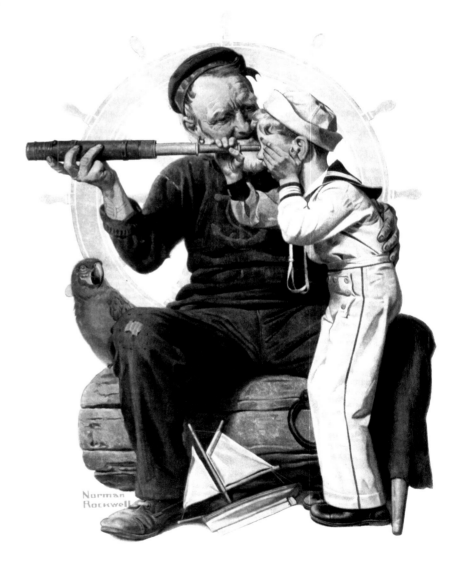

SONG TO BE SUNG BY THE FATHER OF INFANT FEMALE CHILDREN

OGDEN NASH

MY HEART LEAPS up when I behold
A rainbow in the sky;
Contrariwise, my blood runs cold
When little boys go by.
For little boys as little boys,
No special hate I carry,
But now and then they grow to men,
And when they do, they marry.
No matter how they tarry,
Eventually they marry.
And, swine among the pearls,
They marry little girls.

Oh, somewhere, somewhere, an infant plays,
With parents who feed and clothe him.
Their lips are sticky with pride and praise,
But I have begun to loathe him.
Yes, I loathe with loathing shameless
This child who to me is nameless.
This bachelor child in his carriage
Gives never a thought to marriage,
But a person can hardly say knife
Before he will hunt him a wife.

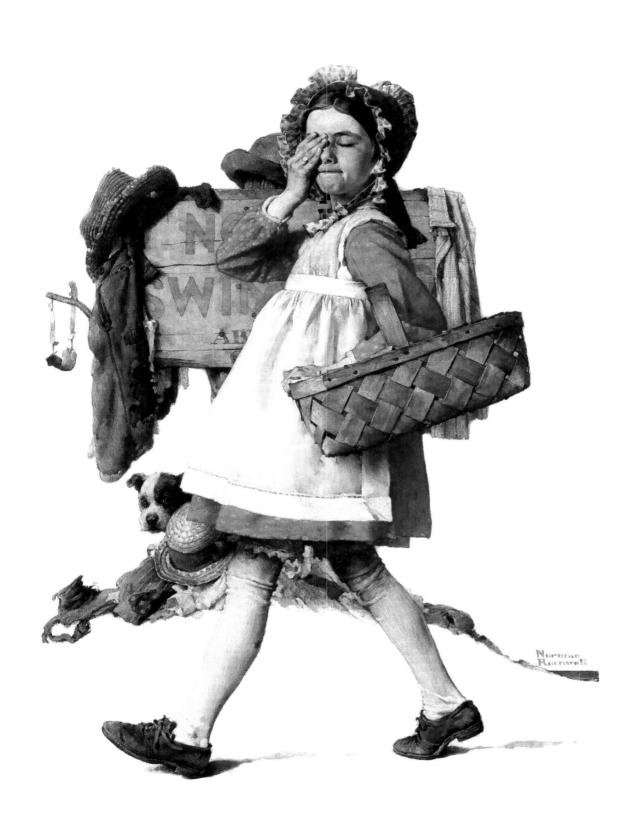

✻ ✻

I never see an infant (male),
A-sleeping in the sun,
Without I turn a trifle pale
And think is he the one?
Oh, first he'll want to crop his curls,
And then he'll want a pony,
And then he'll think of pretty girls,
And holy matrimony.
A cat without a mouse
Is he without a spouse.

Oh, somewhere he bubbles bubbles of milk,
And quietly sucks his thumbs.
His cheeks are roses painted on silk,
And his teeth are tucked in his gums.
But alas the teeth will begin to grow,
And the bubbles will cease to bubble;
Given a score of years or so,
The roses will turn to stubble.
He'll sell a bond, or he'll write a book,
And his eyes will get that acquisitive look,
And raging and ravenous for the kill,
He'll boldly ask for the hand of Jill.
This infant whose middle
Is diapered still
Will want to marry My daughter Jill.

Oh sweet be his slumber and moist his middle!
My dreams, I fear, are infanticiddle.
A fig for embryo Lohengrins!
I'll open all his safety pins,
I'll pepper his powder, and salt his bottle,
And give him readings from Aristotle.
Sand for his spinach I'll gladly bring,
And Tabasco sauce for his teething ring.
Then perhaps he'll struggle through fire and water
To marry somebody else's daughter.

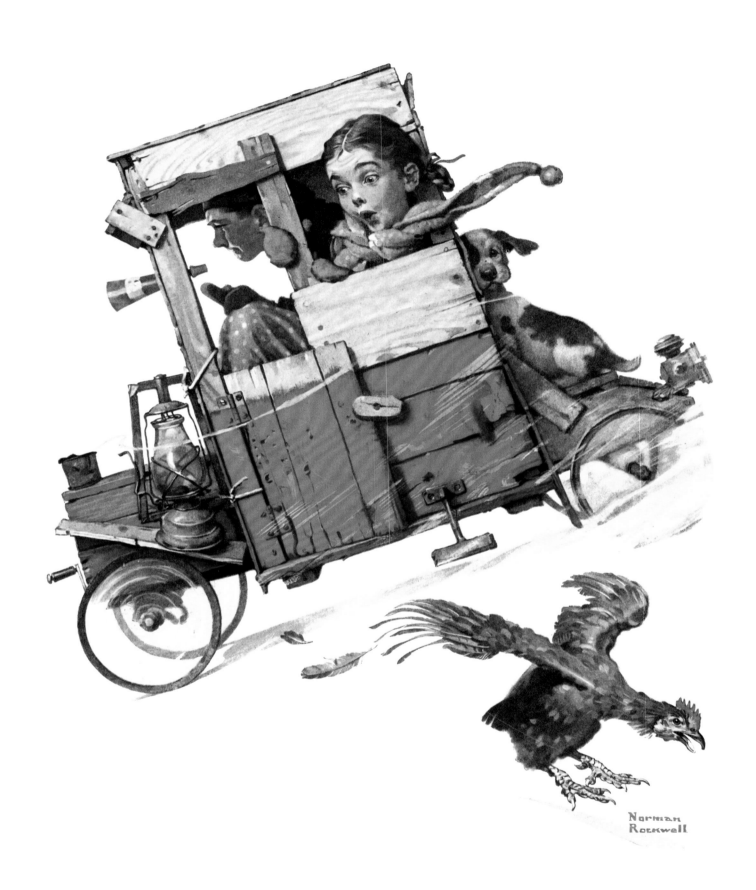

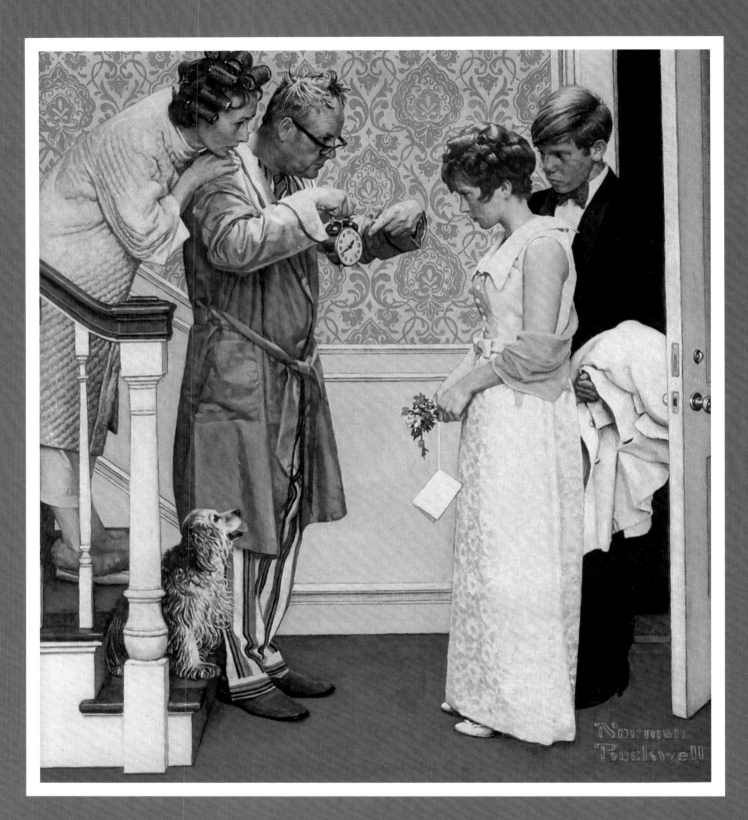

Daddy's Home, See You Tomorrow

Ogden Nash

I ALWAYS FOUND my daughters' beaux
Invisible as the emperor's clothes,
And I could hear of them no more
Than the slamming of an auto door.
My chicks would then slip up to roost;
They were, I finally deduced,
Concealing tactfully, pro tem,
Not boys from me but me from them.

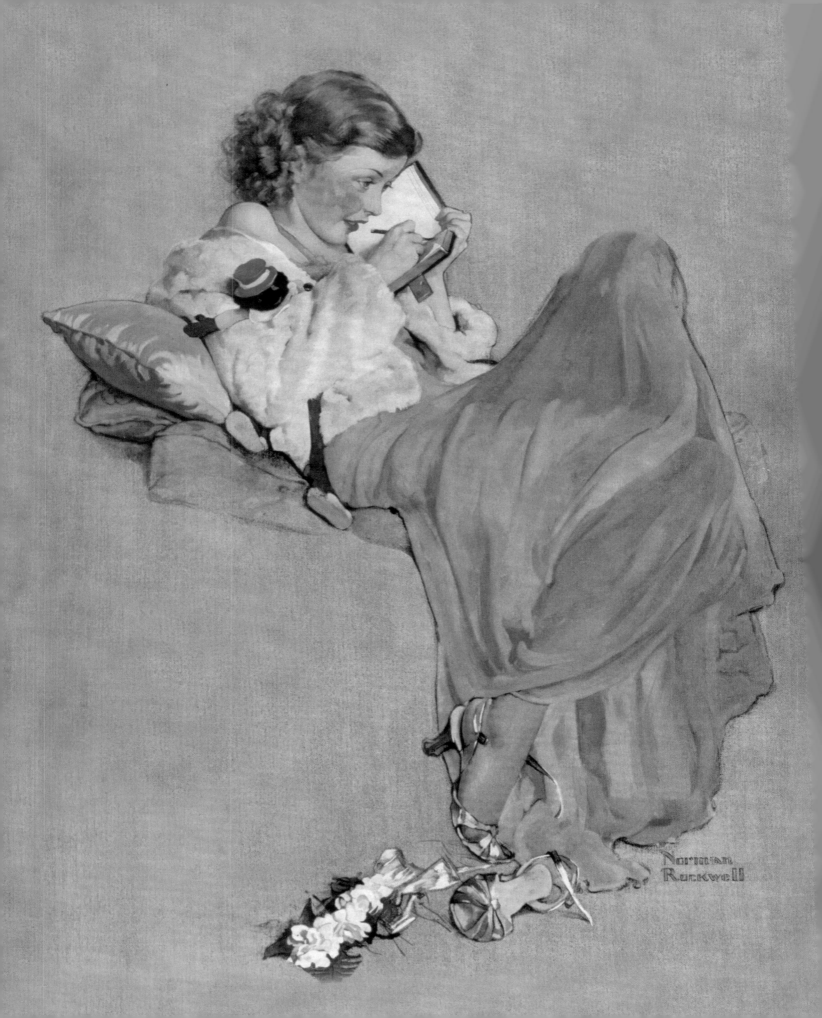

THE WRITER

RICHARD WILBUR

―――――――――⊂○χ○⊃―――――――――

IN HER ROOM at the prow of the house
Where light breaks, and the windows are tossed with linden,
My daughter is writing a story.

I pause in the stairwell, hearing
From her shut door a commotion of typewriter-keys
Like a chain hauled over a gunwale.

Young as she is, the stuff
Of her life is a great cargo, and some of it heavy:
I wish her a lucky passage.

But now it is she who pauses,
As if to reject my thought and its easy figure.
A stillness greatens, in which

The whole house seems to be thinking,
And then she is at it again with a bunched clamor
Of strokes, and again is silent.

I remember the dazed starling
Which was trapped in that very room, two years ago;
How we stole in, lifted a sash

✳ ✳

And retreated, not to affright it;
And how for a helpless hour, through the crack of the door,
We watched the sleek, wild, dark

And iridescent creature
Batter against the brilliance, drop like a glove
To the hard floor, or the desk-top,

And wait then, humped and bloody,
For the wits to try it again; and how our spirits
Rose when, suddenly sure,

It lifted off from a chair-back,
Beating a smooth course for the right window
And clearing the sill of the world.

It is always a matter, my darling,
Of life or death, as I had forgotten. I wish
What I wished you before, but harder.

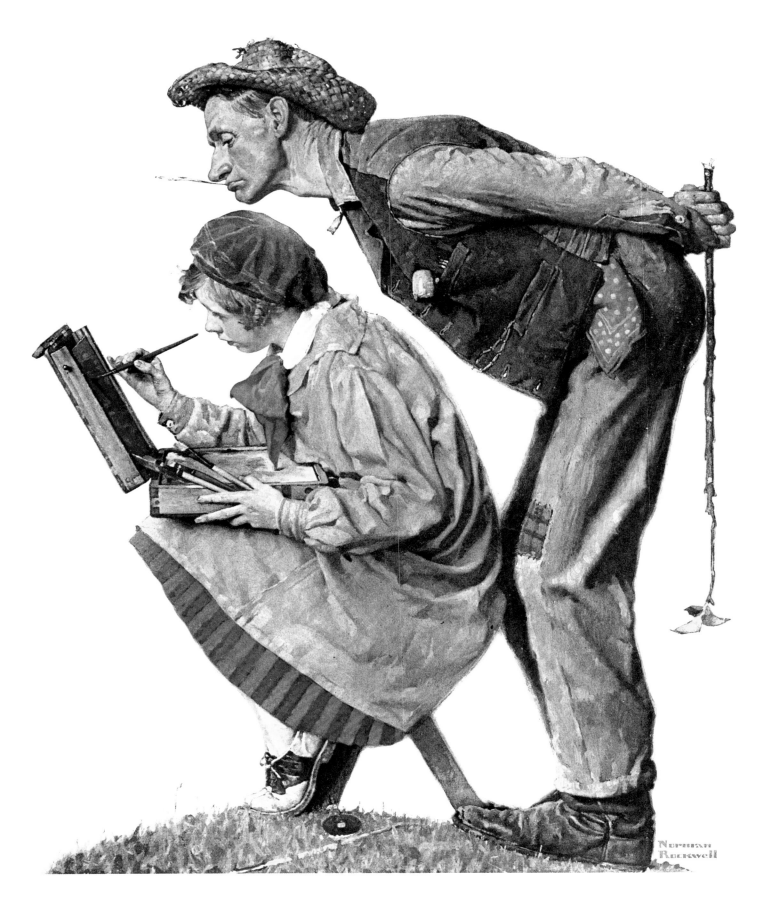

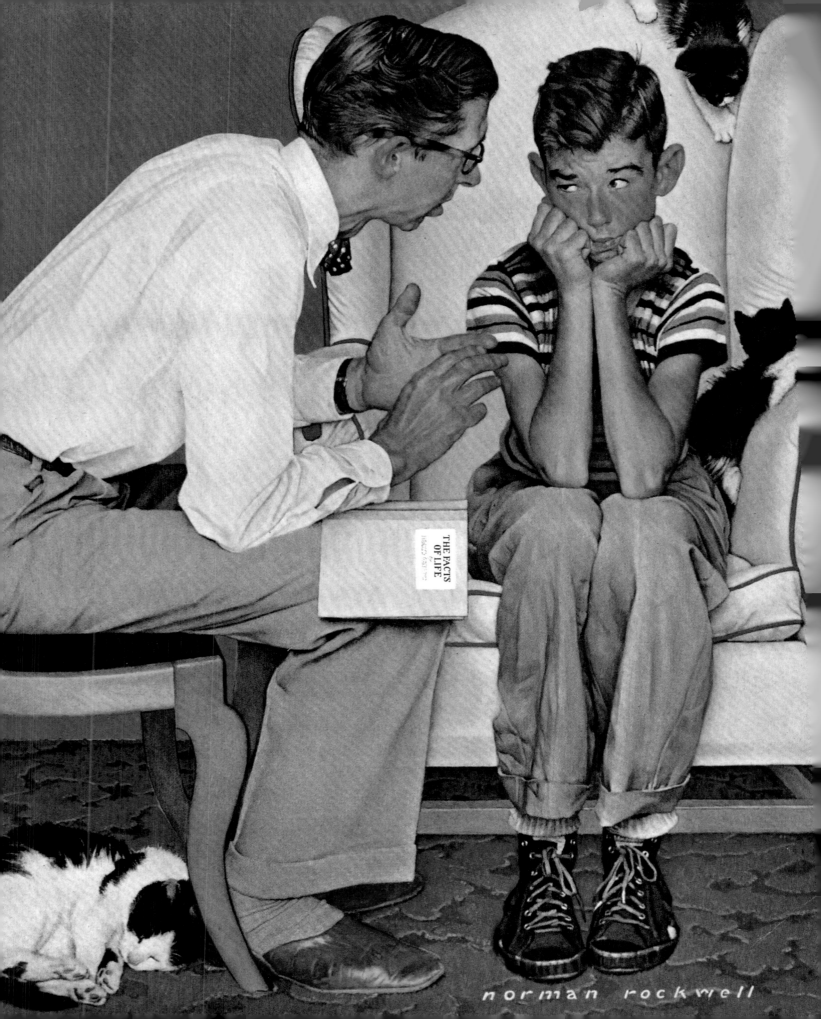

THE FACTS
OF LIFE

norman rockwell

Part Four

FATHERS
AND SONS

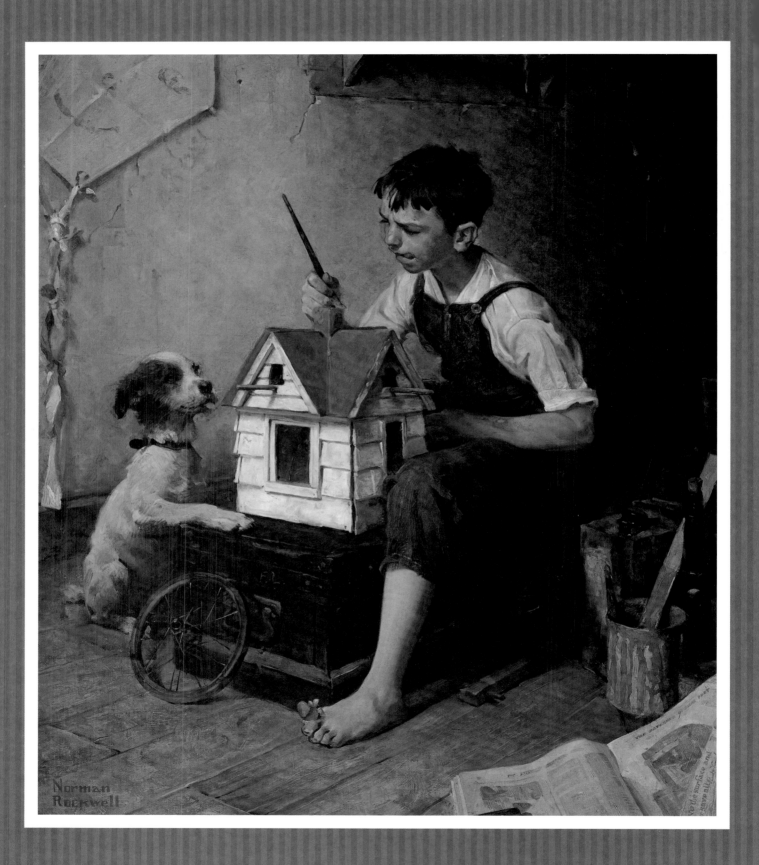

THE CHILD IS
FATHER TO THE MAN

GERARD MANLEY HOPKINS

"THE CHILD IS father to the man."
How can he be? The words are wild.
Suck any sense from that who can:
"The child is father to the man."
No; what the poet did write ran,
"The man is father to the child."
"The child is father to the man!"
How can he be? The words are wild.

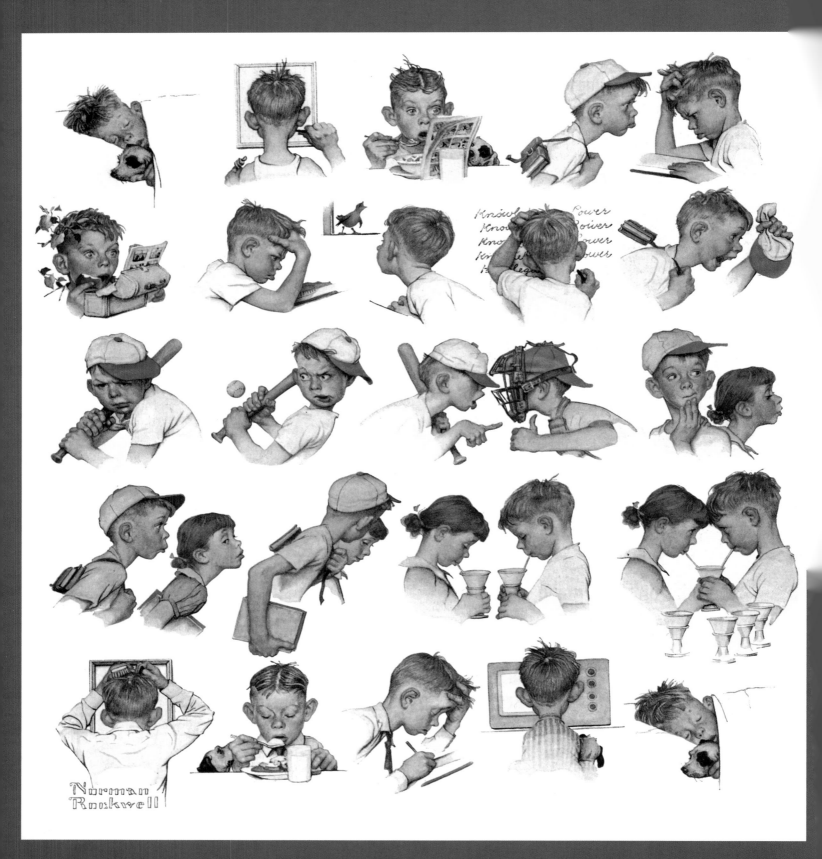

A Prayer for My Son

William Butler Yeats

BID A STRONG GHOST stand at the head
That my Michael may sleep sound,
Nor cry, nor turn in the bed
Till his morning meal come round;
And may departing twilight keep
All dread afar till morning's back.
That his mother may not lack
Her fill of sleep.

Bid the ghost have sword in fist:
Some there are, for I avow
Such devilish things exist,
Who have planned his murder, for they know
Of some most haughty deed or thought
That waits upon his future days,
And would through hatred of the bays
Bring that to nought.

Though You can fashion everything
From nothing every day, and teach
The morning stars to sing,
You have lacked articulate speech
To tell Your simplest want, and known,
Wailing upon a woman's knee,
All of that worst ignominy
Of flesh and bone;

And when through all the town there ran
The servants of Your enemy,
A woman and a man,
Unless the Holy Writings lie,
Hurried through the smooth and rough
And through the fertile and waste,
Protecting, till the danger past,
With human love.

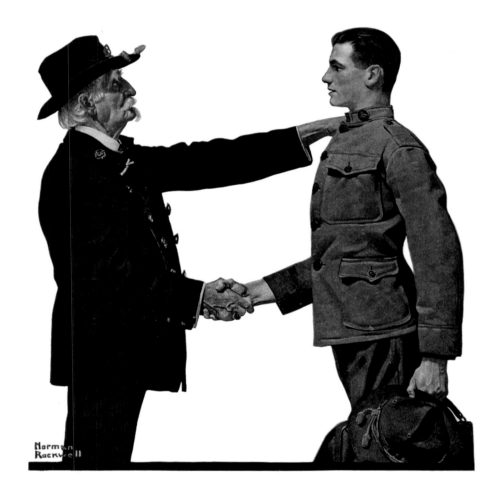

IF

RUDYARD KIPLING

IF YOU CAN keep your head when all about you
Are losing theirs and blaming it on you;
If you can trust yourself when all men doubt you
But make allowance for their doubting too;
If you can wait and not be tired by waiting,
Or, being lied about, don't deal in lies,
Or, being hated, don't give way to hating,
And yet don't look too good, nor talk too wise;

If you can dream—and not make dreams your master;
If you can think—and not make thoughts your aim;
If you can meet with triumph and disaster
And treat those two imposters just the same;
If you can bear to hear the truth you've spoken
Twisted by knaves to make a trap for fools,
Or watch the things you gave your life to, broken
And stoop and build 'em up with worn-out tools;

If you can make one heap of all your winnings
And risk it on one turn of pitch-and-toss,
And lose, and start again at your beginnings
And never breathe a word about your loss;
If you can force your heart and nerve and sinew
To serve your turn long after they are gone,
And so hold on when there is nothing in you
Except the Will which says to them: "Hold on!";

If you can talk with crowds and keep your virtue,
Or walk with kings—nor lose the common touch;
If neither foes nor loving friends can hurt you;
If all men count with you, but none too much;
If you can fill the unforgiving minute
With sixty seconds' worth of distance run—
Yours is the Earth and everything that's in it,
And—which is more—you'll be a Man, my son!

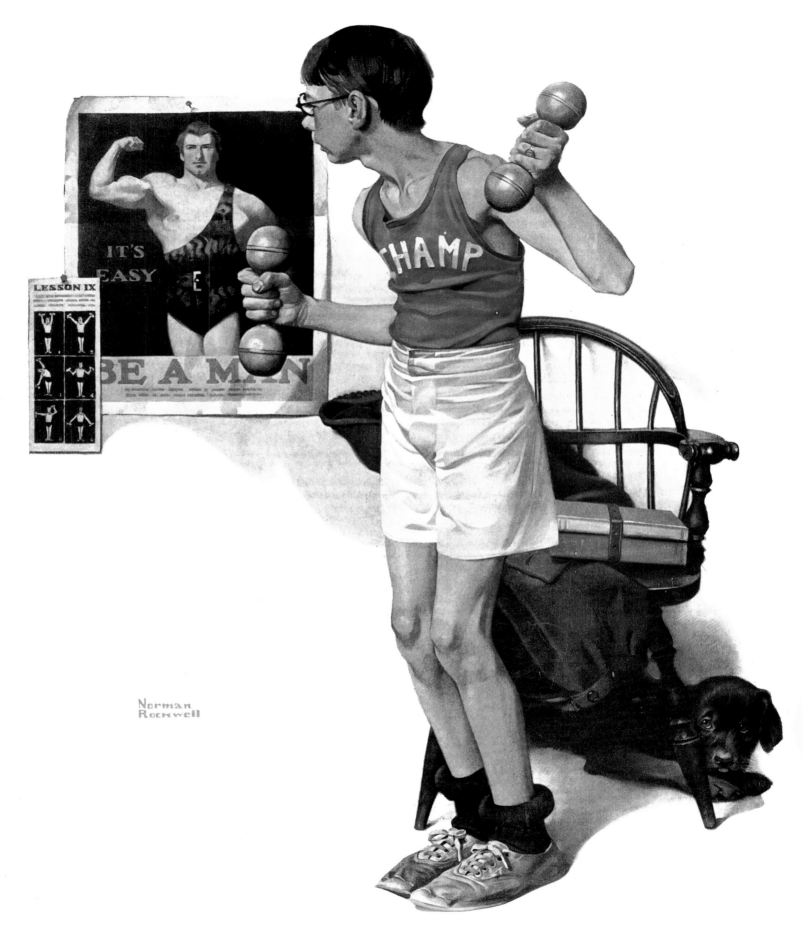

THE MAN TO BE

EDGAR GUEST

SOME DAY THE WORLD will need a man of courage in a time of doubt,
And somewhere, as a little boy, that future hero plays about.
Within some humble home, no doubt, that instrument of greater things
Now climbs upon his father's knee or to his mother's garments clings.
And when shall come that call for him to render service that is fine.
He that shall do God's mission here may be your little boy or mine.

Long years of preparation mark the pathway for the splendid souls,
And generations live and die and seem no nearer to their goals,
And yet the purpose of it all, the fleeting pleasure and the woe,
The laughter and the grief of life that all who come to earth must know
May be to pave the way for one—one man to serve the Will Divine
And it is possible that he may be your little boy or mine.

Some day the world will need a man! I stand beside his cot at night
And wonder if I'm teaching him, as best I can, to know the right.
I am the father of a boy—his life is mine to make or mar—
And he no better can become than what my daily teachings are;
There will be need for someone great—I dare not falter from the line—
The man that is to serve the world may be that little boy of mine.

Perhaps your boy and mine may not ascend the lofty heights of fame;
The orders for their births are hid. We know not why to earth they came.
Yet in some little bed to-night the great man of to-morrow sleeps
And only He who sent him here, the secret of his purpose keeps.
As fathers then our care is this—to keep in mind the Great Design.
The man the world shall need some day may be your little boy or mine.

THE BOY SOLDIER

EDGAR GUEST

EACH EVENING on my lap there climbs
A little boy of three,
And with his dimpled, chubby fists
He pounds me shamefully.
He gives my beard a vicious tug,
He bravely pulls my nose;
And then he tussles with my hair
And then explores my clothes.

He throws my pencils on the floor
My watch is his delight;
He never seems to think that I
Have any private right.
And though he breaks my good cigars,
With all his cunning art,
He works a greater ruin, far,
Deep down within my heart.

This roguish little tyke who sits
Each night upon my knee,
And hammers at his poor old dad,
Is bound to conquer me.
He little knows that long ago,
He forced the gates apart,
And marched triumphantly into
The city of my heart.

Some day perhaps, in years to come,
When he is older grown,
He, too, will be assailed as I,
By youngsters of his own.
And when at last a little lad
Gives battle on his knee,
I know that he'll be captured, too,
Just as he captured me.

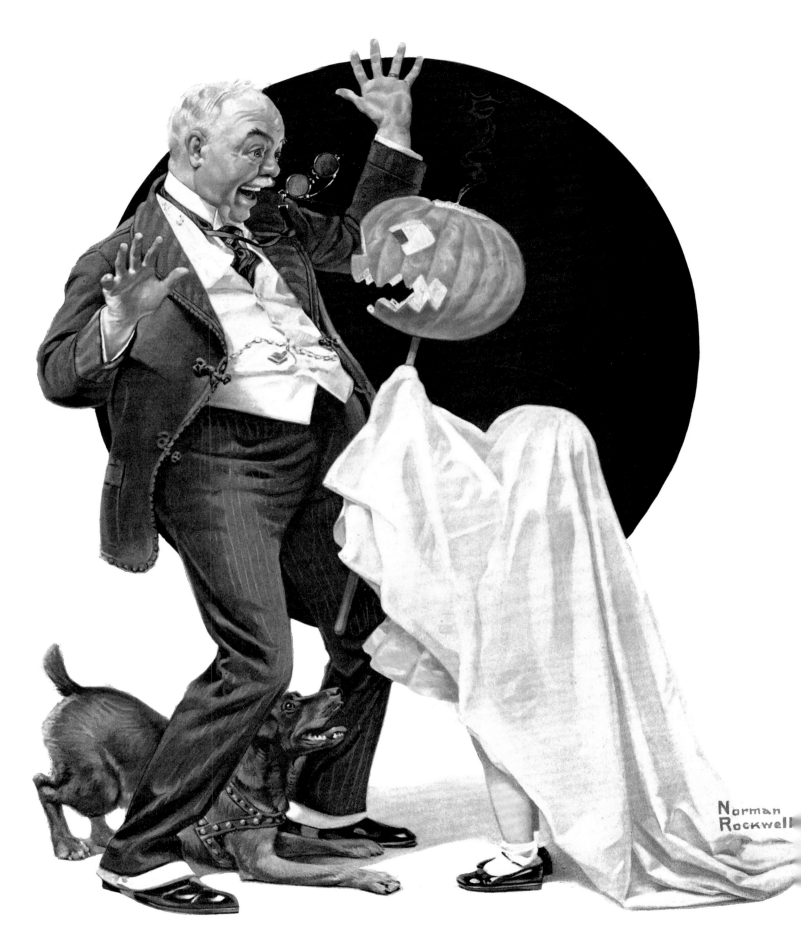

YOU ARE OLD, FATHER WILLIAM

LEWIS CARROLL

———coxoo———

"YOU ARE OLD, Father William," the young man said,
"And your hair has become very white;
And yet you incessantly stand on your head—
Do you think, at your age, it is right?"

"In my youth," Father William replied to his son,
"I feared it might injure the brain;
But now that I'm perfectly sure I have none,
Why, I do it again and again."

"You are old," said the youth, "as I mentioned before,
And you have grown most uncommonly fat;
Yet you turned a back somersault in at the door—
Pray, what is the reason of that?"

"In my youth," said the sage, as he shook his gray locks,
"I kept all my limbs very supple
By the use of this ointment—one shilling a box—
Allow me to sell you a couple."

"You are old," said the youth, "and your jaws are too weak
For anything tougher than suet;
Yet you finished the goose, with the bones and the beak—
Pray, how did you manage to do it?"

"In my youth," said his father, "I took to the law,
And argued each case with my wife;
And the muscular strength, which it gave to my jaw,
Has lasted the rest of my life."

"You are old," said the youth, "one would hardly suppose
That your eyes was as steady as ever;
Yet you balanced an eel on the end of your nose—
What made you so awfully clever?"

"I have answered three questions, and that is enough,"
Said his father; "don't give yourself airs!
Do you think I can listen all day to such stuff?
Be off, or I'll kick you downstairs!"

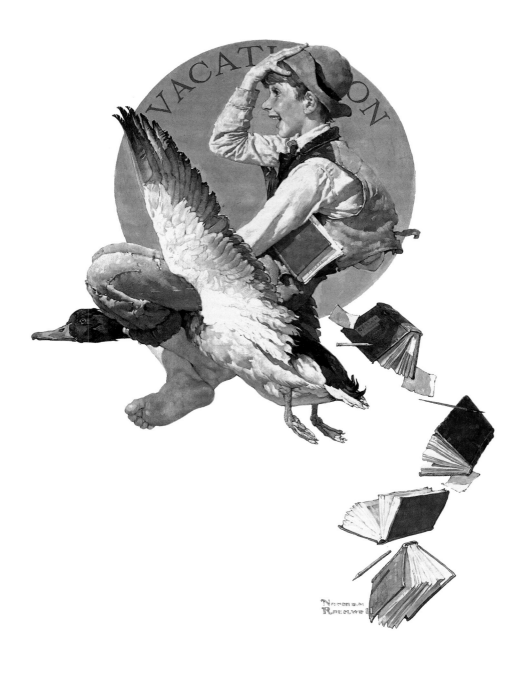

THE OLD MAN DREAMS

OLIVER WENDELL HOLMES

OH FOR ONE HOUR of youthful joy!
Give back my twentieth spring!
I'd rather laugh, a bright-haired boy,
Than reign, a gray-beard king.

Off with the spoils of wrinkled age!
Away with Learning's crown!
Tear out life's Wisdom-written page,
And dash its trophies down!

One moment let my life-blood stream
From boyhood's fount of flame!
Give me one giddy, reeling dream
Of life all love and fame!

* * * *

My listening angel heard the prayer,
And, calmly smiling, said,
"If I but touch thy silvered hair
Thy hasty wish hath sped.

"But is there nothing in thy track,
To bid thee fondly stay,
While the swift seasons hurry back
To find the wished-for day?"

"Ah, truest soul of womankind!
Without thee what were life?
One bliss I cannot leave behind:
I'll take—my—precious—wife!"

The angel took a sapphire pen
And wrote in rainbow dew,
The man would be a boy again,
And be a husband too!

"And is there nothing yet unsaid,
Before the change appears?
Remember, all their gifts have fled
With those dissolving years."

"Why, yes;" for memory would recall
My fond paternal joys;
"I could not bear to leave them all—
I'll take—my—girl—and—boys."

The smiling angel dropped his pen,—
"Why, this will never do;
The man would be a boy again,
And be a father too!"

✳ ✳ ✳ ✳

And so I laughed,— my laughter woke
The household with its noise,—
And wrote my dream, when morning broke,
To please the gray-haired boys.

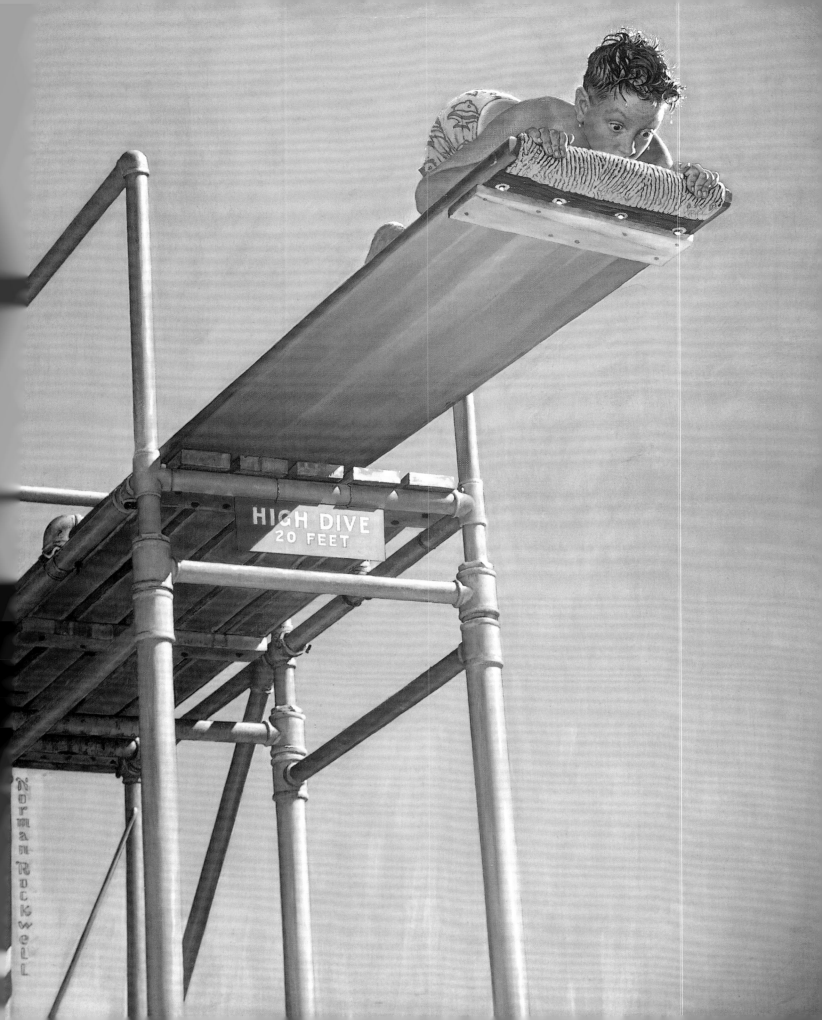

A Boy and His Dad

Edgar Guest

A BOY AND HIS DAD on a fishing-trip—
There is a glorious fellowship!
Father and son and the open sky
And the white clouds lazily drifting by,
And the laughing stream as it runs along
With the clicking reel like a martial song,
And the father teaching the youngster gay
How to land a fish in the sportsman's way.

I fancy I hear them talking there
In an open boat, and the speech is fair.
And the boy is learning the ways of men
From the finest man in his youthful ken.
Kings, to the youngster, cannot compare
With the gentle father who's with him there.
And the greatest mind of the human race
Not for one minute could take his place.

Which is happier, man or boy?
The soul of the father is steeped in joy,
For he's finding out, to his heart's delight,
That his son is fit for the future fight.
He is learning the glorious depths of him,
And the thoughts he thinks and his every whim;
And he shall discover, when night comes on,
How close he has grown to his little son.

A boy and his dad on a fishing-trip—
Builders of life's companionship!
Oh, I envy them, as I see them there

Under the sky in the open air,
For out of the old, old long-ago
Come the summer days that I used to know,
When I learned life's truths from my father's lips
As I shared the joy of his fishing-trips.

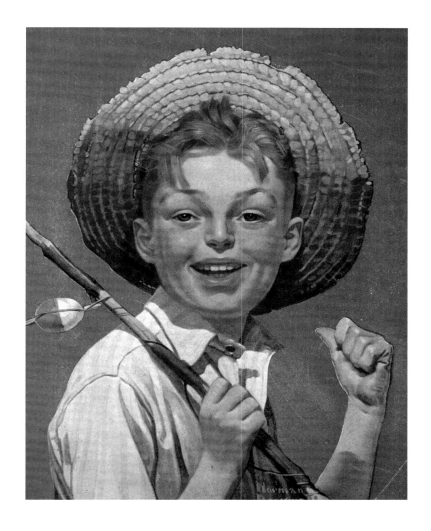

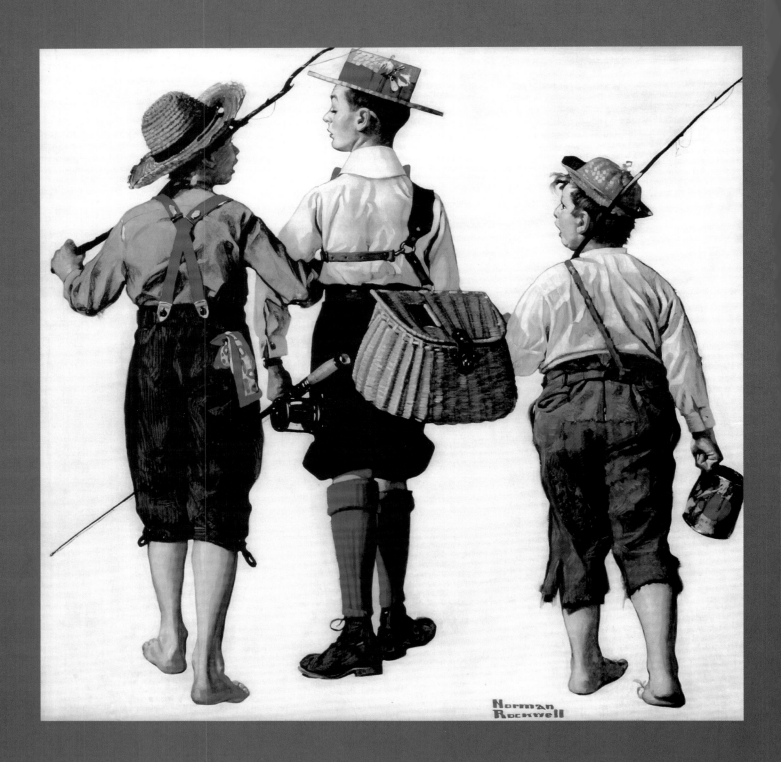

Fun Together

Fishing Secrets

—⁂—

FISHING CAN BE a highly technical hobby—the choice in rods, reels, bait, lures, and lines can be mind-boggling. Remember, when you take your kids out fishing, keep it simple and keep it light. This will keep you from fighting equipment and allow more time for fighting fish.

Light line with small floats, weights, hooks, and bait can help you put some excitement on the end of the line fast. Kids tire quickly and often give up while waiting for lunker bass to bite. Most kids would rather pull in twenty-five minnow-sized bluegill than wait for one trophy catch.

Combining activities can also make family outings more enjoyable. For instance, try making your own fishing rods from willow branches and a length of fishing line. Or find your own bait under rocks or in the weeds around lakes and streams. Make fishing a learning experience and an adventure. And don't forget, fishing is not "catching" fish—it's "trying to catch" fish, while being outdoors with family and friends.

TIPS FOR FISHING WITH KIDS

START SIMPLE.

A cane pole is a good way for little anglers to start fishing. Spin-casting gear is a simple rod and reel for kids. The next step is ultralight spinning gear.

LIGHTEN UP YOUR LINE.

Line that is four- to eight-pound test will do the job; pound test is the amount of force it takes to break the line. Unless you're targeting monster catfish or muskies, light line is your best bet.

BAG THE BIG BOBBERS.

Bobbers (or floats) are used to suspend your bait in the water and to alert you when to set the hook. The harder the bobber is to pull under, the harder it will be to hook a fish. Small floats will help convince the fish to take your tasty bait and run. "Slip" bobbers work well for kids. "Slip" bobber rigs cut down on the amount of line needed at the end of the rod and are easier to cast. Small ice-fishing bobbers can provide a light touch any time of year.

SINK IT WITH SHOT.

Sinkers (or weights) help get your line down to the fish. They can also create "zero buoyancy." Ideally, you want your bobber to just barely float on the top of the water. Squeeze small BB-sized split shot sinkers onto your line, one at a time, until your bobber nearly sinks from the weight. Since there is very little resistance when the fish takes the bait, it is more likely to bite the bait and run.

SMALL HOOKS = BIG CATCHES.

Use hook sizes 6 to 10 (size 6 is larger than size 10). Fish won't readily take large hooks unless they are feeding like crazy. A subtle presentation is often needed to catch wary fish. Tiny hooks also allow small fish to "inhale" the bait, rather than nibble the bait off the hook. If a fish swallows the hook and you want to return the fish to the water, simply cut the line as close to the hook as possible and release the fish. For a safer hook, smash down the barb with pliers or use barbless hooks.

GREAT BIG GOBS OF WORMS WON'T DO.

There's no need to use whole, whopping-big, writhing night crawlers on your hook. Live bait such as red worms, wax worms (bee moth larvae), or crickets work best. Keep the bait approximately the size of your hook, so the fish is less likely to steal your bait. You can also cut the bait to fit your hook. When you're finished with the bait, give it to another angler, bring it home for the next trip, or throw it in the trash—never dump your bait into the water.

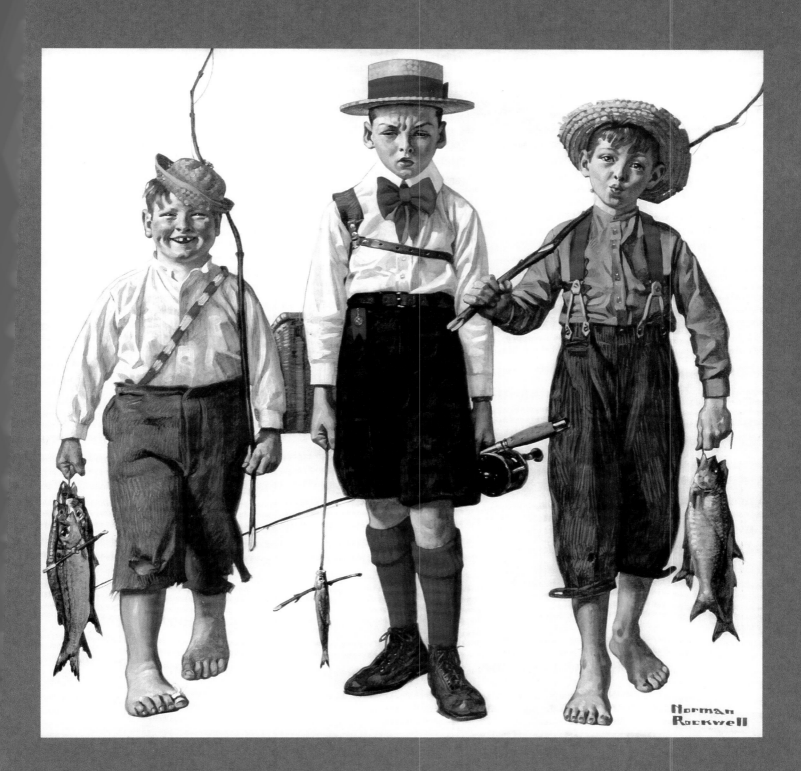

MY FATHER

TED HUGHES

SOME FATHERS work at the office, others work at the store,
Some operate great cranes and build up skyscrapers galore,
Some work in canning factories counting green peas into cans,
Some drive all night in huge and thundering removal vans.

But mine has the strangest job of the lot.
My Father's the Chief Inspector of—What?
O don't tell the mice, don't tell the moles,
My Father's the Chief Inspector of HOLES.

It's a work of the highest importance because you never know
What's in a hole, what fearful thing is creeping from below.
Perhaps it's a hole to the ocean and will soon gush water in tons,
Or maybe it leads to a vast cave full of gold and skeletons.

Though a hole might seem to have nothing but dirt in it,
Somebody's simply got to make certain.
Caves in the mountain, clefts in the wall,
My father has to inspect them all.

That crack in the road looks harmless. My Father knows it's not.
The world may be breaking into two and starting at that spot.
Or maybe world is a great egg, and we live on the shell,
And it's just beginning to split and hatch: you simply cannot tell.

If you see a crack, run to the phone, run;
My father will know just what's to be done.
A rumbling hole, a silent hole,
My father will soon have it under control.

Keeping a check on all these holes he hurries from morning to night.
There might be sounds of marching in one, or an eye shining bright.

A tentacle came groping from a hole that belonged to a mouse,
A floor collapsed and Chinamen swarmed up into the house.

A Hole's an unpredictable thing—
Nobody knows what a Hole might bring.
Caves in the mountain, clefts in the wall,
My father has to inspect them all!

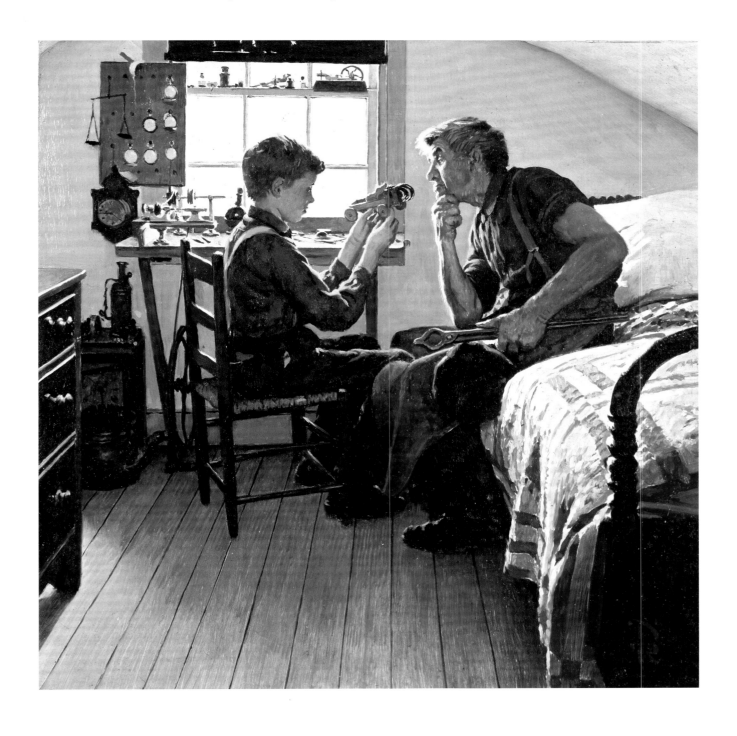

FATHER AND SON

EDGAR GUEST

BE MORE than his dad,
Be a chum to the lad;
Be a part of his life
Every hour of the day;
Find time to talk with him,
Take time to walk with him,
Share in his studies
And share in his play;
Take him to places,
To ball games and races,
Teach him the things
That you want him to know;
Don't live apart from him,
Don't keep your heart from him,
Be his best comrade,
He's needing you so!

Never neglect him,
Though young, still respect him,
Hear his opinions
With patience and pride;
Show him his error,
But be not a terror,
Grim-visaged and fearful,
When he's at your side.
Know what his thoughts are,
Know what his sports are,
Know all his playmates,

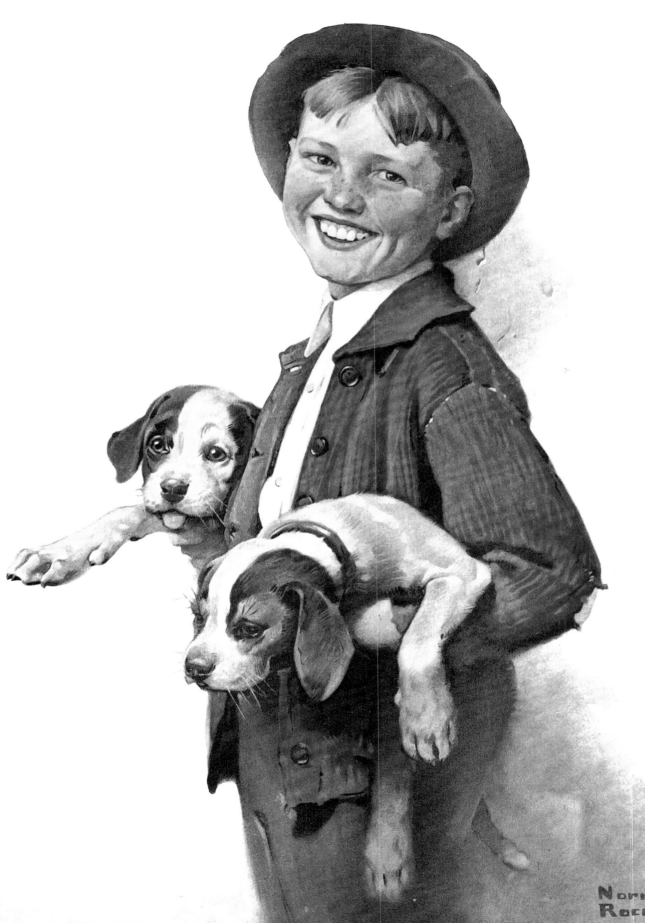

Norman
Rockwell

It's easy to learn to;
Be such a father
That when troubles gather
You'll be the first one
For counsel, he'll turn to.

You can inspire him
With courage, and fire him
Hot with ambition
For deeds that are good;
He'll not betray you
Nor illy repay you,
If you have taught him
The things that you should.
Father and son
Must in all things be one—
Partners in trouble
And comrades in joy.
More than a dad
Was the best pal you had;
Be such a chum
As you knew, to your boy.

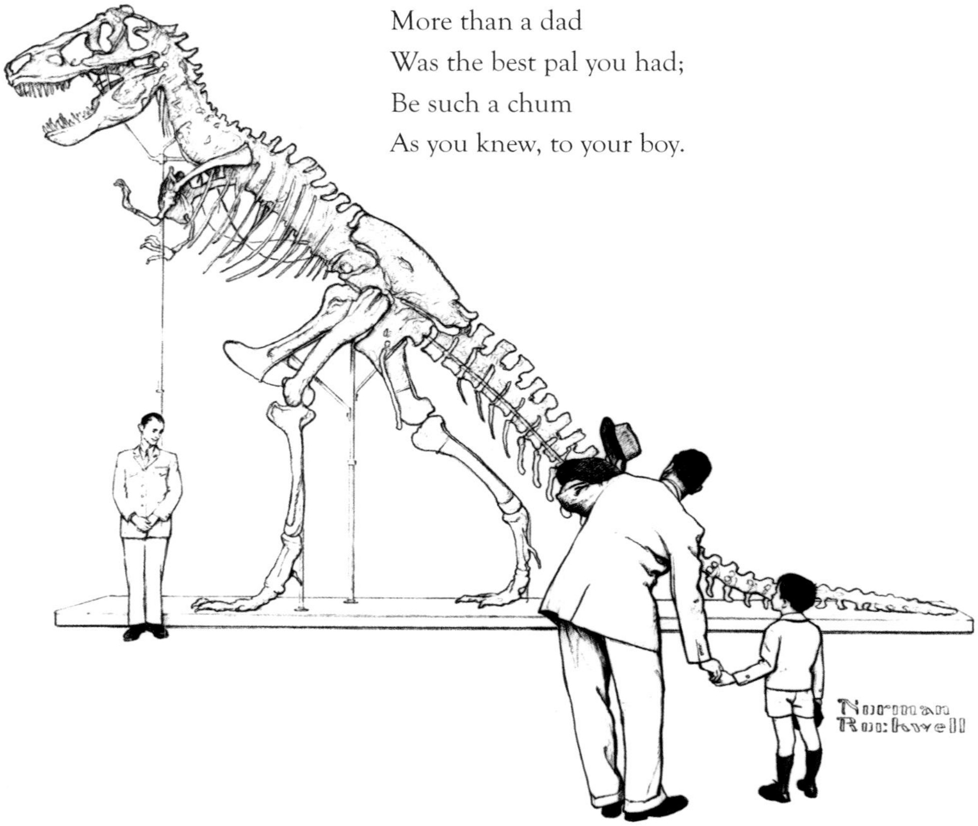

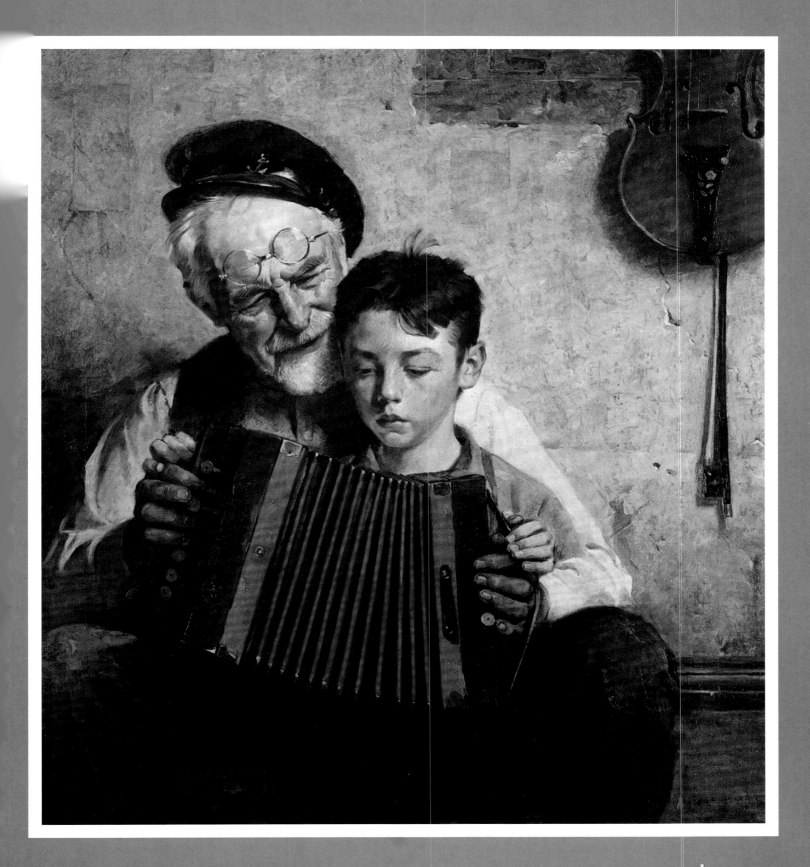

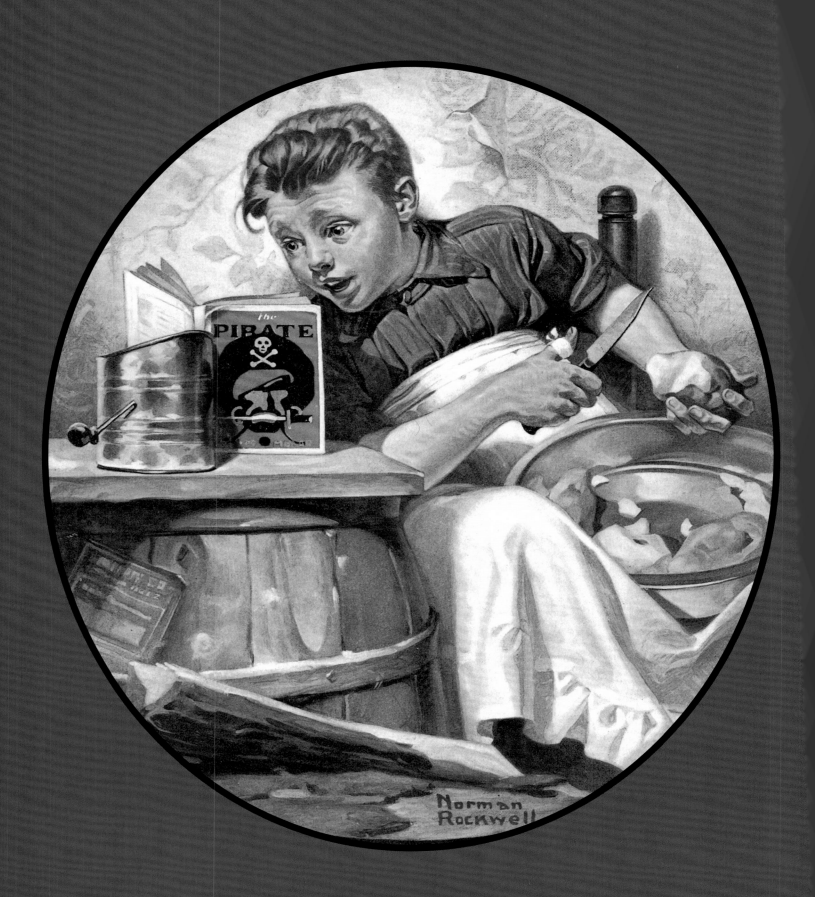

Part Five

FAVORITE STORIES
TO READ ALOUD

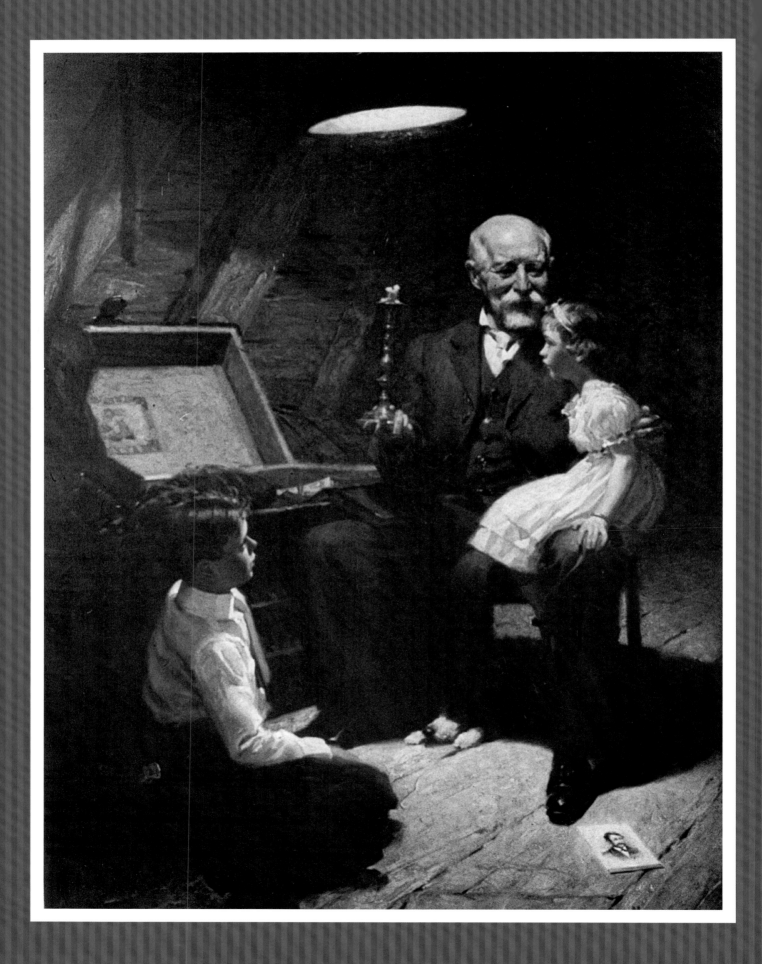

THE GOLDEN TOUCH

NATHANIEL HAWTHORNE

ONCE UPON A TIME, there lived a very rich man, and a king besides, whose name was Midas; and he had a little daughter, whom nobody but myself ever heard of, and whose name I either never knew, or have entirely forgotten. So, because I love odd names for little girls, I choose to call her Marygold.

This King Midas was fonder of gold than of anything else in the world. He valued his royal crown chiefly because it was composed of that precious metal. If he loved anything better, or half so well, it was the one little maiden who played so merrily around her father's footstool. But the more Midas loved his daughter, the more did he desire and seek for wealth. He thought, foolish man! that the best thing he could possibly do for this dear child would be to bequeath her the immensest pile of yellow, glistening coin, that had ever been heaped together since the world was made. Thus, he gave all his thoughts and all his time to this one purpose. If ever he happened to gaze for an instant at the gold-tinted clouds of sunset, he wished that they were real gold, and that they could be squeezed safely into his strong box. When little Marygold ran to meet him, with a bunch of buttercups and dandelions, he used to say, "Poh, poh, child! If these flowers were as golden as they look, they would be worth the plucking!"

And yet, in his earlier days, before he was so entirely possessed of this insane desire for riches, King Midas had shown a great taste for flowers. He had planted a garden, in which grew the biggest and beautifullest and sweetest roses that any mortal ever saw or smelt. These roses were still growing in the garden, as large, as lovely, and as fragrant, as when Midas used to pass whole hours in gazing at them, and inhaling their perfume. But now, if he looked at them at all, it was only to calculate how much the garden would be worth if each of the innumerable rose-petals were a thin plate of gold. And though he once was fond of music (in spite of an idle story about his ears, which were said to resemble those of an ass), the only music for poor Midas, now, was the chink of one coin against another.

At length (as people always grow more and more foolish, unless they take care to grow wiser and wiser), Midas had got to be so exceedingly unreasonable, that he could scarcely bear to see or touch any object that was not gold. He made it his custom, therefore, to pass a large portion of every day in a dark and dreary apartment, underground, at the basement of his palace. It was here

that he kept his wealth. To this dismal hole—for it was little better than a dungeon—Midas betook himself, whenever he wanted to be particularly happy. Here, after carefully locking the door, he would take a bag of gold coin, or a gold cup as big as a washbowl, or a heavy golden bar, or a peck-measure of gold-dust, and bring them from the obscure corners of the room into the one bright and narrow sunbeam that fell from the dungeon-like window. He valued the sunbeam for no other reason but that his treasure would not shine without its help. And then would he reckon over the coins in the bag; toss up the bar, and catch it as it came down; sift the gold-dust through his fingers; look at the funny image of his own face, as reflected in the burnished circumference of the cup; and whisper to himself, "O Midas, rich King Midas, what a happy man art thou!" But it was laughable to see how the image of his face kept grinning at him, out of the polished surface of the cup. It seemed to be aware of his foolish behavior, and to have a naughty inclination to make fun of him.

Midas called himself a happy man, but felt that he was not yet quite so happy as he might be. The very tiptop of enjoyment would never be reached, unless the whole world were to become his treasure-room, and be filled with yellow metal which should be all his own.

Now, I need hardly remind such wise little people as you are, that in the old, old times, when King Midas was alive, a great many things came to pass, which we should consider wonderful if they were to happen in our own day and country. And, on the other hand, a great many things take place nowadays, which seem not only wonderful to us, but at which the people of old times would have stared their eyes out. On the whole, I regard our own times as the strangest of the two; but, however that may be, I must go on with my story.

Midas was enjoying himself in his treasure-room, one day, as usual, when he perceived a shadow fall over the heaps of gold; and, looking suddenly up, what should he behold but the figure of a stranger, standing in the bright and narrow sunbeam! It was a young man, with a cheerful and ruddy face. Whether it was that the imagination of King Midas threw a yellow tinge over everything, or whatever the cause might be, he could not help fancying that the smile with which the stranger regarded him had a kind of golden radiance in it. Certainly, although his figure intercepted the sunshine, there was now a brighter gleam upon all the piled-up treasures than before. Even the remotest corners had their share of it, and were lighted up, when the stranger smiled, as with tips of flame and sparkles of fire.

As Midas knew that he had carefully turned the key in the lock, and that no mortal strength could possibly break into his treasure-room, he, of course, concluded that his visitor must be something more than mortal. It is no matter about telling you who he was. In those days, when the earth was comparatively a new affair, it was supposed to be often the resort of beings endowed with supernatural power, and who used to interest themselves in the joys and sorrows of men, women, and children, half playfully and half seriously. Midas had met such beings before now, and was not sorry to meet one of them again. The stranger's aspect, indeed, was so good-humored and kindly, if not beneficent, that it would have been unreasonable to suspect him of intending any mischief. It was far more probable that he came to do Midas a favor. And what could that favor be, unless to multiply his heaps of treasure?

The stranger gazed about the room; and when his lustrous smile had glistened upon all the golden objects that were there, he turned again to Midas.

"You are a wealthy man, friend Midas!" he observed. "I doubt whether any other four walls, on earth, contain so much gold as you have contrived to pile up in this room."

"I have done pretty well,—pretty well," answered Midas, in a discontented tone. "But, after all, it is but a trifle, when you consider that it has taken me my whole life to get it together. If one could live a thousand years, he might have time to grow rich!"

"What!" exclaimed the stranger. "Then you are not satisfied?"

Midas shook his head.

"And pray what would satisfy you?" asked the stranger. "Merely for the curiosity of the thing, I should be glad to know."

Midas paused and meditated. He felt a presentiment that this stranger, with such a golden lustre in his good-humored smile, had come hither with both the power and the purpose of gratifying his utmost wishes. Now, therefore, was the fortunate moment, when he had but to speak, and obtain whatever possible, or seemingly impossible thing, it might come into his head to ask. So he thought, and thought, and thought, and heaped up one golden mountain upon another, in his imagination, without being able to imagine them big enough. At last, a bright idea occurred to King Midas. It seemed really as bright as the glistening metal which he loved so much.

Raising his head, he looked the lustrous stranger in the face.

"Well, Midas," observed his visitor, "I see that you have at length hit upon something that will satisfy you. Tell me your wish."

"It is only this," replied Midas. "I am weary of collecting my treasures with so much trouble, and beholding the heap so diminutive, after I have done my best. I wish everything that I touch to be changed to gold!"

The stranger's smile grew so very broad, that it seemed to fill the room like an outburst of the sun, gleaming into a shadowy dell, where the yellow autumnal leaves—for so looked the lumps and particles of gold—lie strewn in the glow of light.

"The Golden Touch!" exclaimed he. "You certainly deserve credit, friend Midas, for striking out so brilliant a conception. But are you quite sure that this will satisfy you?"

"How could it fail?" said Midas.

"And will you never regret the possession of it?"

"What could induce me?" asked Midas. "I ask nothing else, to render me perfectly happy."

"Be it as you wish, then," replied the stranger, waving his hand in token of farewell. "To-morrow, at sunrise, you will find yourself gifted with the Golden Touch."

The figure of the stranger then became exceedingly bright, and Midas involuntarily closed his eyes. On opening them again, he beheld only one yellow sunbeam in the room, and, all around him, the glistening of the precious metal which he had spent his life in hoarding up.

Whether Midas slept as usual that night, the story does not say. Asleep or awake, however, his mind was probably in the state of a child's, to whom a beautiful new plaything has been promised in the morning. At any rate, day had hardly peeped over the hills, when King Midas was broad awake, and, stretching his arms out of bed, began to touch the objects that were within reach. He was anxious to prove whether the Golden Touch had really come, according to the stranger's promise. So he laid his finger on a chair by the bedside, and on various other things, but was grievously disappointed to perceive that they remained of exactly the same substance as before. Indeed, he felt very much afraid that he had only dreamed about the lustrous stranger, or else that the latter had been making game of him. And what a miserable affair would it be, if, after all his hopes, Midas must content himself with what little gold he could scrape together by ordinary means, instead of creating it by a touch!

All this while, it was only the gray of the morning, with but a streak of brightness along the edge of the sky, where Midas could not see it. He lay in a very disconsolate mood, regretting the downfall of his hopes, and kept growing sadder and sadder, until the earliest sunbeam shone through the window, and gilded the ceiling over his head. It seemed to Midas that this bright yellow sunbeam was reflected in rather a singular way on the white covering of the bed. Looking more closely, what was his astonishment and delight, when he found that this linen fabric had been transmuted to what seemed a woven texture of the purest and brightest gold! The Golden Touch had come to him with the first sunbeam!

Midas started up, in a kind of joyful frenzy, and ran about the room, grasping at everything that happened to be in his way. He seized one of the bed-posts, and it became immediately a fluted golden pillar. He pulled aside a window-curtain, in order to admit a clear spectacle of the wonders which he was performing; and the tassel grew heavy in his hand,—a mass of gold.

He took up a book from the table. At his first touch, it assumed the appearance of such a splendidly bound and gilt-edged volume as one often meets with, nowadays; but, on running his fingers through the leaves, behold! it was a bundle of thin golden plates, in which all the wisdom of the book had grown illegible. He hurriedly put on his clothes, and was enraptured to see himself in a magnificent suit of gold cloth, which retained its flexibility and softness, although it burdened him a little with its weight. He drew out his handkerchief, which little Marygold had hemmed for him. That was likewise gold, with the dear child's neat and pretty stitches running all along the border, in gold thread!

Somehow or other, this last transformation did not quite please King Midas. He would rather that his little daughter's handiwork should have remained just the same as when she climbed his knee and put it into his hand.

But it was not worth while to vex himself about a trifle. Midas now took his spectacles from his pocket, and put them on his nose, in order that he might see more distinctly what he was about. In those days, spectacles for common people had not been invented, but were already worn by kings; else, how could Midas have had any? To his great perplexity, however, excellent as the glasses were, he discovered that he could not possibly see through them. But this was the most natural thing in the world; for, on taking them off, the transparent crystal turned out to be plates of yellow metal, and, of course, were worthless as spectacles, though valuable as gold. It struck Midas as rather inconvenient that, with all his wealth, he could never again be rich enough to own a pair of serviceable spectacles.

"It is no great matter, nevertheless," said he to himself, very philosophically. "We cannot expect any great good, without its being accompanied with some small inconvenience. The Golden Touch is worth the sacrifice of a pair of spectacles, at least, if not of one's very eyesight. My own eyes will serve for ordinary purposes, and little Marygold will soon be old enough to read to me."

Wise King Midas was so exalted by his good fortune, that the palace seemed not sufficiently spacious to contain him. He therefore went downstairs, and smiled, on observing that the balustrade of the staircase became a bar of burnished gold, as his hand passed over it, in his descent. He lifted the door-latch (it was brass only a moment ago, but golden when his fingers quitted it), and emerged into the garden. Here, as it happened, he found a great number of beautiful roses in full bloom, and others in all the stages of lovely bud and blossom. Very delicious was their fragrance in the morning breeze. Their delicate blush was one of the fairest sights in the world; so gentle, so modest, and so full of sweet tranquillity, did these roses seem to be.

But Midas knew a way to make them far more precious, according to his way of thinking, than roses had ever been before. So he took great pains in going from bush to bush, and exercised his magic touch most indefatigably; until every individual flower and bud, and even the worms at the heart of some of them, were changed to gold. By the time this good work was completed, King Midas was summoned to breakfast; and as the morning air had given him an excellent appetite, he made haste back to the palace.

What was usually a king's breakfast in the days of Midas, I really do not know, and cannot stop now to investigate. To the best of my belief, however, on this particular morning, the breakfast consisted of hot cakes, some nice little brook trout, roasted potatoes, fresh boiled eggs, and coffee, for King Midas himself, and a bowl of bread and milk for his daughter Marygold. At all events, this is a breakfast fit to set before a king; and, whether he had it or not, King Midas could not have had a better.

Little Marygold had not yet made her appearance. Her father ordered her to be called, and, seating himself at table, awaited the child's coming, in order to begin his own breakfast. To do Midas justice, he really loved his daughter, and loved her so much the more this morning, on account of the good fortune which had befallen him. It was not a great while before he heard her coming along the passageway crying bitterly. This circumstance surprised him, because Marygold was one of the cheerfullest little people whom you would see in a summer's day, and

hardly shed a thimbleful of tears in a twelvemonth. When Midas heard her sobs, he determined to put little Marygold into better spirits, by an agreeable surprise; so, leaning across the table, he touched his daughter's bowl (which was a China one, with pretty figures all around it), and transmuted it to gleaming gold.

Meanwhile, Marygold slowly and disconsolately opened the door, and showed herself with her apron at her eyes, still sobbing as if her heart would break.

"How now, my little lady!" cried Midas. "Pray what is the matter with you, this bright morning?"

Marygold, without taking the apron from her eyes, held out her hand, in which was one of the roses which Midas had so recently transmuted.

"Beautiful!" exclaimed her father. "And what is there in this magnificent golden rose to make you cry?"

"Ah, dear father!" answered the child, as well as her sobs would let her; "it is not beautiful, but the ugliest flower that ever grew! As soon as I was dressed I ran into the garden to gather some roses for you; because I know you like them, and like them the better when gathered by your little daughter. But, oh dear, dear me! What do you think has happened? Such a misfortune! All the beautiful roses, that smelled so sweetly and had so many lovely blushes, are blighted and spoilt! They are grown quite yellow, as you see this one, and have no longer any fragrance! What can have been the matter with them?"

"Poh, my dear little girl,—pray don't cry about it!" said Midas, who was ashamed to confess that he himself had wrought the change which so greatly afflicted her. "Sit down and eat your bread and milk! You will find it easy enough to exchange a golden rose like that (which will last hundreds of years) for an ordinary one which would wither in a day."

"I don't care for such roses as this!" cried Marygold, tossing it contemptuously away. "It has no smell, and the hard petals prick my nose!"

The child now sat down to table, but was so occupied with her grief for the blighted roses that she did not even notice the wonderful transmutation of her China bowl. Perhaps this was all the better; for Marygold was accustomed to take pleasure in looking at the queer figures, and strange trees and houses, that were painted on the circumference of the bowl; and these ornaments were now entirely lost in the yellow hue of the metal.

Midas, meanwhile, had poured out a cup of coffee, and, as a matter of course, the coffee-pot, whatever metal it may have been when he took it up, was gold when he set it down. He thought to himself, that it was rather an extravagant style of splendor, in a king of his simple habits, to breakfast off a service of gold, and began to be puzzled with the difficulty of keeping his treasures safe. The cupboard and the kitchen would no longer be a secure place of deposit for articles so valuable as golden bowls and coffee-pots.

Amid these thoughts, he lifted a spoonful of coffee to his lips, and, sipping it, was astonished to perceive that, the instant his lips touched the liquid, it became molten gold, and, the next moment, hardened into a lump!

"Ha!" exclaimed Midas, rather aghast.

"What is the matter, father?" asked little Marygold, gazing at him, with the tears still standing in her eyes.

"Nothing, child, nothing!" said Midas. "Eat your milk, before it gets quite cold."

He took one of the nice little trouts on his plate, and, by way of experiment, touched its tail with his finger. To his horror, it was immediately transmuted from an admirably fried brook-trout into a gold-fish, though not one of those gold-fishes which people often keep in glass globes, as ornaments for the parlor. No; but it was really a metallic fish, and looked as if it had been very cunningly made by the nicest goldsmith in the world. Its little bones were now golden wires; its fins and tail were thin plates of gold; and there were the marks of the fork in it, and all the delicate, frothy appearance of a nicely fried fish, exactly imitated in metal. A very pretty piece of work, as you may suppose; only King Midas, just at that moment, would much rather have had a real trout in his dish than this elaborate and valuable imitation of one.

"I don't quite see," thought he to himself, "how I am to get any breakfast."

He took one of the smoking-hot cakes, and had scarcely broken it, when, to his cruel mortification, though, a moment before, it had been of the whitest wheat, it assumed the yellow hue of Indian meal. To say the truth, if it had really been a hot Indian cake, Midas would have prized it a good deal more than he now did, when its solidity and increased weight made him too bitterly sensible that it was gold. Almost in despair, he helped himself to a boiled egg, which immediately underwent a change similar to those of the trout and the cake. The egg, indeed, might have been mistaken for one of those which the famous goose, in the story-book, was in the habit of laying; but King Midas was the only goose that had anything to do with the matter.

"Well, this is a quandary!" thought he, leaning back in his chair, and looking quite enviously at little Marygold, who was now eating her bread and milk with great satisfaction. "Such a costly breakfast before me, and nothing that can be eaten!"

Hoping that, by dint of great dispatch, he might avoid what he now felt to be a considerable inconvenience, King Midas next snatched a hot potato, and attempted to cram it into his mouth, and swallow it in a hurry. But the Golden Touch was too nimble for him. He found his mouth full, not of mealy potato, but of solid metal, which so burnt his tongue that he roared aloud, and, jumping up from the table, began to dance and stamp about the room, both with pain and affright.

"Father, dear father!" cried little Marygold, who was a very affectionate child, "pray what is the matter? Have you burnt your mouth?"

"Ah, dear child," groaned Midas, dolefully, "I don't know what is to become of your poor father!"

And, truly, my dear little folks, did you ever hear of such a pitiable case in all your lives? Here was literally the richest breakfast that could be set before a king, and its very richness made it absolutely good for nothing. The poorest laborer, sitting down to his crust of bread and cup of water, was far better off than King Midas, whose delicate food was really worth its weight in gold. And what was to be done? Already, at breakfast, Midas was excessively hungry. Would he be less so by dinner time? And how ravenous would be his appetite for supper, which must undoubtedly consist of the same sort of indigestible dishes as those now before him! How many days, think you, would he survive a continuance of this rich fare?

These reflections so troubled wise King Midas, that he began to doubt whether, after all, riches are the one desirable thing in the world, or even the most desirable. But this was only a passing thought. So fascinated was Midas with the glitter of the yellow metal, that he would still have refused to give up the Golden Touch for so paltry a consideration as a breakfast. Just imagine what a price for one meal's victuals! It would have been the same as paying millions and millions of money (and as many millions more as would take forever to reckon up) for some fried trout, an egg, a potato, a hot cake, and a cup of coffee!

"It would be quite too dear," thought Midas.

Nevertheless, so great was his hunger, and the perplexity of his situation, that he again groaned aloud, and very grievously too. Our pretty Marygold could endure it no longer. She sat, a moment, gazing at her father, and trying, with all the might of her little wits, to find out what was the matter with him. Then, with a sweet and sorrowful impulse to comfort him, she started from her chair, and, running to Midas, threw her arms affectionately about his knees. He bent down and kissed her. He felt that his little daughter's love was worth a thousand times more than he had gained by the Golden Touch.

"My precious, precious Marygold!" cried he.

But Marygold made no answer.

Alas, what had he done? How fatal was the gift which the stranger bestowed! The moment the lips of Midas touched Marygold's forehead, a change had taken place. Her sweet, rosy face, so full of affection as it had been, assumed a glittering yellow color, with yellow tear-drops congealing on her cheeks. Her beautiful brown ringlets

took the same tint. Her soft and tender little form grew hard and inflexible within her father's encircling arms. Oh, terrible misfortune! The victim of his insatiable desire for wealth, little Marygold was a human child no longer, but a golden statue!

Yes, there she was, with the questioning look of love, grief, and pity, hardened into her face. It was the prettiest and most woeful sight that ever mortal saw. All the features and tokens of Marygold were there; even the beloved little dimple remained in her golden chin. But the more perfect was the resemblance, the greater was the father's agony at beholding this golden image, which was all that was left him of a daughter. It had been a favorite phrase of Midas, whenever he felt particularly fond of the child, to say that she was worth her weight in gold. And now the phrase had become literally true. And now, at last, when it was too late, he felt how infinitely a warm and tender heart, that loved him, exceeded in value all the wealth that could be piled up betwixt the earth and sky!

It would be too sad a story, if I were to tell you how Midas, in the fullness of all his gratified desires, began to wring his hands and bemoan himself; and how he could neither bear to look at Marygold, nor yet to look away from her. Except when his eyes were fixed on the image, he could not possibly believe that she was changed to gold. But, stealing another glance, there was the precious little figure, with a yellow tear-drop on its yellow cheek, and a look so piteous and tender, that it seemed as if that very expression must needs soften the gold, and make it flesh again. This, however, could not be. So Midas had only to wring his hands, and to wish that he were the poorest man in the wide world, if the loss of all his wealth might bring back the faintest rose-color to his dear child's face.

While he was in this tumult of despair, he suddenly beheld a stranger standing near the door. Midas bent down his head, without speaking; for he recognized the same figure which had appeared to him, the day before, in the treasure-room, and had bestowed on him this disastrous faculty of the Golden Touch. The stranger's countenance still wore a smile, which seemed to shed a yellow lustre all about the room, and gleamed on little Marygold's image, and on the other objects that had been transmuted by the touch of Midas.

"Well, friend Midas," said the stranger, "pray how do you succeed with the Golden Touch?"

Midas shook his head.

"I am very miserable," said he.

"Very miserable, indeed!" exclaimed the stranger. "And how happens that? Have I not faithfully kept my promise with you? Have you not everything that your heart desired?"

"Gold is not everything," answered Midas. "And I have lost all that my heart really cared for."

"Ah! So you have made a discovery, since yesterday?" observed the stranger. "Let us see, then. Which of these two things do you think is really worth the most,—the gift of the Golden Touch, or one cup of clear cold water?"

"O blessed water!" exclaimed Midas. "It will never moisten my parched throat again!"

"The Golden Touch," continued the stranger, "or a crust of bread?"

"A piece of bread," answered Midas, "is worth all the gold on earth!"

"The Golden Touch," asked the stranger, "or your own little Marygold, warm, soft, and loving as she was an hour ago?"

"Oh, my child, my dear child!" cried poor Midas, wringing his hands. "I would not have given that one small dimple in her chin for the power of changing this whole big earth into a solid lump of gold!"

"You are wiser than you were, King Midas!" said the stranger, looking seriously at him. "Your own heart, I perceive, has not been entirely changed from flesh to gold. Were it so, your case would indeed be desperate. But you appear to be still capable of understanding that the commonest things, such as lie within everybody's grasp, are more valuable than the riches which so many mortals sigh and struggle after. Tell me, now, do you sincerely desire to rid yourself of this Golden Touch?"

"It is hateful to me!" replied Midas.

A fly settled on his nose, but immediately fell to the floor; for it, too, had become gold. Midas shuddered.

"Go, then," said the stranger, "and plunge into the river that glides past the bottom of your garden. Take likewise a vase of the same water, and sprinkle it over any object that you may desire to change back again from gold into its former substance. If you do this in earnestness and sincerity, it may possibly repair the mischief which your avarice has occasioned."

King Midas bowed low; and when he lifted his head, the lustrous stranger had vanished.

You will easily believe that Midas lost no time in snatching up a great earthen pitcher (but, alas me! it was no longer earthen after he touched it), and hastening to the river-side. As he scampered along, and forced his way through the shrubbery, it was positively marvelous to see how the foliage turned yellow behind him, as if the autumn had been there, and nowhere else. On reaching the river's brink, he plunged headlong in, without waiting so much as to pull off his shoes.

"Poof! poof! poof!" snorted King Midas, as his head emerged out of the water. "Well; this is really a refreshing bath, and I think it must have quite washed away the Golden Touch. And now for filling my pitcher!"

As he dipped the pitcher into the water, it gladdened his very heart to see it change from gold into the same good, honest earthen vessel which it had been before he touched it. He was conscious, also, of a change within himself. A cold, hard, and heavy weight seemed to have gone out of his bosom. No doubt, his heart had been gradually losing its human substance, and transmuting itself into insensible metal, but had now softened back again into flesh. Perceiving a violet, that grew on the bank of the river, Midas touched it with his finger, and was overjoyed to find that the delicate flower retained its purple hue, instead of undergoing a yellow blight. The curse of the Golden Touch had, therefore, really been removed from him.

King Midas hastened back to the palace; and, I suppose, the servants knew not what to make of it when they saw their royal master so carefully bringing home an earthen pitcher of water. But that water, which was to undo all the mischief that his folly had wrought, was more precious to Midas than an ocean of molten gold could have been. The first thing he did, as you need hardly be told, was to sprinkle it by handfuls over the golden figure of little Marygold.

No sooner did it fall on her than you would have laughed to see how the rosy color came back to the dear child's cheek! and how she began to sneeze and sputter!—and how astonished she was to find herself dripping wet, and her father still throwing more water over her!

"Pray do not, dear father!" cried she. "See how you have wet my nice frock, which I put on only this morning!"

For Marygold did not know that she had been a little golden statue; nor could she remember anything that had happened since the moment when she ran with outstretched arms to comfort poor King Midas.

Her father did not think it necessary to tell his beloved child how very foolish he had been, but contented himself with showing how much wiser he had now grown. For this purpose, he led little Marygold into the garden, where he sprinkled all the remainder of the water over the rose-bushes, and with such good effect that above five thousand roses recovered their beautiful bloom. There were two circumstances, however, which, as long as he lived, used to put King Midas in mind of the Golden Touch. One was, that the sands of the river sparkled like gold; the other, that little Marygold's hair had now a golden tinge, which he had never observed in it before she had been transmuted by the effect of his kiss. This change of hue was really an improvement, and made Marygold's hair richer than in her babyhood.

When King Midas had grown quite an old man, and used to trot Marygold's children on his knee, he was fond of telling them this marvelous story, pretty much as I have now told it to you. And then would he stroke their glossy ringlets, and tell them that their hair, likewise, had a rich shade of gold, which they had inherited from their mother.

"And to tell you the truth, my precious little folks," quoth King Midas, diligently trotting the children all the while, "ever since that morning, I have hated the very sight of all other gold, save this!"

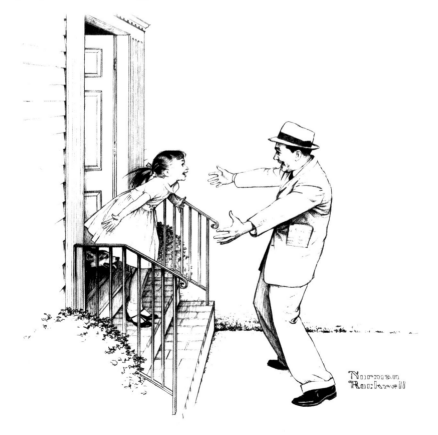

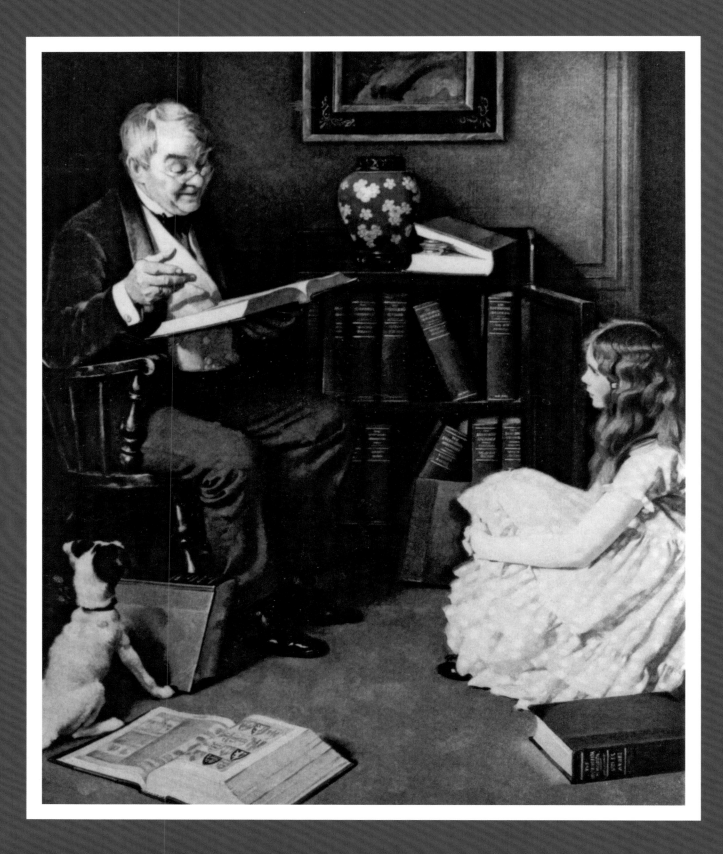

Playing Pilgrims

from *Little Women*

Louisa May Alcott

"CHRISTMAS WON'T BE Christmas without any presents," grumbled Jo, lying on the rug.

"It's so dreadful to be poor!" sighed Meg, looking down at her old dress.

"I don't think it's fair for some girls to have plenty of pretty things, and other girls nothing at all," added little Amy, with an injured sniff.

"We've got Father and Mother, and each other," said Beth contentedly from her corner.

The four young faces on which the firelight shone brightened at the cheerful words, but darkened again as Jo said sadly, "We haven't got Father, and shall not have him for a long time." She didn't say "perhaps never," but each silently added it, thinking of Father far away, where the fighting was.

Nobody spoke for a minute; then Meg said in an altered tone, "You know the reason Mother proposed not having any presents this Christmas was because it is going to be a hard winter for everyone; and she thinks we ought not to spend money for pleasure, when our men are suffering so in the army. We can't do much, but we can make our little sacrifices, and ought to do it gladly. But I am afraid I don't." And Meg shook her head, as she thought regretfully of all the pretty things she wanted.

"But I don't think the little we should spend would do any good. We've each got a dollar, and the army wouldn't be much helped by our giving that. I agree not to expect anything from Mother or you, but I do want to buy *Undine and Sintram* for myself. I've wanted it so long," said Jo, who was a bookworm.

"I planned to spend mine in new music," said Beth, with a little sigh, which no one heard but the hearth brush and kettle holder.

"I shall get a nice box of Faber's drawing pencils. I really need them," said Amy decidedly.

"Mother didn't say anything about our money, and she won't wish us to give up everything. Let's each buy what we want, and have a little fun. I'm sure we work hard enough to earn it," cried Jo, examining the heels of her shoes in a gentlemanly manner.

"I know I do—teaching those tiresome children nearly all day, when I'm longing to enjoy myself at home," began Meg, in the complaining tone again.

"You don't have half such a hard time as I do," said Jo. "How would you like to be shut up for hours with a nervous, fussy old lady, who keeps you trotting, is never satisfied, and worries you till you're ready to fly out the window or cry?"

"It's naughty to fret, but I do think washing dishes and keeping things tidy is the worst work in the world. It makes me cross, and my hands get so stiff, I can't practice well at all." And Beth looked at her rough hands with a sigh that any one could hear that time.

"I don't believe any of you suffer as I do," cried Amy, "for you don't have to go to school with impertinent girls, who plague you if you don't know your lessons, and laugh at your dresses, and label your father if he isn't rich, and insult you when your nose isn't nice."

"If you mean *libel*, I'd say so, and not talk about *labels*, as if Papa was a pickle bottle," advised Jo, laughing.

"I know what I mean, and you needn't be *statirical* about it. It's proper to use good words, and improve your *vocabilary*," returned Amy, with dignity.

"Don't peck at one another, children. Don't you wish we had the money Papa lost when we were little, Jo? Dear me! How happy and good we'd be, if we had no worries!" said Meg, who could remember better times.

"You said the other day you thought we were a deal happier than the King children, for they were fighting and fretting all the time, in spite of their money."

"So I did, Beth. Well, I think we are. For though we do have to work, we make fun of ourselves, and are a pretty jolly set, as Jo would say."

"Jo does use such slang words!" observed Amy, with a reproving look at the long figure stretched on the rug.

Jo immediately sat up, put her hands in her pockets, and began to whistle.

"Don't, Jo. It's so boyish!"

"That's why I do it."

"I detest rude, unladylike girls!"

"I hate affected, niminy-piminy chits!"

"Birds in their little nests agree," sang Beth, the peacemaker, with such a funny face that both sharp voices softened to a laugh, and the "pecking" ended for that time.

"Really, girls, you are both to be blamed," said Meg, beginning to lecture in her elder-sisterly fashion. "You are old enough to leave off boyish tricks, and to behave better, Josephine. It didn't matter so much when you were a little girl, but now you are so tall, and turn up your hair, you should remember that you are a young lady."

"I'm not! And if turning up my hair makes me one, I'll wear it in two tails till I'm twenty," cried Jo, pulling off her net, and shaking down a chestnut mane. "I hate to think I've got to grow up, and be Miss March, and wear long gowns, and look as prim as a China Aster! It's bad enough to be a girl, anyway, when I like boy's games and work and manners! I can't get over my disappointment in not being a boy. And it's worse than ever now, for I'm dying to go and fight with Papa. And I can only stay home and knit, like a poky old woman!"

And Jo shook the blue army sock till the needles rattled like castanets, and her ball bounded across the room.

"Poor Jo! It's too bad, but it can't be helped. So you must try to be contented with making your name boyish, and playing brother to us girls," said Beth, stroking the rough head with a hand that all the dish washing and dusting in the world could not make ungentle in its touch.

"As for you, Amy," continued Meg, "you are altogether too particular and prim. Your airs are funny now, but you'll grow up an affected little goose, if you don't take care. I like your nice manners and refined ways of speaking, when you don't try to be elegant. But your absurd words are as bad as Jo's slang."

"If Jo is a tomboy and Amy a goose, what am I, please?" asked Beth, ready to share the lecture.

"You're a dear, and nothing else," answered Meg warmly, and no one contradicted her, for the "Mouse" was the pet of the family.

As young readers like to know "how people look," we will take this moment to give them a little sketch of the four sisters, who sat knitting away in the twilight, while the December snow fell quietly without, and the fire crackled cheerfully within. It was a comfortable room, though the carpet was faded and the furniture very plain, for a good picture or two hung on the walls, books filled the recesses, chrysanthemums and Christmas roses

bloomed in the windows, and a pleasant atmosphere of home peace pervaded it.

Margaret, the eldest of the four, was sixteen, and very pretty, being plump and fair, with large eyes, plenty of soft brown hair, a sweet mouth, and white hands, of which she was rather vain. Fifteen-year-old Jo was very tall, thin, and brown, and reminded one of a colt, for she never seemed to know what to do with her long limbs, which were very much in her way. She had a decided mouth, a comical nose, and sharp, gray eyes, which appeared to see everything, and were by turns fierce, funny, or thoughtful. Her long, thick hair was her one beauty, but it was usually bundled into a net, to be out of her way. Round shoulders had Jo, big hands and feet, a fly-away look to her clothes, and the uncomfortable appearance of a girl who was rapidly shooting up into a woman and didn't like it. Elizabeth, or Beth, as everyone called her, was a rosy, smooth-haired, bright-eyed girl of thirteen, with a shy manner, a timid voice, and a peaceful expression which was seldom disturbed. Her father called her "Little Miss Tranquillity," and the name suited her excellently, for she seemed to live in a happy world of her own, only venturing out to meet the few whom she trusted and loved. Amy, though the youngest, was a most important person, in her own opinion at least. A regular snow maiden, with blue eyes, and yellow hair curling on her shoulders, pale and slender, and always carrying herself like a young lady mindful of her manners. What the characters of the four sisters were we will leave to be found out.

The clock struck six and, having swept up the hearth, Beth put a pair of slippers down to warm. Somehow the sight of the old shoes had a good effect upon the girls, for Mother was coming, and everyone brightened to welcome her. Meg stopped lecturing, and lighted the lamp, Amy got out of the easy chair without being asked, and Jo forgot how tired she was as she sat up to hold the slippers nearer to the blaze.

"They are quite worn out. Marmee must have a new pair."

"I thought I'd get her some with my dollar," said Beth.

"No, I shall!" cried Amy.

"I'm the oldest," began Meg, but Jo cut in with a decided—

"I'm the man of the family now Papa is away, and I shall provide the slippers, for he told me to take special care of Mother while he was gone."

"I'll tell you what we'll do," said Beth, "let's each get her something for Christmas, and not get anything for ourselves."

"That's like you, dear! What will we get?" exclaimed Jo.

Everyone thought soberly for a minute, then Meg announced, as if the idea was suggested by the sight of her own pretty hands, "I shall give her a nice pair of gloves."

"Army shoes, best to be had," cried Jo.

"Some handkerchiefs, all hemmed," said Beth.

"I'll get a little bottle of cologne. She likes it, and it won't cost much, so I'll have some left to buy my pencils," added Amy.

"How will we give the things?" asked Meg.

"Put them on the table, and bring her in and see her open the bundles. Don't you remember how we used to do on our birthdays?" answered Jo.

"I used to be so frightened when it was my turn to sit in the chair with the crown on, and see you all come marching round to give the presents, with a kiss. I liked the things and the kisses, but it was dreadful to have you sit looking at me while I opened the bundles," said Beth, who was toasting her face and the bread for tea at the same time.

"Let Marmee think we are getting things for ourselves, and then surprise her. We must go shopping tomorrow afternoon, Meg. There is so much to do about the play for Christmas night," said Jo, marching up and down, with her hands behind her back, and her nose in the air.

"I don't mean to act any more after this time. I'm getting too old for such things," observed Meg, who was as much a child as ever about "dressing-up" frolics.

"You won't stop, I know, as long as you can trail round in a white gown with your hair down, and wear gold-paper jewelry. You are the best actress we've got, and there'll be an end of everything if you quit the boards," said Jo. "We

ought to rehearse tonight. Come here, Amy, and do the fainting scene, for you are as stiff as a poker in that."

"I can't help it. I never saw anyone faint, and I don't choose to make myself all black and blue, tumbling flat as you do. If I can go down easily, I'll drop. If I can't, I shall fall into a chair and be graceful. I don't care if Hugo does come at me with a pistol," returned Amy, who was not gifted with dramatic power, but was chosen because she was small enough to be borne out shrieking by the villain of the piece.

"Do it this way. Clasp your hands so, and stagger across the room, crying frantically, 'Roderigo! save me! save me!'" and away went Jo, with a melodramatic scream which was truly thrilling.

Amy followed, but she poked her hands out stiffly before her, and jerked herself along as if she went by machinery, and her "Ow!" was more suggestive of pins being run into her than of fear and anguish. Jo gave a despairing groan, and Meg laughed outright, while Beth let her bread burn as she watched the fun with interest.

"It's no use! Do the best you can when the time comes, and if the audience laughs, don't blame me. Come on, Meg."

Then things went smoothly, for Don Pedro defied the world in a speech of two pages without a single break. Hagar, the witch, chanted an awful incantation over her kettleful of simmering toads, with weird effect. Roderigo rent his chains asunder manfully, and Hugo died in agonies of remorse and arsenic, with a wild, "Ha! ha!"

"It's the best we've had yet," said Meg, as the dead villain sat up and rubbed his elbows.

"I don't see how you can write and act such splendid things, Jo. You're a regular Shakespeare!" exclaimed Beth, who firmly believed that her sisters were gifted with wonderful genius in all things.

"Not quite," replied Jo modestly. "I do think *The Witches Curse, an Operatic Tragedy* is rather a nice thing, but I'd like to try *Macbeth*, if we only had a trapdoor for Banquo. I always wanted to do the killing part. 'Is that a dagger that I see before me?'" muttered Jo, rolling her eyes and clutching at the air, as she had seen a famous tragedian do.

"No, it's the toasting fork, with Mother's shoe on it instead of the bread. Beth's stage-struck!" cried Meg, and the rehearsal ended in a general burst of laughter.

"Glad to find you so merry, my girls," said a cheery voice at the door, and actors and audience turned to welcome a tall, motherly lady with a "can I help you" look about her which was truly delightful. She was not elegantly dressed, but a noble-looking woman, and the girls thought the gray cloak and unfashionable bonnet covered the most splendid mother in the world.

"Well, dearies, how have you got on today? There was so much to do, getting the boxes ready to go tomorrow, that I didn't come home to dinner. Has anyone called, Beth? How is your cold, Meg? Jo, you look tired to death. Come and kiss me, baby."

While making these maternal inquiries Mrs. March got her wet things off, her warm slippers on, and sitting down in the easy chair, drew Amy to her lap, preparing to enjoy the happiest hour of her busy day. The girls flew about, trying to make things comfortable, each in her own way. Meg arranged the tea table, Jo brought wood and set chairs, dropping, overturning, and clattering everything she touched. Beth trotted to and fro between parlor kitchen, quiet and busy, while Amy gave directions to everyone, as she sat with her hands folded.

As they gathered about the table, Mrs. March said, with a particularly happy face, "I've got a treat for you after supper."

A quick, bright smile went round like a streak of sunshine. Beth clapped her hands, regardless of the biscuit she held, and Jo tossed up her napkin, crying, "A letter! A letter! Three cheers for Father!"

"Yes, a nice long letter. He is well, and thinks he shall get through the cold season better than we feared. He sends all sorts of loving wishes for Christmas, and an especial message to you girls," said Mrs. March, patting her pocket as if she had got a treasure there.

"Hurry and get done! Don't stop to quirk your little finger and simper over your plate, Amy," cried Jo, choking on her tea and dropping her bread, butter side down, on the carpet in her haste to get at the treat.

Beth ate no more, but crept away to sit in her shadowy corner and brood over the delight to come, till the others were ready.

"I think it was so splendid in Father to go as chaplain when he was too old to be drafted, and not strong enough for a soldier," said Meg warmly.

"Don't I wish I could go as a drummer, a *vivan*—what's its name? Or a nurse, so I could be near him and help him," exclaimed Jo, with a groan.

"It must be very disagreeable to sleep in a tent, and eat all sorts of bad-tasting things, and drink out of a tin mug," sighed Amy.

"When will he come home, Marmee?" asked Beth, with a little quiver in her voice.

"Not for many months, dear, unless he is sick. He will stay and do his work faithfully as long as he can, and we won't ask for him back a minute sooner than he can be spared. Now come and hear the letter."

They all drew to the fire, Mother in the big chair with Beth at her feet, Meg and Amy perched on either arm of the chair, and Jo leaning on the back, where no one would see any sign of emotion if the letter should happen to be touching. Very few letters were written in those hard times that were not touching, especially those which fathers sent home. In this one little was said of the hardships endured, the dangers faced, or the homesickness conquered. It was a cheerful, hopeful letter, full of lively descriptions of camp life, marches, and military news, and only at the end did the writer's heart over-flow with fatherly love and longing for the little girls at home.

"Give them all of my dear love and a kiss. Tell them I think of them by day, pray for them by night, and find my best comfort in their affection at all times. A year seems very long to wait before I see them, but remind them that while we wait we may all work, so that these hard days need not be wasted. I know they will remember all I said to them, that they will be loving children to you, will do their duty faithfully, fight their bosom enemies bravely, and conquer themselves so beautifully that when I come back to them I may be fonder and prouder than ever of my little women."

Everybody sniffed when they came to that part. Jo wasn't ashamed of the great tear that dropped off the end of her nose, and Amy never minded the rumpling of her curls as she hid her face on her mother's shoulder and sobbed out, "I *am* a selfish girl! But I'll truly try to be better, so he mayn't be disappointed in me by-and-by."

"We all will!" cried Meg. "I think too much of my looks and hate to work, but won't any more, if I can help it."

"I'll try and be what he loves to call me, 'a little woman,' and not be rough and wild, but do my duty here instead of wanting to be somewhere else," said Jo, thinking that keeping her temper at home was a much harder task than facing a rebel or two down South.

Beth said nothing, but wiped away her tears with the blue army sock and began to knit with all her might, losing no time in doing the duty that lay nearest her, while she resolved in her quiet little soul to be all that Father hoped to find her when the year brought round the happy coming home.

Mrs. March broke the silence that followed Jo's words, by saying in her cheery voice, "Do you remember how you used to play Pilgrim's Progress when you were little things? Nothing delighted you more than to have me tie my piece bags on your backs for burdens, give you hats and sticks and rolls of paper, and let you travel through the house from the cellar, which was the City of Destruction, up, up, to the housetop, where you had all the lovely things you could collect to make a Celestial City."

"What fun it was, especially going by the lions, fighting Apollyon, and passing through the valley where the hobgoblins were!" said Jo.

"I liked the place where the bundles fell off and tumbled downstairs," said Meg.

"I don't remember much about it, except that I was afraid of the cellar and the dark entry, and always liked the cake and milk we had up at the top. If I wasn't too old for such things, I'd rather like to play it over again," said Amy, who began to talk of renouncing childish things at the mature age of twelve.

"We never are too old for this, my dear, because it is a play we are playing all the time in one way or another. Out burdens are here, our road is before us, and the longing for goodness and happiness is the guide that leads us through many troubles and mistakes to the peace which is a true Celestial City. Now, my little pilgrims, suppose you begin again, not in play, but in earnest, and see how far on you can get before Father comes home."

"Really, Mother? Where are our bundles?" asked Amy, who was a very literal young lady.

"Each of you told what your burden was just now, except Beth. I rather think she hasn't got any," said her mother.

"Yes, I have. Mine is dishes and dusters, and envying girls with nice pianos, and being afraid of people."

Beth's bundle was such a funny one that everybody wanted to laugh, but nobody did, for it would have hurt her feelings very much.

"Let us do it," said Meg thoughtfully. "It is only another name for trying to be good, and the story may help us, for though we do want to be good, it's hard work and we forget, and don't do our best."

"We were in the Slough of Despond tonight, and Mother came and pulled us out as Help did in the book. We ought to have our roll of directions, like Christian. What shall we do about that?" asked Jo, delighted with the fancy which lent a little romance to the very dull task of doing her duty.

"Look under your pillows Christmas morning, and you will find your guidebook," replied Mrs. March.

They talked over the new plan while old Hannah cleared the table, then out came the four little work baskets, and the needles flew as the girls made sheets for Aunt March. It was uninteresting sewing, but tonight no one grumbled. They adopted Jo's plan of dividing the long seams into four parts, and calling the quarters

Europe, Asia, Africa, and America, and in that way got on capitally, especially when they talked about the different countries as they stitched their way through them.

At nine they stopped work, and sang, as usual, before they went to bed. No one but Beth could get much music out of the old piano, but she had a way of softly touching the yellow keys and making a pleasant accompaniment to the simple songs they sang. Meg had a voice like a flute, and she and her mother led the little choir. Amy chirped like a cricket, and Jo wandered through the airs at her own sweet will, always coming out at the wrong place with a croak or a quaver that spoiled the most pensive tune. They had always done this from the time they could lisp . . .

Crinkle, crinkle, 'ittle 'tar, and it had become a household custom, for the mother was a born singer. The first sound in the morning was her voice as she went about the house singing like a lark, and the last sound at night was the same cheery sound, for the girls never grew too old for that familiar lullaby.

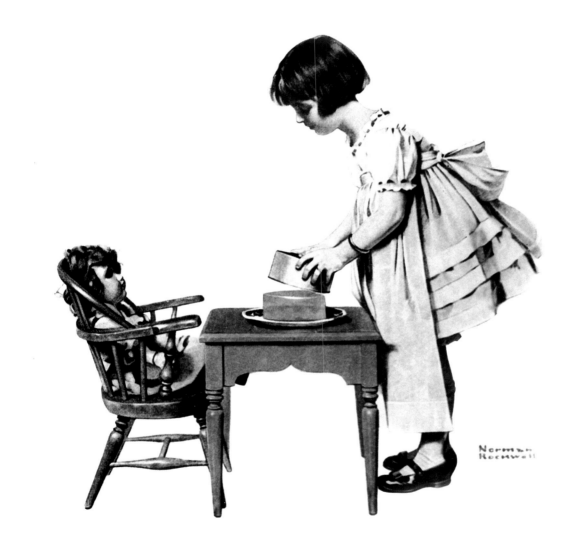

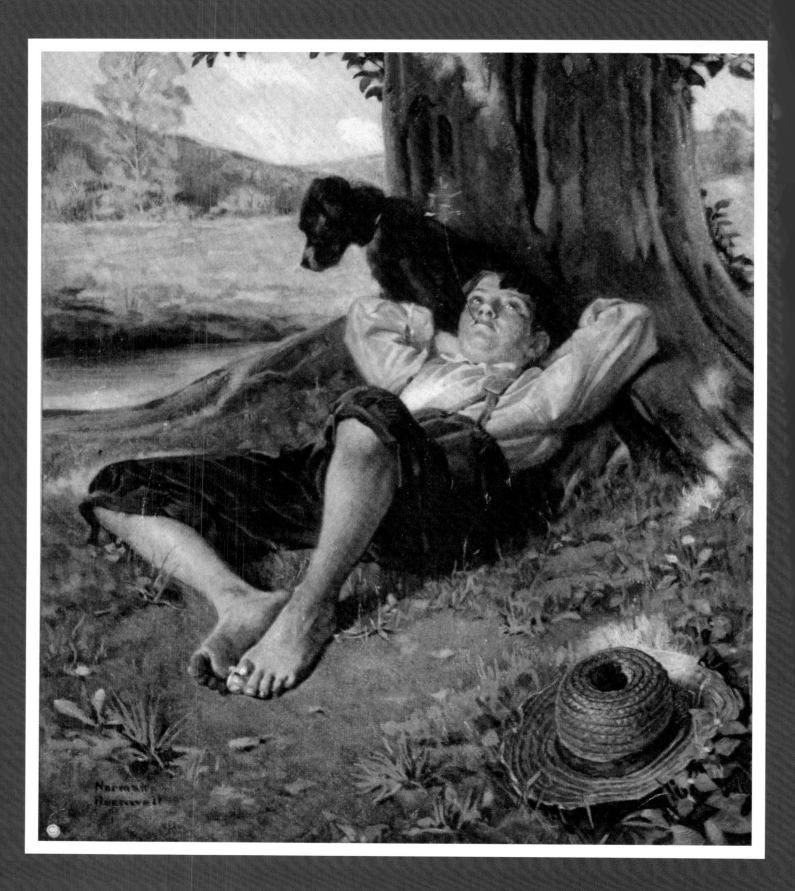

PREFACE &
TOM'S MEETING WITH THE PRINCE

from *The Prince and the Pauper*

MARK TWAIN

I WILL SET DOWN a tale as it was told to me by one who had it of his father, which latter had it of *his* father, this last having in like manner had it of *his* father—and so on, back and still back, three hundred years and more, the fathers transmitting it to the sons and so preserving it. It may be history, it may be only a legend, a tradition. It may have happened, it may not have happened: but it *could* have happened. It may be that the wise and the learned believed it in the old days; it may be that only the unlearned and the simple loved it and credited it.

* * *

Tom got up hungry, and sauntered hungry away, but with his thoughts busy with the shadowy splendors of his night's dreams. He wandered here and there in the city, hardly noticing where he was going, or what was happening around him. People jostled him, and some gave him rough speech; but it was all lost on the musing boy. By and by he found himself at Temple Bar, the farthest from home he had ever traveled in that direction. He stopped and considered a moment, then fell into his imaginings again, and passed on outside the walls of London. The Strand had ceased to be a country-road then, and regarded itself as a street, but by a strained construction; for, though there was a tolerably compact row of houses on one side of it, there were only some scattered great buildings on the other, these being palaces of rich nobles, with ample and beautiful grounds stretching to the river—grounds that are now closely packed with grim acres of brick and stone.

Tom discovered Charing Village presently, and rested himself at the beautiful cross built there by a bereaved king of earlier days; then idled down a quiet, lovely road, past the great cardinal's stately palace, toward a far more mighty and majestic palace beyond—Westminster. Tom stared in glad wonder at the vast pile of masonry, the wide-spreading wings, the frowning bastions and turrets, the huge stone gateway, with its gilded bars and its magnificent array of colossal granite lions, and other the signs and symbols of English royalty. Was the desire of his soul to be satisfied at last? Here, indeed, was a king's palace. Might he not hope to see a prince now—a prince of flesh and blood, if Heaven were willing?

At each side of the gilded gate stood a living statue— that is to say, an erect and stately and motionless man-at-arms, clad from head to heel in shining steel armor. At a respectful distance were many country folk, and people from the city, waiting for any chance glimpse of royalty that might offer. Splendid carriages, with splendid people in them and splendid servants outside, were arriving and departing by several other noble gateways that pierced the royal enclosure.

Poor little Tom, in his rags, approached, and was moving slowly and timidly past the sentinels, with a beating heart and a rising hope, when all at once he caught sight through the golden bars of a spectacle that almost made him shout for joy. Within was a comely boy, tanned and brown with sturdy outdoor sports and exercises, whose clothing was all of lovely silks and satins, shining with jewels; at his hip a little jeweled sword and dagger; dainty buskins on his feet, with red heels; and on his head a jaunty crimson cap, with drooping plumes fastened with a great sparkling gem. Several gorgeous gentlemen stood near—his servants, without a doubt. Oh! he was a prince—a prince, a living prince, a real prince— without the shadow of a question; and the prayer of the pauper-boy's heart was answered at last.

Tom's breath came quick and short with excitement, and his eyes grew big with wonder and delight. Everything gave way in his mind instantly to one desire: that was to get close to the prince, and have a good, devouring look at him. Before he knew what he was about, he had his face against the gate-bars. The next instant one of the soldiers snatched him rudely away, and sent him spinning among the gaping crowd of country gawks and London idlers. The soldier said:

"Mind thy manners, thou young beggar!"

The crowd jeered and laughed; but the young prince sprang to the gate with his face flushed, and his eyes flashing with indignation, and cried out:

"How dar'st thou use a poor lad like that? How dar'st thou use the King my father's meanest subject so? Open the gates, and let him in!"

You should have seen that fickle crowd snatch off their hats then. You should have heard them cheer, and shout, "Long live the Prince of Wales!"

The soldiers presented arms with their halberds, opened the gates, and presented again as the little Prince of Poverty passed in, in his fluttering rags, to join hands with the Prince of Limitless Plenty.

Edward Tudor said:

"Thou lookest tired and hungry: thou'st been treated ill. Come with me."

Half a dozen attendants sprang forward to—I don't know what; interfere, no doubt. But they were waved aside with a right royal gesture, and they stopped stock still where they were, like so many statues. Edward took Tom to a rich apartment in the palace, which he called his cabinet. By his command a repast was brought such as Tom had never encountered before except in books. The prince, with princely delicacy and breeding, sent away the servants, so that his humble guest might not be embarrassed by their critical presence; then he sat near by, and asked questions while Tom ate.

"What is thy name, lad?"

"Tom Canty, an' it please thee, sir."

"'Tis an odd one. Where dost live?"

"In the city, please thee, sir. Offal Court, out of Pudding Lane."

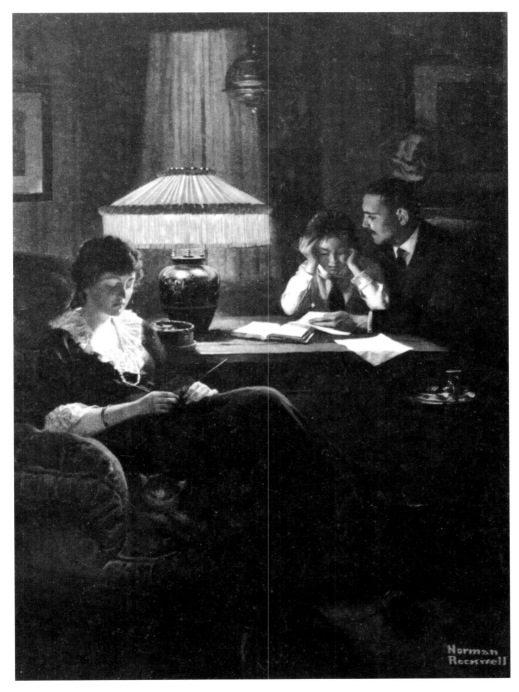

"Offal Court! Truly 'tis another odd one. Hast parents?"

"Parents have I, sir, and a grand-dam likewise that is but indifferently precious to me, God forgive me if it be offence to say it—also twin sisters, Nan and Bet."

"Then is thy grand-dam not overkind to thee, I take it?"

"Neither to any other is she, so please your worship. She hath a wicked heart, and worketh evil all her days."

"Doth she mistreat thee?"

"There be times that she stayeth her hand, being asleep or overcome with drink; but when she hath her judgment clear again, she maketh it up to me with goodly beatings."

A fierce look came into the little prince's eyes, and he cried out:

"What! Beatings?"

"Oh, indeed, yes, please you, sir."

"*Beatings!*—and thou so frail and little. Hark ye: before the night come, she shall hie her to the Tower. The King my father"—

"In sooth, you forget, sir, her low degree. The Tower is for the great alone."

"True, indeed. I had not thought of that. I will consider of her punishment. Is thy father kind to thee?"

"Not more than Gammer Canty, sir."

"Fathers be alike, mayhap. Mine hath not a doll's temper. He smiteth with a heavy hand, yet spareth me: he spareth me not always with his tongue, though, sooth to say. How doth thy mother use thee?"

"She is good, sir, and giveth me neither sorrow nor pain of any sort. And Nan and Bet are like to her in this."

"How old be these?"

"Fifteen, an' it please you, sir."

"The Lady Elizabeth, my sister, is fourteen, and the Lady Jane Grey, my cousin, is of mine own age, and comely and gracious withal; but my sister the Lady Mary, with her gloomy mien and—Look you: do thy sisters forbid their servants to smile, lest the sin destroy their souls?"

"They? Oh, dost think, sir, that *they* have servants?"

The little prince contemplated the little pauper gravely a moment, then said:

"And prithee, why not? Who helpeth them undress at night? Who attireth them when they rise?"

"None, sir. Would'st have them take off their garment, and sleep without—like the beasts?"

"Their garment! Have they but one?"

"Ah, good your worship, what would they do with more? Truly they have not two bodies each."

"It is a quaint and marvelous thought! Thy pardon, I had not meant to laugh. But thy good Nan and thy Bet shall have raiment and lackeys enow, and that soon, too: my cofferer shall look to it. No, thank me not; 'tis nothing. Thou speakest well; thou hast an easy grace in it. Art learned?"

"I know not if I am or not, sir. The good priest that is called Father Andrew taught me, of his kindness, from his books."

"Know'st thou the Latin?"

"But scantly, sir, I doubt."

"Learn it, lad: 'tis hard only at first. The Greek is harder; but neither these nor any tongues else, I think, are hard to the Lady Elizabeth and my cousin. Thou should'st hear those damsels at it! But tell me of thy Offal Court. Hast thou a pleasant life there?"

"In truth, yes, so please you, sir, save when one is hungry. There be Punch-and-Judy shows, and monkeys—oh such antic creatures! and so bravely dressed!—and there be plays wherein they that play do shout and fight till all are slain, and 'tis so fine to see, and costeth but a farthing—albeit 'tis main hard to get the farthing, please your worship."

"Tell me more."

"We lads of Offal Court do strive against each other with the cudgel, like to the fashion of the 'prentices, sometimes."

The prince's eyes flashed. Said he:

"Marry, that would not I mislike. Tell me more."

"We strive in races, sir, to see who of us shall be fleetest."

"That would I like also. Speak on."

"In summer, sir, we wade and swim in the canals and in the river, and each doth duck his neighbor, and splatter him with water, and dive and shout and tumble and—"

"'Twould be worth my father's kingdom but to enjoy it once! Prithee go on."

"We dance and sing about the Maypole in Cheapside; we play in the sand, each covering his neighbor up; and times we make mud pastry—oh the lovely mud, it hath not its like for delightfulness in all the world!—we do fairly wallow in the mud, sir, saving your worship's presence."

"Oh, prithee, say no more, 'tis glorious! If that I could but clothe me in raiment like to thine, and strip my feet, and revel in the mud once, just once, with none to rebuke me or forbid, meseemeth I could forego the crown!"

"And if that I could clothe me once, sweet sir, as thou art clad—just once—"

"Oho, would'st like it? Then so shall it be. Doff thy rags, and don these splendors, lad! It is a brief happiness, but will be not less keen for that. We will have it while we may, and change again before any come to molest."

A few minutes later the little Prince of Wales was garlanded with Tom's fluttering odds and ends, and the little Prince of Pauperdom was tricked out in the gaudy plumage of royalty. The two went and stood side by side before a great mirror, and lo, a miracle: there did not seem to have been any change made! They stared at each other, then at the glass, then at each other again. At last the puzzled princeling said:

"What dost thou make of this?"

"Ah, good your worship, require me not to answer. It is not meet that one of my degree should utter the thing."

"Then will I utter it. Thou hast the same hair, the same eyes, the same voice and manner, the same form and stature, the same face and countenance that I bear. Fared we forth naked, there is none could say which was you, and which the Prince of Wales. And, now that I am clothed as thou wert clothed, it seemeth I should be able the more nearly to feel as thou didst when the brute soldier—Hark ye, is not this a bruise upon your hand?"

"Yes; but it is a slight thing, and your worship knoweth that the poor man-at-arms—"

"Peace! It was a shameful thing and a cruel!" cried the little prince, stamping his bare foot. "If the King—Stir not a step till I come again! It is a command!"

In a moment he had snatched up and put away an article of national importance that lay upon a table, and was out at the door and flying through the palace grounds in his bannered rags, with a hot face and glowing eyes. As soon as he reached the great gate, he seized the bars, and tried to shake them, shouting:

"Open! Unbar the gates!"

The soldier that had maltreated Tom obeyed promptly; and as the prince burst through the portal, half-smothered with royal wrath, the soldier fetched him a sounding box on the ear that sent him whirling to the roadway, and said:

"Take that, thou beggar's spawn, for what thou got'st me from his Highness!"

The crowd roared with laughter. The prince picked himself out of the mud, and made fiercely at the sentry, shouting:

"I am the Prince of Wales, my person is sacred; and thou shalt hang for laying thy hand upon me!"

The soldier brought his halberd to a present-arms and said mockingly:

"I salute your gracious Highness." Then angrily, "Be off, thou crazy rubbish!"

Here the jeering crowd closed round the poor little prince, and hustled him far down the road, hooting him, and shouting, "Way for his Royal Highness! way for the Prince of Wales!"

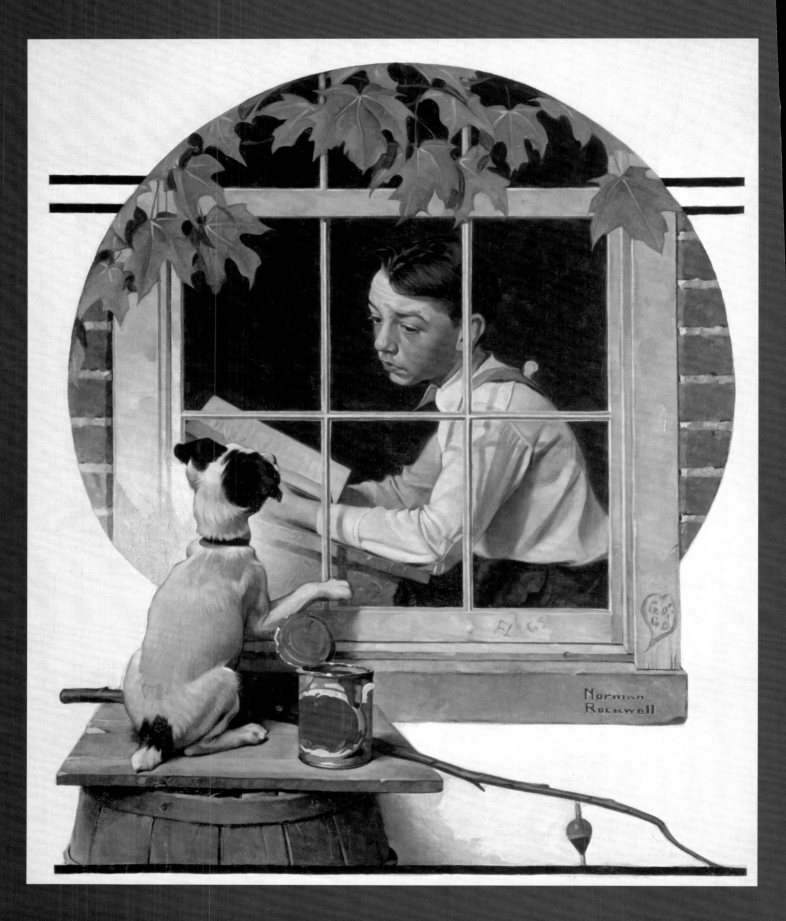

A Grand Transformation Scene

from *Vice Versa or A Lesson to Fathers*

F. Anstey

———∞∞∞———

"*MAGNAQUE numinibus vota exaudita malignis.*"

Paul Bultitude put on his glasses to examine the stone more carefully, for it was some time since he had last seen or thought about it. Then he looked up and said once more, "What use would a thing like this be to you?"

Dick would have considered it a very valuable prize indeed; he could have exhibited it to admiring friends—during lessons, of course, when it would prove a most agreeable distraction; he could have played with and fingered it incessantly, invented astonishing legends of its powers and virtues; and, at last, when he had grown tired of it, have bartered it for any more desirable article that might take his fancy. All these advantages were present to his mind in a vague shifting form, but he could not find either courage or words to explain them.

Consequently he only said awkwardly, "Oh, I don't know, I should like it."

"Well, any way," said Paul, "you certainly won't have it. It's worth keeping, whatever it is, as the only thing your uncle Marmaduke was ever known to give to anybody."

Marmaduke Paradine, his brother-in-law, was not a connection of whom he had much reason to feel particularly proud. One of those persons endowed with what are known as "insinuating manners and address," he had, after some futile attempts to enter the army, been sent out to Bombay as agent for a Manchester firm, and in that capacity had contrived to be mixed up in some more than shady transactions with rival exporters and native dealers up the country, which led to an unceremonious dismissal by his employers.

He had brought home the stone from India as a propitiatory token of remembrance, more portable and less expensive than the lacquered cabinets, brasses, stuffs and carved work which are expected from friends at such a distance, and he had been received with pardon and started once more, until certain other proceedings of his, shadier still, had obliged Paul to forbid him the house at Westbourne Terrace.

Since then little had been heard of him, and the reports which reached Mr. Bultitude of his disreputable relative's connection with the promotion of a series of companies of the kind affected by the widow and curate, and exposed in money articles and law courts, gave him no desire to renew his acquaintance.

"Isn't it a talisman, though?" said Dick, rather unfortunately for any hopes he might have of persuading his father to entrust him with the coveted treasure.

"I'm sure I can't tell you," yawned Paul, "how do you mean?"

"I don't know, only Uncle Duke once said something about it. Barbara heard him tell mamma. I say, perhaps it's like the one in Scott, and cures people of things, though I don't think it's that sort of talisman either, because I tried it once on my chilblains, and it wasn't a bit of good. If you would only let me have it, perhaps I might find out, you know."

"You might," said his father drily, apparently not much influenced by this inducement, "but you won't have the chance. If it has a secret, I will find it out for myself" (he little knew how literally he was to be taken at his word), "and, by the way, there's your cab—at last."

There was a sound of wheels outside, and, as Dick heard them, he grew desperate in his extremity; a wish he had long secretly cherished unspoken, without ever hoping for courage to give it words, rose to his lips now; he got up and moved timidly towards his father.

"Father," he said, "there's something I want to say to you so much before I go. Do let me ask you now."

"Well, what is it?" said Paul. "Make haste, you haven't much time."

"It's this. I want you to—to let me leave Grimstone's at the end of the term."

Paul stared at him, angry and incredulous, "Let you leave Dr. Grimstone's (oblige me by giving him his full title when you speak of him)," he said slowly. "Why, what do you mean? It's an excellent school—never saw a better expressed prospectus in my life. And my old friend Bangle, Sir Benjamin Bangle, who's a member of the School Board, and ought to know something about schools, strongly recommended it—would have sent his own son there, if he hadn't entered him at Eton. And when I pay for most of the extras for you too. Dancing, by Gad, and meat for breakfast. I'm sure I don't know what you would have."

"I'd like to go to Marlborough, or Harrow, or somewhere," whimpered Dick. "Jolland's going to Harrow at Easter. (Jolland's one of the fellows at Grimstone's—Dr. Grimstone's I mean.) And what does old Bangle know about it? He hasn't got to go there himself! And—and Grimstone's jolly enough to fellows he likes, but he doesn't like me—he's always sitting on me for something—and I hate some of the fellows there, and altogether it's beastly. Do let me leave! If you don't want me to go to a public school, I—I could stop at home and have a private tutor—like Joe Twitterley!"

"It's all ridiculous nonsense, I tell you," said Paul angrily, "ridiculous nonsense! And, once for all, I'll put a stop to it. I don't approve of public schools for boys like you, and, what's more, I can't afford it. As for private tutors, that's absurd! So you will just make up your mind to stay at Crichton House as long as I think proper to keep you there, and there's an end of that!"

At this final blow to all his hopes, Dick began to sob in a subdued hopeless kind of way, which was more than his father could bear. To do Paul justice, he had not meant to be quite so harsh when the boy was about to set out for school, and, a little ashamed of his irritation, he sought to justify his decision.

He chose to do this by delivering a short homily on the advantages of school, by which he might lead Dick to look on the matter in the calm light of reason and common sense, and commonplaces on the subject began to rise to the surface of his mind, from the rather muddy depths to which they had long since sunk.

He began to give Dick the benefit of all this stagnant wisdom, with a feeling of surprise as he went on, at his own powerful and original way of putting things.

"Now, you know, it's no use to cry like that," he began. "It's—ah—the usual thing for boys at school, I'm quite aware, to go about fancying they're very ill-used, and miserable, and all the rest of it, just as if people in my position had their sons educated out of spite! It's one of those petty troubles all boys have to go through. And you mark my words, my boy, when they go out into the world and have real trials to put up with, and grow middle-aged men, like me, why, they see what fools they've been, Dick; they see what fools they've been. All the—hum, the innocent games and delights of boyhood, and that sort of thing, you know—come back to them—and then they look back to those hours passed at school as the happiest, aye, the very happiest time of their life!"

"Well," said Dick, "then I hope it won't be the happiest time in mine, that's all! And you may have been happy at the school you went to, perhaps, but I don't believe you would very much care about being a boy again like me, and going back to Grimstone's, you know you wouldn't!"

This put Paul on his mettle; he had warmed well to his subject, and could not let this open challenge pass unnoticed—it gave him such an opening for a cheap and easy effect.

He still had the stone in his hand as he sank back into his chair, smiling with a tolerant superiority.

"Perhaps you will believe me," he said, impressively, "when I tell you, old as I am and much as you envy me, I only wish, at this very moment, I could be a boy again, like you. Going back to school wouldn't make me unhappy, I can tell you."

It is so fatally easy to say more than we mean in the desire to make as strong an impression as possible. Well for most of us that—more fortunate than Mr. Bultitude—we can generally do so without fear of being taken too strictly at our word.

As he spoke these unlucky words, he felt a slight shiver, followed by a curious shrinking sensation all over him. It was odd, too, but the arm-chair in which he sat seemed to have grown so much bigger all at once. He felt a passing surprise, but concluded it must be fancy, and went on as comfortably as before.

"I should like it, my boy, but what's the good of wishing? I only mention it to prove that I was not speaking at random. I'm an old man and you're a young boy, and, that being so, why, of course—What the dooce are you giggling about?"

For Dick, after some seconds of half-frightened open-mouthed staring, had suddenly burst into a violent fit of almost hysterical giggling, which he seemed trying vainly to suppress.

This naturally annoyed Mr. Bultitude, and he went on with immense dignity, "I—ah—I'm not aware that I've been saying anything particularly ridiculous. You seem to be amused?"

"Don't!" gasped Dick. "It, it isn't anything you're saying—it's, it's—oh, can't you feel any difference?"

"The sooner you go back to school the better!" said Paul angrily. "I wash my hands of you. When I do take the trouble to give you any advice, it's received with ridicule. You always were an ill-mannered little cub. I've had quite enough of this. Leave the room, sir!"

The wheels must have belonged to some other cab, for none had stopped at the pavement as yet; but Mr. Bultitude was justly indignant, and could stand the interview no longer. Dick, however, made no attempt to move; he remained there, choking and shaking with laughter, while his father sat stiffly on his chair, trying to ignore his son's unmannerly conduct, but only partially succeeding.

No one can calmly endure watching other people laughing at him like idiots, while he is left perfectly incapable of guessing what he has said or done to amuse them. Even when this is known, it requires a peculiarly keen sense of humour to see the point of a joke against oneself.

At last his patience gave out, and he said coldly, "Now, perhaps, if you are quite yourself again, you will be good enough to let me know what the joke is?"

Dick, looking flushed and half-ashamed, tried again and again to speak, but each time the attempt was too much for him. After a time he did succeed, but his voice was hoarse and shaken with laughter as he spoke. "Haven't you found it out yet? Go and look at yourself in the glass—it will make you roar!"

There was the usual narrow sheet of plate glass at the back of the sideboard, and to this Mr. Bultitude walked, almost under protest, and with a cold dignity. It occurred to him that he might have a smudge on his face or something

wrong with his collar and tie—something to account to some extent for his son's frivolous and insulting behavior. No suspicion of the terrible truth crossed his mind as yet.

Meanwhile Dick was looking on eagerly with a chuckle of anticipation, as one who watches the dawning appreciation of an excellent joke.

But no sooner had Paul met the reflection in the glass than he started back in incredulous horror—then returned and stared again and again.

Surely, surely, this could not be he!

He had expected to see his own familiar portly bow-windowed presence there—but somehow, look as he would, the mirror insisted upon reflecting the figure of his son Dick. Could he possibly have become invisible and have lost the power of casting a reflection—or how was it that Dick, and only Dick, was to be seen there?

How was it, too, when he looked round, there was the boy still sitting there? It could not be Dick, evidently, that he saw in the glass. Besides, the reflection opposite him moved when he moved, returned when he returned, copied his every gesture!

He turned round upon his son with angry and yet hopeful suspicion. "You, you've been playing some of your infernal tricks with this mirror, sir," he cried fiercely. "What have you done to it?"

"Done! how could I do anything to it? As if you didn't know that!"

"Then," stammered Paul, determined to know the worst, "then do you, do you mean to tell me you can see any—alteration in me? Tell me the truth now!"

"I should just think I could!" said Dick emphatically. "It's very queer, but just look here," and he came up to the sideboard and placed himself by the side of his horrified father. "Why," he said, with another giggle, "we're—he-he—as like as two peas!"

They were indeed; the glass reflected now two small boys, each with chubby cheeks and auburn hair, both dressed, too, exactly alike, in Eton jackets and broad white collars; the only difference to be seen between them was that, while one face wore an expression of intense glee and satisfaction, the other—the one which Mr. Bultitude was beginning to fear must belong to him—was lengthened and drawn with dismay and bewilderment.

"Dick," said Paul faintly, "what is all this? Who has been, been taking these liberties with me?"

"I'm sure I don't know," protested Dick. "It wasn't me. I believe you did it all yourself."

"Did it all myself!" repeated Paul indignantly. "Is it likely I should? It's some trickery, I tell you, some villainous plot. The worst of it is," he added plaintively, "I don't understand who I'm supposed to be now. Dick, who am I?"

"You can't be me," said Dick, "because here I am, you know. And you're not yourself, that's very plain. You must be *somebody*, I suppose," he added dubiously.

"Of course I am. What do you mean?" said Paul angrily. "Never mind who I am. I feel just the same as I always did. Tell me when you first began to notice any change. Could you see it coming on at all, eh?"

"It was all at once, just as you were talking about school and all that. You said you only wished—Why of course; look here, it must be the stone that did it!"

"Stone! what stone?" said Paul. "I don't know what you're talking about."

"Yes, you do—the Garudâ Stone! You've got it in your hand still. Don't you see? It's a real talisman after all! How jolly!"

"I didn't do anything to set it off; and besides, oh, it's perfectly absurd! How can there be such things as talismans nowadays, eh? Tell me that."

"Well, something's happened to you, hasn't it? And it must have been done somehow," argued Dick.

"I was holding the confounded thing, certainly," said Paul, "here it is. But what could I have said to start it? What has it done this to me for?"

"I know!" cried Dick. "Don't you remember? You said you wished you were a boy again, like me. So you are, you see, exactly like me! What a lark it is, isn't it? But, I say, you can't go up to business like that, you know, can you? I tell you what, you'd better come to Grimstone's with me

now, and see how you like it. I shouldn't mind so much if you came too. Grimstone's face would be splendid when he saw two of us. Do come!"

"That's ridiculous nonsense you're talking," said Paul, "and you know it. What should I do at school at my age? I tell you I'm the same as ever inside, though I may have shrunk into a little rascally boy to look at. And it's simply an abominable nuisance, Dick, that's what it is! Why on earth couldn't you let the stone alone? Just see what mischief you've done by meddling now—put me to all this inconvenience!"

"You shouldn't have wished," said Dick.

"Wished!" echoed Mr. Bultitude. "Why, to be sure," he said, with a gleam of returning hopefulness, "of course—I never thought of that. The thing's a wishing stone; it must be! You have to hold it, I suppose, and then say what you wish aloud, and there you are. If that's the case, I can soon put it all right by simply wishing myself back again. I—I shall have a good laugh at all this by and by—I know I shall!"

He took the stone, and got into a corner by himself where he began repeating the words, "I wish I was back again," "I wish I was the man I was five minutes ago," "I wish all this had not happened," and so on, until he was very exhausted and red in the face. He tried with the stone held in his left hand, as well as his right, sitting and standing, under all the various conditions he could think of, but absolutely nothing came of it; he was just as exasperatingly boyish and youthful as ever at the end of it.

"I don't like this," he said at last, giving it up with a rather crestfallen air. "It seems to me that this diabolical invention has got out of order somehow; I can't make it work any more!"

"Perhaps," suggested Dick, who had shown throughout the most unsympathetic cheerfulness, "perhaps it's one of those talismans that only give you one wish, and you've had it, you know?"

"Then it's all over!" groaned Paul. "What the dooce am I to do? What shall I do? Suggest something, for Heaven's sake; don't stand cackling there in that unfeeling manner. Can't you see what a terrible, mess I've got into? Suppose—only suppose your sister or one of the servants were to come in, and see me like this!"

This suggestion simply enchanted Dick. "Let's have 'em all up," he laughed; "it would be such fun! How they will laugh when we tell them!" And he rushed to the bell.

"Touch that bell if you dare!" screamed Paul. "I won't be seen in this condition by anybody! What on earth could have induced that scoundrelly uncle of yours to bring such a horrible thing as this over I can't imagine! I never heard of such a situation as this in my life. I can't stay like this, you know—it's not to be thought of! I—I wonder whether it would be any use to send over to Dr. Bustard and ask him to step in; he might give me something to bring me round. But then the whole neighbourhood would hear about it! If I don't see my way out of this soon, I shall go raving mad!"

And he paced restlessly up and down the room with his brain on fire.

All at once, as he became able to think more coherently, there occurred to him a chance, slender and desperate enough, but still a chance, of escaping even yet the consequences of his folly.

He was forced to conclude that, however improbable and fantastic it might appear in this rationalistic age, there must be some hidden power in this Garudâ Stone which had put him in his present very unpleasant position. It was plain too that the virtues of the talisman refused to exert themselves any more at his bidding.

But it did not follow that in another's hands the spell would remain as powerless. At all events, it was an experiment well worth the trial, and he lost no time in explaining the notion to Dick, who, by the sparkle in his eyes and suppressed excitement in his manner, seemed to think there might be something in it.

"I may as well try," he said, "give it to me."

"Take it, my dear boy," said Paul, with a paternal air that sorely tried Dick's recovered gravity, it contrasted so absurdly with his altered appearance. "Take it, and wish your poor old father himself again!"

Dick took it, and held it thoughtfully for some moments, while Paul waited in nervous impatience. "Isn't it any use?" he said dolefully at last, as nothing happened.

"I don't know," said Dick calmly, "I haven't wished yet."

"Then do so at once," said Paul fussily, "do so at once. There's no time to waste, every moment is of importance—your cab will be here directly. Although, although I'm altered in this ridiculous way, I hope I still retain my authority as a father, and as a father, by Gad, I expect you to obey me, sir!"

"Oh, all right," said Dick indifferently, "you may keep the authority if you like."

"Then do what I tell you. Can't you see how urgent it is that a scandal like this shouldn't get about? I should be the laughing-stock of the city. Not a soul must ever guess that such a thing has happened. You must see that yourself."

"Yes," said Dick, who all this time was sitting on a corner of the table, swinging his legs, "I see that. It will be all right. I'm going to wish in a minute, and no one will guess there has been anything the matter."

"That's a good boy!" said Paul, much relieved, "I know your heart is in the right place—only do make haste."

"I suppose," Dick asked, "when you are yourself again, things would go on just as usual?"

"I—I hope so."

"I mean you will go on sitting here, and I shall go off to Grimstone's?"

"Of course, of course," said Paul; "don't ask so many questions. I'm sure you quite understand what has to be done, so get on. We might be found like this any minute."

"That settles it," said Dick, "any fellow would do it after that."

"Yes, yes, but you're so slow about it!"

"Don't be in a hurry," said Dick, "you mayn't like it after all when I've done it."

"Done what?" asked Mr. Bultitude sharply, struck by something sinister and peculiar in the boy's manner.

"Well, I don't mind telling you," said Dick, "it's fairer. You see, you wished to be a boy just like me, didn't you?"

"I didn't mean it," protested Paul.

"Ah, you couldn't expect a stone to know that; at any rate, it made you into a boy like me directly. Now, if I wish myself a man just like you were ten minutes ago, before you took the stone, that will put things all right again, won't it?"

"Is the boy mad?" cried Paul, horrified at this proposal. "Why, why, that would be worse than ever!"

"I don't see that," objected Dick, stubbornly. "No one would know anything about it then."

"But, you little blockhead, can't I make you understand? It wouldn't do at all. We should both of us be wrong then—each with the other's personal appearance."

"Well," said Dick blandly, "I shouldn't mind that."

"But I should—I mind very much. I object strongly to such a—such a preposterous arrangement. And what's more, I won't have it. Do you hear, I forbid you to think of any such thing. Give me back that stone. I can't trust you with it after this."

"I can't help it," said Dick doggedly. "You've had your wish, and I don't see why I shouldn't have mine. I mean to have it, too."

"Why, you unnatural little rascal!" cried the justly-enraged father, "do you mean to defy me? I tell you I will have that stone! Give it up this instant!" and he made a movement towards his son, as if he meant to recover the talisman by main force.

But Dick was too quick for him. Slipping off the table with great agility, he planted himself firmly on the hearth-rug, with the hand that held the stone clenched behind his back, and the other raised in self-defence.

"I'd much rather you wouldn't make me hit you, you know," he said, "because, in spite of what's happened, you're still my father, I suppose. But if you interfere with me before I've done with this stone, I'm afraid I shall have to punch your head."

Mr. Bultitude retreated a few steps apprehensively, feeling himself no match for his son, except in size and general appearance; and for some moments of really frightful intensity they stood panting on the hearth-rug, each cautiously watching the other, on his guard against stratagem and surprise.

It was one of those painful domestic scenes which are fortunately rare between father and son.

Overhead, the latest rollicking French polka was being rattled out, with a savage irony of which pianos, even by the best makers, can at times be capable.

Suddenly Dick drew himself up. "Stand out of my way!" he cried excitedly, "I am going to do it. I wish I was a man like you were just now!"

And as he spoke, Mr. Bultitude had the bitterness of seeing his unscrupulous son swell out like the frog in the fable, till he stood there before him the exact duplicate of what Paul had so lately been!

The transformed Dick began to skip and dance round the room in high glee, with as much agility as his increased bulk would allow. "It's all right, you see," he said. "The old stone's as good as ever. You can't say anyone would ever know, to look at us."

And then he threw himself panting into a chair, and began to laugh excitedly at the success of his unprincipled manoeuvres.

As for Paul, he was perfectly furious at having been so outwitted and overreached. It was a long time before he could command his voice sufficiently to say, savagely: "Well, you've had your way, and a pretty mess you've made of it. We're both of us in false positions now. I hope you're satisfied, I'm sure. Do you think you'll care about going back to Crichton House in that state?"

"No," said Dick, very decidedly: "I'm quite sure I shouldn't."

"Well, I can't help it. You've brought it on yourself; and, provided the Doctor sees no objection to take you back as you are and receive you as one of his pupils, I shall most certainly send you there."

Paul did not really mean this, he only meant to frighten him; for he still trusted that, by letting Boaler into the secret, the charm might be set in motion once more, and the difficulty comfortably overcome. But his threat had a most unfortunate effect upon Dick; it hardened him to take a course he might otherwise have shrunk from.

"Oh," he said, "you're going to do that? But doesn't it strike you that things are rather altered with us now?"

"They are, to a certain extent, of course," said Paul, "through my folly and your wicked cunning; but a word or two of explanation from me—"

"You'll find it will take more explanation than you think," said Dick; "but, of course, you can try, if you think it worth while—when you get to Grimstone's."

"When I,—I don't understand. When I,—what did you say?" gasped Paul.

"Why, you see," exclaimed Dick, "it would never have done for us both to go back; the chaps would have humbugged us so, and as I hate the place and you seem so fond of being a boy and going back to school and that, I thought perhaps it would be best for you to go and see how you liked it!"

"I never will! I'll not stir from this room! I dare you to try to move me!" cried Paul. And just then there was the sound of wheels outside once more. They stopped before the house, the bell rang sharply—the long-expected cab had come at last.

"You've no time to lose," said Dick, "get your coat on."

Mr. Bultitude tried to treat the affair as a joke. He laughed a ghastly little laugh.

"Ha! ha! you've fairly caught your poor father this time; you've proved him in the wrong. I admit I said more than I exactly meant. But that's enough. Don't drive a good joke too far; shake hands, and let us see if we can't find a way out of this!"

But Dick only warmed his coat tails at the fire as he said, with a very ungenerous reminiscence of his father's manner: "You are going back to an excellent establishment, where you will enjoy all the comforts of home—I can specially recommend the stickjaw; look out for it on Tuesdays and Fridays. You will once more take part in the games and lessons of happy boyhood. (Did you ever play 'chevy' when you were a boy before? You'll enjoy chevy.) And you will find your companions easy enough to get on with, if you don't go giving yourself airs; they won't stand airs. Now good-bye, my boy, and bless you!"

Paul stood staring stupidly at this outrageous assumption; he could scarcely believe yet that it was meant in cruel earnest. Before he could answer, the door opened and Boaler appeared.

"Had a deal of trouble to find a keb, sir, on a night like this," he said to the false Dick, "but the luggage is all on top, and the man says there's plenty of time still."

"Good-bye then, my boy," said Dick, with well-assumed tenderness, but a rather dangerous light in his eye. "My compliments to the Doctor, remember."

Paul turned indignantly from him to the butler; he, at least, would stand by him. Boaler would not see a master who had always been fair, if not indulgent, to him driven from his home in this cold-blooded manner!

He made two or three attempts to speak, for his brain whirled so with scathing, burning things to say. He would expose the fraud then and there, and defy the impudent usurper; he would warn every one against this spurious pinchbeck imitation of himself. The whole household should be summoned and called upon to judge between the two!

No doubt, if he had had enough self-command to do all this effectually, while Dick had as yet not had the time thoroughly to adapt himself to his altered circumstances, he might have turned the situation at the outset, and spared himself some very painful experiences.

But it is very often precisely those words which are the most vitally important to be said that refuse to pass our lips on a sudden emergency. We feel all the necessity of saying something at once, but the necessary words unaccountably desert us at the critical moment.

Mr. Bultitude felt himself in this unfortunate position. He made more wild efforts to explain, but the sense of his danger only petrified his mind instead of stimulating it. Then he was spared further conflict. A dark mist rose before his eyes; the walls of the room receded into infinite space; and, with a loud singing in his ears, he fell, and seemed to himself to be sinking down, down, through the earth to the very crust of the antipodes. Then the blackness closed over him—and he knew no more.

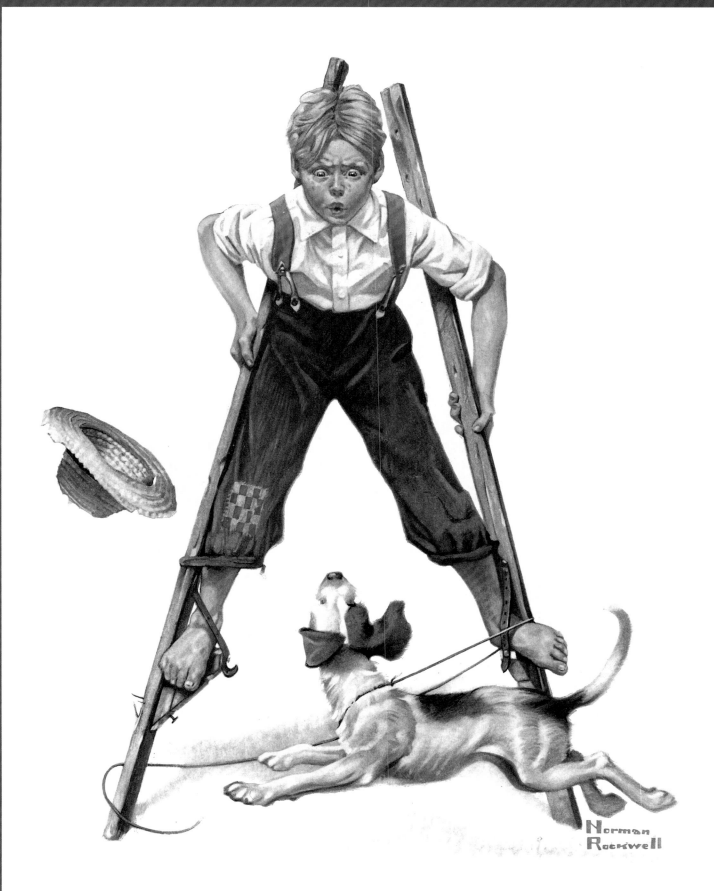

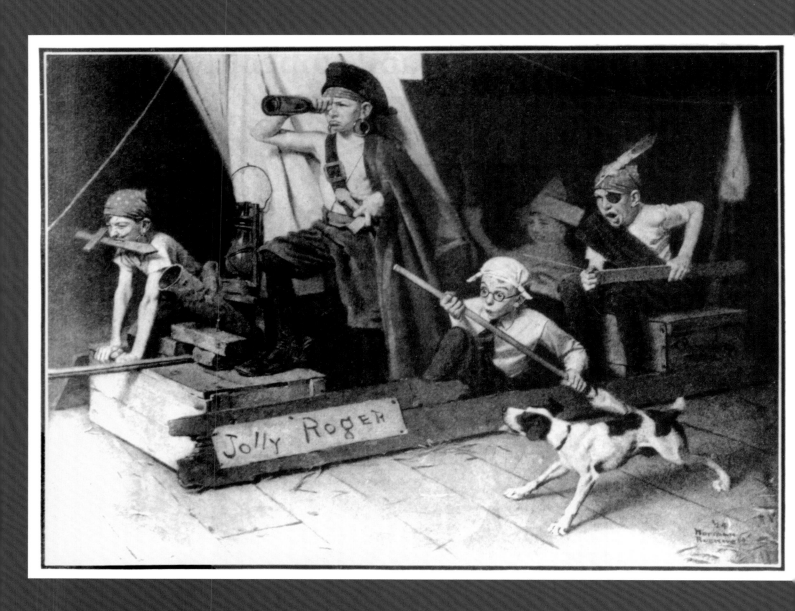

The Captain's Papers

from *Treasure Island*

Robert Louis Stevenson

—⚬✕⚬—

WE RODE HARD all the way till we drew up before Dr. Livesey's door. The house was all dark to the front.

Mr. Dance told me to jump down and knock, and Dogger gave me a stirrup to descend by. The door was opened almost at once by the maid.

"Is Dr. Livesey in?" I asked.

No, she said, he had come home in the afternoon but had gone up to the hall to dine and pass the evening with the squire.

"So there we go, boys," said Mr. Dance.

This time, as the distance was short, I did not mount, but ran with Dogger's stirrup-leather to the lodge gates and up the long, leafless, moonlit avenue to where the white line of the hall buildings looked on either hand on great old gardens. Here Mr. Dance dismounted, and taking me along with him, was admitted at a word into the house.

The servant led us down a matted passage and showed us at the end into a great library, all lined with bookcases and busts upon the top of them, where the squire and Dr. Livesey sat, pipe in hand, on either side of a bright fire.

I had never seen the squire so near at hand. He was a tall man, over six feet high, and broad in proportion, and he had a bluff, rough-and-ready face, all roughened and reddened and lined in his long travels. His eyebrows were very black, and moved readily, and this gave him a look of some temper, not bad, you would say, but quick and high.

"Come in, Mr. Dance," says he, very stately and condescending.

"Good evening, Dance," says the doctor with a nod. "And good evening to you, friend Jim. What good wind brings you here?"

The supervisor stood up straight and stiff and told his story like a lesson; and you should have seen how the two gentlemen leaned forward and looked at each other, and forgot to smoke in their surprise and interest. When they heard how my mother went back to the inn, Dr. Livesey fairly slapped his thigh, and the squire cried "Bravo!" and broke his long pipe against the grate. Long before it was done, Mr. Trelawney (that, you will remember, was the squire's name) had got up from his seat and was striding about the room, and the doctor, as if to hear the better, had taken off his powdered wig and sat there looking very strange indeed with his own close-cropped black poll.

At last Mr. Dance finished the story.

"Mr. Dance," said the squire, "you are a very noble fellow. And as for riding down that black, atrocious miscreant, I regard it as an act of virtue, sir, like stamping on a cockroach. This lad Hawkins is a trump, I perceive. Hawkins, will you ring that bell? Mr. Dance must have some ale."

"And so, Jim," said the doctor, "you have the thing that they were after, have you?"

"Here it is, sir," said I, and gave him the oilskin packet.

The doctor looked it all over, as if his fingers were itching to open it; but instead of doing that, he put it quietly in the pocket of his coat.

"Squire," said he, "when Dance has had his ale he must, of course, be off on his Majesty's service; but I mean to keep Jim Hawkins here to sleep at my house, and with your permission, I propose we should have up the cold pie and let him sup."

"As you will, Livesey," said the squire; "Hawkins has earned better than cold pie."

So a big pigeon pie was brought in and put on a side table, and I made a hearty supper, for I was as hungry as a hawk, while Mr. Dance was further complimented and at last dismissed.

"And now, squire," said the doctor.

"And now, Livesey," said the squire in the same breath.

"One at a time, one at a time," laughed Dr. Livesey. "You have heard of this Flint, I suppose?"

"Heard of him!" cried the squire. "Heard of him, you say! He was the bloodthirstiest buccaneer that sailed. Blackbeard was a child to Flint. The Spaniards were so prodigiously afraid of him that, I tell you, sir, I was sometimes proud he was an Englishman. I've seen his top-sails with these eyes, off Trinidad, and the cowardly son of a rum-puncheon that I sailed with put back—put back, sir, into Port of Spain."

"Well, I've heard of him myself, in England," said the doctor. "But the point is, had he money?"

"Money!" cried the squire. "Have you heard the story? What were these villains after but money? What do they care for but money? For what would they risk their rascal carcasses but money?"

"That we shall soon know," replied the doctor. "But you are so confoundedly hot-headed and exclamatory that I cannot get a word in. What I want to know is this: Supposing that I have here in my pocket some clue to where Flint buried his treasure, will that treasure amount to much?"

"Amount, sir!" cried the squire. "It will amount to this: If we have the clue you talk about, I fit out a ship in Bristol dock, and take you and Hawkins here along, and I'll have that treasure if I search a year."

"Very well," said the doctor. "Now, then, if Jim is agreeable, we'll open the packet"; and he laid it before him on the table.

The bundle was sewn together, and the doctor had to get out his instrument case and cut the stitches with his medical scissors. It contained two things—a book and a sealed paper.

"First of all we'll try the book," observed the doctor.

The squire and I were both peering over his shoulder as he opened it, for Dr. Livesey had kindly motioned me to come round from the side-table, where I had been eating, to enjoy the sport of the search. On the first page there were only some scraps of writing, such as a man with a pen in his hand might make for idleness or practice. One was the same as the tattoo mark, "Billy Bones his fancy"; then there was "Mr. W. Bones, mate," "No more rum," "Off Palm Key he got itt," and some other snatches, mostly single words and unintelligible. I could not help wondering who it was that had "got itt," and what "itt" was that he got. A knife in his back as like as not.

"Not much instruction there," said Dr. Livesey as he passed on.

The next ten or twelve pages were filled with a curious series of entries. There was a date at one end of the line and at the other a sum of money, as in common account-books, but instead of explanatory writing, only a varying number of crosses between the two. On the 12th of June, 1745, for instance, a sum of seventy pounds had plainly become due to someone, and there was nothing but six crosses to explain the cause. In a few cases, to be sure, the name of a place would be added, as "Offe Caraccas," or a mere entry of latitude and longitude, as "62° 17' 20", 19° 2' 40"."

The record lasted over nearly twenty years, the amount of the separate entries growing larger as time went on, and at the end a grand total had been made out after five or six wrong additions, and these words appended, "Bones, his pile."

"I can't make head or tail of this," said Dr. Livesey.

"The thing is as clear as noonday," cried the squire. "This is the black-hearted hound's account-book. These crosses stand for the names of ships or towns that they sank or plundered. The sums are the scoundrel's share, and where he feared an ambiguity, you see he added something clearer. 'Offe Caraccas,' now; you see, here was some unhappy vessel boarded off that coast. God help the poor souls that manned her—coral long ago."

"Right!" said the doctor. "See what it is to be a traveler. Right! And the amounts increase, you see, as he rose in rank."

There was little else in the volume but a few bearings of places noted in the blank leaves towards the end and a table for reducing French, English, and Spanish moneys to a common value.

"Thrifty man!" cried the doctor. "He wasn't the one to be cheated."

"And now," said the squire, "for the other."

The paper had been sealed in several places with a thimble by way of seal; the very thimble, perhaps, that I had found in the captain's pocket. The doctor opened the seals with great care, and there fell out the map of an island, with latitude and longitude, soundings, names of hills and bays and inlets, and every particular that would be needed to bring a ship to a safe anchorage upon its shores. It was about nine miles long and five across, shaped, you might say, like a fat dragon standing up, and had two fine land-locked harbors, and a hill in the center part marked "The Spy-glass." There were several additions of a later date, but above all, three crosses of red ink—two on the north part of the island, one in the southwest—and beside this last, in the same red ink, and in a small, neat hand, very different from the captain's tottery characters, these words: "Bulk of treasure here."

Over on the back the same hand had written this further information:

Tall tree, Spy-glass shoulder, bearing a point to the N. of N.N.E.

Skeleton Island E.S.E. and by E.

Ten feet.

The bar silver is in the north cache; you can find it by the trend of the east hummock, ten fathoms south of the black crag with the face on it.

The arms are easy found, in the sand-hill, N. point of north inlet cape, bearing E. and a quarter N.

J.F.

That was all; but brief as it was, and to me incomprehensible, it filled the squire and Dr. Livesey with delight.

"Livesey," said the squire, "you will give up this wretched practice at once. Tomorrow I start for Bristol. In three weeks' time—three weeks!—two weeks—ten days—we'll have the best ship, sir, and the choicest crew in England. Hawkins shall come as cabin-boy. You'll make a famous cabin-boy, Hawkins. You, Livesey, are ship's doctor; I am admiral. We'll take Redruth, Joyce, and Hunter. We'll have favorable winds, a quick passage, and not the least difficulty in finding the spot, and money to eat, to roll in, to play duck and drake with ever after."

"Trelawney," said the doctor, "I'll go with you; and I'll go bail for it, so will Jim, and be a credit to the undertaking. There's only one man I'm afraid of."

"And who's that?" cried the squire. "Name the dog, sir!"

"You," replied the doctor; "for you cannot hold your tongue. We are not the only men who know of this paper. These fellows who attacked the inn tonight—bold, desperate blades, for sure—and the rest who stayed aboard that lugger, and more, I dare say, not far off, are, one and all, through thick and thin, bound that they'll get that money. We must none of us go alone till we get to sea. Jim and I shall stick together in the meanwhile; you'll take Joyce and Hunter when you ride to Bristol, and from first to last, not one of us must breathe a word of what we've found."

"Livesey," returned the squire, "you are always in the right of it. I'll be as silent as the grave."

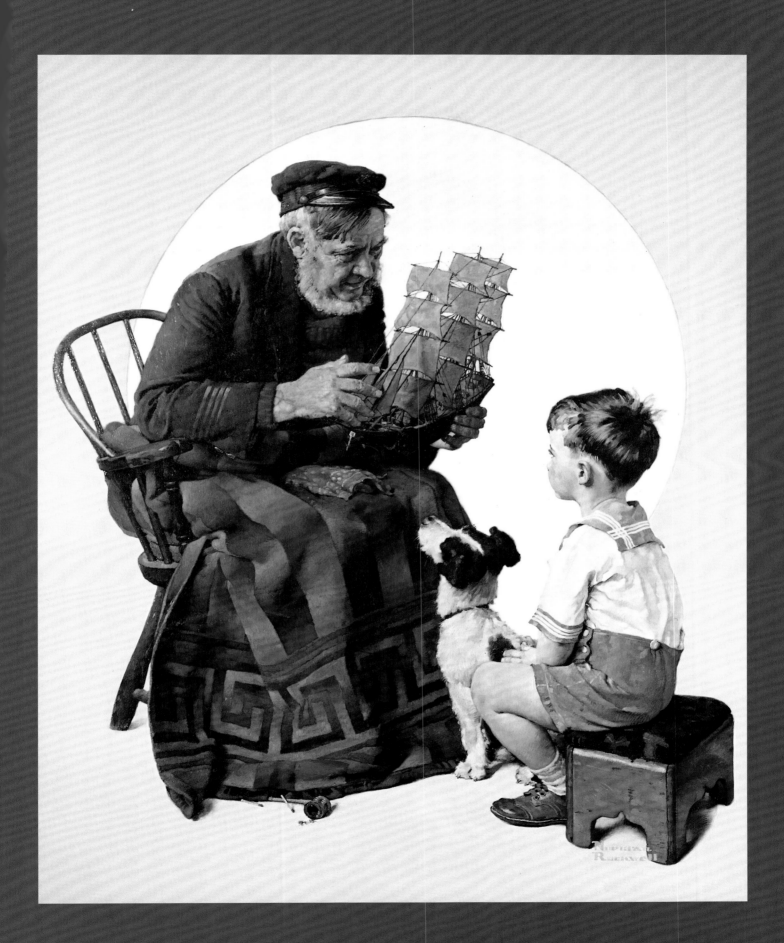

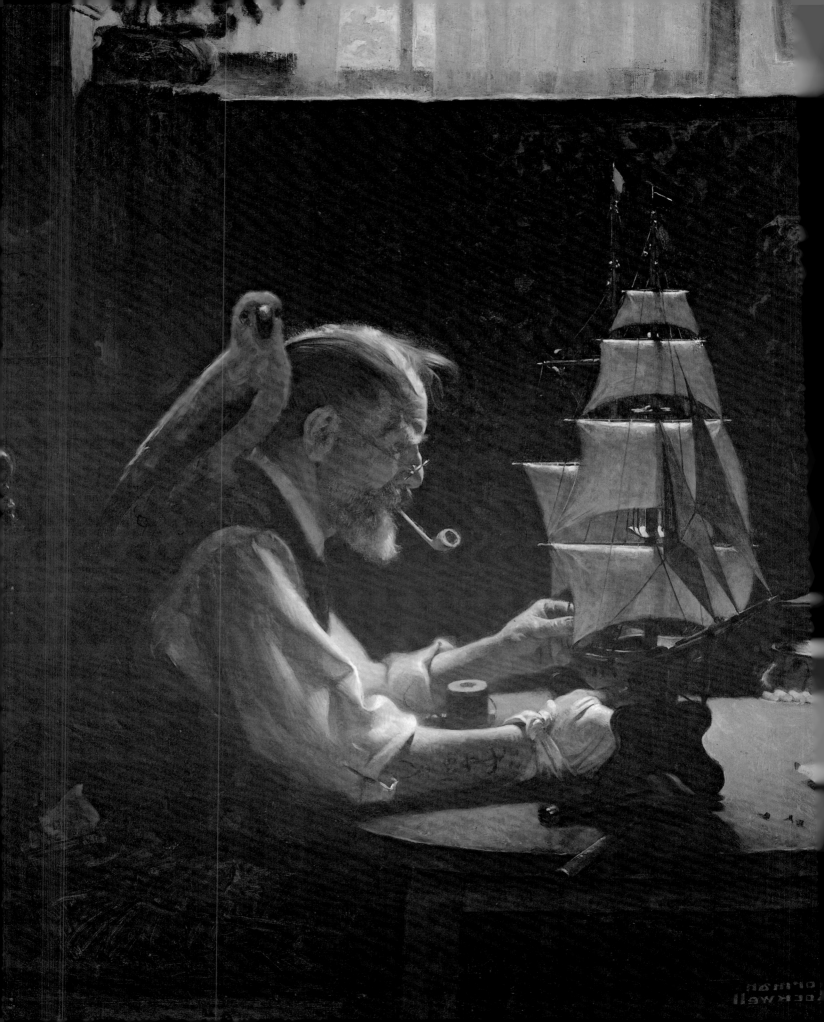

Fun Together

Making a Treasure Map

CUT OPEN the seams of a brown-paper grocery bag and lay the bag flat. Gently tear the bag into the shape of a map. The torn edges will give your map a rough, weathered feel.

Pencil in landmarks like paths, trees, rocks, bodies of water, and other important elements. Once these basic components are laid in, embellish them with permanent markers. Don't forget to add a compass rose to show north, south, east, and west.

Mark the spot where your treasure is hidden (or will be hidden) with a big red X. Draw a dotted line leading to the X. In fancy letters, write "Treasure Map" somewhere on the map.

Age your map by crumpling it into a ball. Open it up and crumple it again, repeating the process until it is as weathered as you'd like. Then soak it in coffee or tea. After a couple of minutes, pull it out and lay it in the sun to dry.

Fold the map in half, roll it up, and tie it with a ribbon. Your pirate's map can be hidden in a bottle, in a box, in a book, or anywhere you think might be fun!

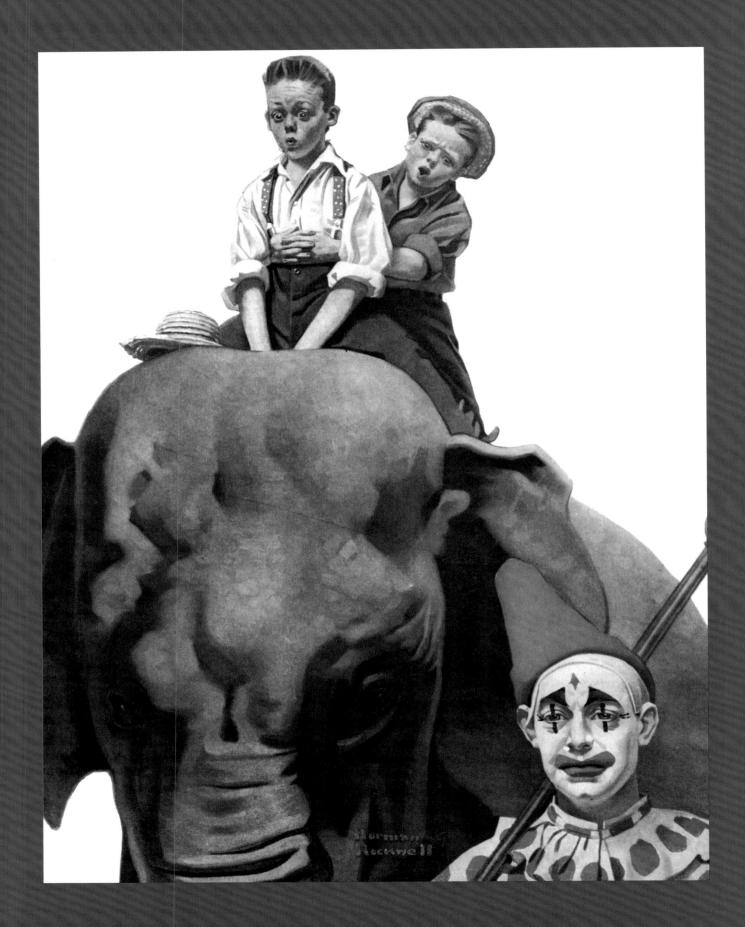

THE ELEPHANT'S CHILD

Just So Stories

RUDYARD KIPLING

—⟨o⟩⟨o⟩—

IN THE HIGH and Far-Off Times the Elephant, O Best Beloved, had no trunk. He had only a blackish, bulgy nose, as big as a boot, that he could wriggle about from side to side; but he couldn't pick up things with it. But there was one Elephant—a new Elephant—an Elephant's Child—who was full of 'satiable curtiosity, and that means he asked ever so many questions. *And* he lived in Africa, and he filled all Africa with his 'satiable curtiosities. He asked his tall aunt, the Ostrich, why her tail-feathers grew just so, and his tall aunt the Ostrich spanked him with her hard, hard claw.

He asked his tall uncle, the Giraffe, what made his skin spotty, and his tall uncle, the Giraffe, spanked him with his hard, hard hoof. And still he was full of 'satiable curtiosity! He asked his broad aunt, the Hippopotamus, why her eyes were red, and his broad aunt, the Hippopotamus, spanked him with her broad, broad hoof; and he asked his hairy uncle, the Baboon, why melons tasted just so, and his hairy uncle, the Baboon, spanked him with his hairy, hairy paw. And *still* he was full of 'satiable curtiosity! He asked questions about everything that he saw, or heard, or felt, or smelt, or touched, and all his uncles and his aunts spanked him. And still he was full of 'satiable curtiosity!

One fine morning in the middle of the Precession of the Equinoxes this 'satiable Elephant's Child asked a new fine question that he had never asked before. He asked, "What does the Crocodile have for dinner?" Then everybody said, "Hush!" in a loud and dretful tone, and they spanked him immediately and directly, without stopping, for a long time.

By and by, when that was finished, he came upon Kolokolo Bird sitting in the middle of a wait-a-bit thorn-bush, and he said, "My father has spanked me, and my mother has spanked me; all my aunts and uncles have spanked me for my 'satiable curtiosity; and *still* I want to know what the Crocodile has for dinner!"

Then Kolokolo Bird said, with a mournful cry, "Go to the banks of the great grey-green, greasy Limpopo River, all set about with fever-trees, and find out."

That very next morning, when there was nothing left of the Equinoxes, because the Precession had preceded according to precedent, this 'satiable Elephant's Child took a hundred pounds of bananas (the little short red kind), and a hundred pounds of sugar-cane (the long purple kind), and seventeen melons (the greeny-crackly kind), and said to all his dear families, "Goodbye. I am going to the great grey-green, greasy Limpopo River, all set about with fever-trees, to find out what the Crocodile has for dinner." And they all spanked him once more for luck, though he asked them most politely to stop.

Then he went away, a little warm, but not at all astonished, eating melons, and throwing the rind about, because he could not pick it up.

He went from Graham's Town to Kimberley, and from Kimberley to Khama's Country, and from Khama's Country he went east by north, eating melons all the time, till at last he came to the banks of the great grey-green, greasy Limpopo River, all set about with fever-trees, precisely as Kolokolo Bird had said.

Now you must know and understand, O Best Beloved, that till that very week, and day, and hour, and minute, this 'satiable Elephant's Child had never seen a Crocodile, and did not know what one was like. It was all his 'satiable curtiosity.

The first thing that he found was a Bi-Coloured-Python-Rock-Snake curled round a rock.

"'Scuse me," said the Elephant's Child most politely, "but have you seen such a thing as a Crocodile in these promiscuous parts?"

"Have I seen a Crocodile?" said the Bi-Coloured-Python-Rock-Snake, in a voice of dretful scorn. "What will you ask me next?"

"'Scuse me," said the Elephant's Child, "but could you kindly tell me what he has for dinner?"

Then the Bi-Coloured-Python-Rock-Snake uncoiled himself very quickly from the rock, and spanked the Elephant's Child with his scalesome, flailsome tail.

"That is odd," said the Elephant's Child, "because my father and my mother, and my uncle and my aunt, not to mention my other aunt, the Hippopotamus, and my other uncle, the Baboon, have all spanked me for my 'satiable curtiosity—and I suppose this is the same thing."

So he said good-bye very politely to the Bi-Coloured-Python-Rock-Snake, and helped to coil him up on the rock again, and went on, a little warm, but not at all astonished, eating melons, and throwing the rind about, because he could not pick it up, till he trod on what he thought was a log of wood at the very edge of the great grey-green, greasy Limpopo River, all set about with fever-trees.

But it was really the Crocodile, O Best Beloved, and the Crocodile winked one eye—like this!

"'Scuse me," said the Elephant's Child most politely, "but do you happen to have seen a Crocodile in these promiscuous parts?"

Then the Crocodile winked the other eye, and lifted half his tail out of the mud; and the Elephant's Child stepped back most politely, because he did not wish to be spanked again.

"Come hither, Little One," said the Crocodile. "Why do you ask such things?"

"'Scuse me," said the Elephant's Child most politely, "but my father has spanked me, my mother has spanked me, not to mention my tall aunt, the Ostrich, and my tall uncle, the Giraffe, who can kick ever so hard, as well as my broad aunt, the Hippopotamus, and my hairy uncle, the Baboon, *and* including the Bi-Coloured-Python-Rock-Snake, with the scalesome, flailsome tail, just up the bank, who spanks harder than any of them; and *so*, if it's quite all the same to you, I don't want to be spanked any more."

"Come hither, Little One," said the Crocodile, "for I am the Crocodile," and he wept crocodile-tears to show it was quite true.

Then the Elephant's Child grew all breathless, and panted, and kneeled down on the bank and said, "You are the very person I have been looking for all these long days. Will you please tell me what you have for dinner?"

"Come hither, Little One," said the Crocodile, "and I'll whisper."

Then the Elephant's Child put his head down close to the Crocodile's musky, tusky mouth, and the Crocodile caught him by his little nose, which up to that very week, day, hour, and minute, had been no bigger than a boot, though much more useful.

"I think," said the Crocodile—and he said it between his teeth, like this—"I think to-day I will begin with Elephant's Child!"

At this, O Best Beloved, the Elephant's Child was much annoyed, and he said, speaking through his nose, like this, "Led go! You are hurtig be!"

Then the Bi-Coloured-Python-Rock-Snake scuffled down from the bank and said, "My young friend, if you do not now, immediately and instantly, pull as hard as ever you can, it is my opinion that your acquaintance in the large-pattern leather ulster" (and by this he meant the Crocodile) "will jerk you into yonder limpid stream before you can say Jack Robinson."

This is the way Bi-Coloured-Python-Rock-Snakes always talk.

Then the Elephant's Child sat back on his little haunches, and pulled, and pulled, and pulled, and his nose began to stretch. And the Crocodile floundered into the water, making it all creamy with great sweeps of his tail, and *he* pulled, and pulled, and pulled.

And the Elephant's Child's nose kept on stretching; and the Elephant's Child spread all his little four legs and pulled, and pulled, and pulled, and his nose kept on stretching; and the Crocodile threshed his tail like an oar, and he pulled, and pulled, and pulled, and at each pull the Elephant's Child's nose grew longer and longer—and it hurt him hijjus!

Then the Elephant's Child felt his legs slipping, and he said through his nose, which was now nearly five feet long, "This is too butch for be!"

Then the Bi-Coloured-Python-Rock-Snake came down from the bank, and knotted himself in a double-clove-hitch round the Elephant's Child's hind legs, and said, "Rash and inexperienced traveller, we will now seriously devote ourselves to a little high tension, because if we do not, it is my impression that yonder self-propelling man-of-war with the armour-plated upper deck" (and by this, O Best Beloved, he meant the Crocodile), "will permanently vitiate your future career."

That is the way all Bi-Coloured-Python-Rock-Snakes always talk.

So he pulled, and the Elephant's Child pulled, and the Crocodile pulled; but the Elephant's Child and the Bi-Coloured-Python-Rock-Snake pulled hardest; and at last the Crocodile let go of the Elephant's Child's nose with a plop that you could hear all up and down the Limpopo.

Then the Elephant's Child sat down most hard and sudden; but first he was careful to say "Thank you" to the Bi-Coloured-Python-Rock-Snake; and next he was kind to his poor pulled nose, and wrapped it all up in cool banana leaves, and hung it in the great grey-green, greasy Limpopo to cool.

"What are you doing that for?" said the Bi-Coloured-Python-Rock-Snake.

"'Scuse me," said the Elephant's Child, "but my nose is badly out of shape, and I am waiting for it to shrink."

"Then you will have to wait a long time," said the Bi-Coloured-Python-Rock-Snake. "Some people do not know what is good for them."

The Elephant's Child sat there for three days waiting for his nose to shrink. But it never grew any shorter, and, besides, it made him squint. For, O Best Beloved, you will see and understand that the Crocodile had pulled it out into a really truly trunk same as all Elephants have to-day.

At the end of the third day a fly came and stung him on the shoulder, and before he knew what he was doing he lifted up his trunk and hit that fly dead with the end of it.

"'Vantage number one!" said the Bi-Coloured-Python-Rock-Snake. "You couldn't have done that with a mere-smear nose. Try and eat a little now."

Before he thought what he was doing the Elephant's Child put out his trunk and plucked a large bundle of grass, dusted it clean against his fore-legs, and stuffed it into his own mouth.

"'Vantage number two!" said the Bi-Coloured-Python-Rock-Snake. "You couldn't have done that with a mear-smear nose. Don't you think the sun is very hot here?"

"It is," said the Elephant's Child, and before he thought what he was doing he schlooped up a schloop of mud from the banks of the great grey-green, greasy Limpopo, and slapped it on his head, where it made a cool schloopy-sloshy mud-cap all trickly behind his ears.

"'Vantage number three!" said the Bi-Coloured-Python-Rock-Snake. "You couldn't have done that with a mere-smear nose. Now how do you feel about being spanked again?"

"'Scuse me," said the Elephant's Child, "but I should not like it at all."

"How would you like to spank somebody?" said the Bi-Coloured-Python-Rock-Snake.

"I should like it very much indeed," said the Elephant's Child.

"Well," said the Bi-Coloured-Python-Rock-Snake, "you will find that new nose of yours very useful to spank people with."

"Thank you," said the Elephant's Child, "I'll remember that; and now I think I'll go home to all my dear families and try."

So the Elephant's Child went home across Africa frisking and whisking his trunk. When he wanted fruit to eat he pulled fruit down from a tree, instead of waiting for it to fall as he used to do. When he wanted grass he plucked grass up from the ground, instead of going on his knees as he used to do. When the flies bit him he broke off the branch of a tree and used it as fly-whisk; and he made himself a new, cool, slushy-squshy mud-cap whenever the sun was hot. When he felt lonely walking through Africa he sang to himself down his trunk, and the noise was louder than several brass bands.

He went especially out of his way to find a broad Hippopotamus (she was no relation of his), and he spanked her very hard, to make sure that the Bi-Coloured-Python-Rock-Snake had spoken the truth about his new trunk. The rest of the time he picked up the melon rinds that he had dropped on his way to the Limpopo—for he was a Tidy Pachyderm.

One dark evening he came back to all his dear families, and he coiled up his trunk and said, "How do you do?" They were very glad to see him, and immediately said, "Come here and be spanked for your 'satiable curtiosity."

"Pooh," said the Elephant's Child. "I don't think you peoples know anything about spanking; but I do, and I'll show you." Then he uncurled his trunk and knocked two of his dear brothers head over heels.

"O Bananas!" said they, "where did you learn that trick, and what have you done to your nose?"

"I got a new one from the Crocodile on the banks of the great grey-green, greasy Limpopo River," said the Elephant's Child. "I asked him what he had for dinner, and he gave me this to keep."

"It looks very ugly," said his hairy uncle, the Baboon.

"It does," said the Elephant's Child. "But it's very useful," and he picked up his hairy uncle, the Baboon, by one hairy leg, and hove him into a hornet's nest.

Then that bad Elephant's Child spanked all his dear families for a long time, till they were very warm and greatly astonished. He pulled out his tall Ostrich aunt's tail-feathers; and he caught his tall uncle, the Giraffe, by the hind-leg, and dragged him through a thorn-bush; and he shouted at his broad aunt, the Hippopotamus, and blew bubbles into her ear when she was sleeping in the water after meals; but he never let any one touch Kolokolo Bird.

At last things grew so exciting that his dear families went off one by one in a hurry to the banks of the great grey-green, greasy Limpopo River, all set about with fever-trees, to borrow new noses from the Crocodile. When they came back nobody spanked anybody any more; and ever since that day, O Best Beloved, all the Elephants you will ever see, besides all those that you won't, have trunks precisely like the trunk of the 'satiable Elephant's Child.

> I Keep six honest serving-men
>   (They taught me all I knew);

> Their names are What and Where and When
>   And How and Why and Who.
> I send them over land and sea,
>   I send them east and west;
> But after they have worked for me,
>   I give them all a rest.

> I let them rest from nine till five.
>   For I am busy then,
> As well as breakfast, lunch, and tea,
>   For they are hungry men:
> But different folk have different views:
>   I know a person small—
> She keeps ten million serving-men,
>   Who get no rest at all!
> She sends 'em abroad on her own affairs,
>   From the second she opens her eyes—
> One million Hows, two million Wheres,
>   And seven million Whys!

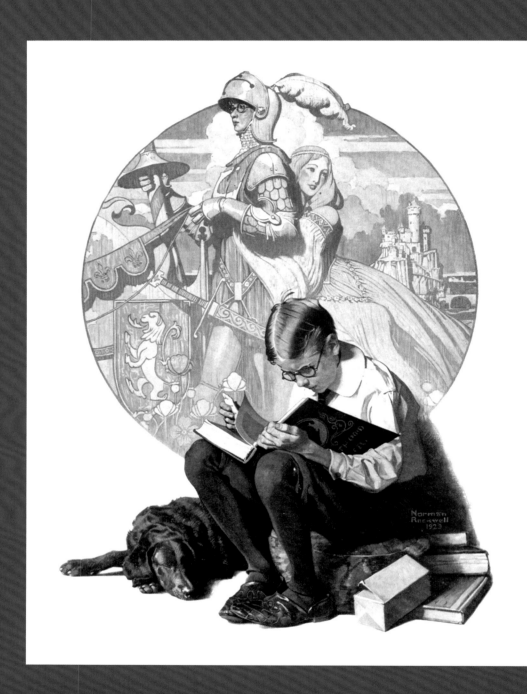

THE RETURN HOME

from *Peter Pan*

JAMES M. BARRIE

BY THREE BELLS that morning they were all stirring their stumps [legs]; for there was a big sea running; and Tootles, the bo'sun, was among them, with a rope's end in his hand and chewing tobacco. They all donned pirate clothes cut off at the knee, shaved smartly, and tumbled up, with the true nautical roll and hitching their trousers.

It need not be said who was the captain. Nibs and John were first and second mate. There was a woman aboard. The rest were tars [sailors] before the mast, and lived in the fo'c'sle. Peter had already lashed himself to the wheel; but he piped all hands and delivered a short address to them; said he hoped they would do their duty like gallant hearties, but that he knew they were the scum of Rio and the Gold Coast, and if they snapped at him he would tear them. The bluff strident words struck the note sailors understood, and they cheered him lustily. Then a few sharp orders were given, and they turned the ship round, and nosed her for the mainland.

Captain Pan calculated, after consulting the ship's chart, that if this weather lasted they should strike the Azores about the 21st of June, after which it would save time to fly.

Some of them wanted it to be an honest ship and others were in favour of keeping it a pirate; but the captain treated them as dogs, and they dared not express their wishes to him even in a round robin [one person after another, as they had to Cpt. Hook]. Instant obedience was the only safe thing. Slightly got a dozen for looking perplexed when told to take soundings. The general feeling was that Peter was honest just now to lull Wendy's suspicions, but that there might be a change when the new suit was ready, which, against her will, she was making for him out of some of Hook's wickedest garments. It was afterwards whispered among them that on the first night he wore this suit he sat long in the cabin with Hook's cigar-holder in his mouth and one hand clenched, all but for the forefinger, which he bent and held threateningly aloft like a hook.

Instead of watching the ship, however, we must now return to that desolate home from which three of our characters had taken heartless flight so long ago. It seems a shame to have neglected No. 14 all this time; and yet we may be sure that Mrs. Darling does not blame us. If we had returned sooner to look with sorrowful sympathy at her, she would probably have cried, "Don't be silly; what do I matter? Do go back and keep an eye on the children." So long as mothers are like this their children

will take advantage of them; and they may lay to [bet on] that.

Even now we venture into that familiar nursery only because its lawful occupants are on their way home; we are merely hurrying on in advance of them to see that their beds are properly aired and that Mr. and Mrs. Darling do not go out for the evening. We are no more than servants. Why on earth should their beds be properly aired, seeing that they left them in such a thankless hurry? Would it not serve them jolly well right if they came back and found that their parents were spending the weekend in the country? It would be the moral lesson they have been in need of ever since we met them; but if we contrived things in this way Mrs. Darling would never forgive us.

One thing I should like to do immensely, and that is to tell her, in the way authors have, that the children are coming back, that indeed they will be here on Thursday week. This would spoil so completely the surprise to which Wendy and John and Michael are looking forward. They have been planning it out on the ship: mother's rapture, father's shout of joy, Nana's leap through the air to embrace them first, when what they ought to be prepared for is a good hiding. How delicious to spoil it all by breaking the news in advance; so that when they enter grandly Mrs. Darling may not even offer Wendy her mouth, and Mr. Darling may exclaim pettishly, "Dash it all, here are those boys again." However, we should get no thanks even for this. We are beginning to know Mrs. Darling by this time, and may be sure that she would upbraid us for depriving the children of their little pleasure.

"But, my dear madam, it is ten days till Thursday week; so that by telling you what's what, we can save you ten days of unhappiness."

"Yes, but at what a cost! By depriving the children of ten minutes of delight."

"Oh, if you look at it in that way!"

"What other way is there in which to look at it?"

You see, the woman had no proper spirit. I had meant to say extraordinarily nice things about her; but I despise her, and not one of them will I say now. She does not really need to be told to have things ready, for they are ready. All the beds are aired, and she never leaves the house, and observe, the window is open. For all the use we are to her, we might well go back to the ship. However, as we are here we may as well stay and look on. That is all we are, lookers-on. Nobody really wants us. So let us watch and say jaggy things, in the hope that some of them will hurt.

The only change to be seen in the night-nursery is that between nine and six the kennel is no longer there. When the children flew away, Mr. Darling felt in his bones that all the blame was his for having chained Nana up, and that from first to last she had been wiser than he. Of course, as we have seen, he was quite a simple man; indeed he might have passed for a boy again if he had been able to take his baldness off; but he had also a noble sense of justice and a lion's courage to do what seemed right to him; and having thought the matter out with anxious care after the flight of the children, he went down on all fours and crawled into the kennel. To all Mrs. Darling's dear invitations to him to come out he replied sadly but firmly:

"No, my own one, this is the place for me."

In the bitterness of his remorse he swore that he would never leave the kennel until his children came back. Of course this was a pity; but whatever Mr. Darling did he had to do in excess, otherwise he soon gave up doing it. And there never was a more humble man than the once proud George Darling, as he sat in the kennel of an evening talking with his wife of their children and all their pretty ways.

Very touching was his deference to Nana. He would not let her come into the kennel, but on all other matters he followed her wishes implicitly.

Every morning the kennel was carried with Mr. Darling in it to a cab, which conveyed him to his office, and he returned home in the same way at six. Something of the strength of character of the man will be seen if we remember how sensitive he was to the opinion of neighbours: this man whose every movement now attracted surprised attention. Inwardly he must have suffered torture; but he preserved a calm exterior even when the young criticised his little home, and he always lifted his hat courteously to any lady who looked inside.

It may have been quixotic, but it was magnificent. Soon the inward meaning of it leaked out, and the great heart of the public was touched. Crowds followed the cab, cheering it lustily; charming girls scaled it to get his autograph; interviews appeared in the better class of papers, and society invited him to dinner and added, "Do come in the kennel."

On that eventful Thursday week, Mrs. Darling was in the night-nursery awaiting George's return home; a very sad-eyed woman. Now that we look at her closely and remember the gaiety of her in the old days, all gone now just because she has lost her babes, I find I won't be able to say nasty things about her after all. If she was too fond of her rubbishy children, she couldn't help it. Look at her in her chair, where she has fallen asleep. The corner of her mouth, where one looks first, is almost withered up. Her hand moves restlessly on her breast as if she had a pain there. Some like Peter best, and some like Wendy best, but I like her best. Suppose, to make her happy, we whisper to her in her sleep that the brats are coming back. They are really within two miles of the window now, and flying strong, but all we need whisper is that they are on the way. Let's.

It is a pity we did it, for she has started up, calling their names; and there is no one in the room but Nana.

"O Nana, I dreamt my dear ones had come back."

Nana had filmy eyes, but all she could do was put her paw gently on her mistress's lap; and they were sitting together thus when the kennel was brought back. As Mr. Darling puts his head out to kiss his wife, we see that his face is more worn than of yore, but has a softer expression.

He gave his hat to Liza, who took it scornfully; for she had no imagination, and was quite incapable of understanding the motives of such a man. Outside, the crowd who had accompanied the cab home were still cheering, and he was naturally not unmoved.

"Listen to them," he said; "it is very gratifying."

"Lots of little boys," sneered Liza.

"There were several adults today," he assured her with a faint flush; but when she tossed her head he had not a word of reproof for her. Social success had not spoilt him; it had made him sweeter. For some time he sat with his head out of the kennel, talking with Mrs. Darling of this success, and pressing her hand reassuringly when she said she hoped his head would not be turned by it.

"But if I had been a weak man," he said. "Good heavens, if I had been a weak man!"

"And, George," she said timidly, "you are as full of remorse as ever, aren't you?"

"Full of remorse as ever, dearest! See my punishment: living in a kennel."

"But it is punishment, isn't it, George? You are sure you are not enjoying it?"

"My love!"

You may be sure she begged his pardon; and then, feeling drowsy, he curled round in the kennel.

"Won't you play me to sleep," he asked, "on the nursery piano?" and as she was crossing to the day-nursery he added thoughtlessly, "And shut that window. I feel a draught."

"O George, never ask me to do that. The window must always be left open for them, always, always."

Now it was his turn to beg her pardon; and she went into the day-nursery and played, and soon he was asleep; and while he slept, Wendy and John and Michael flew into the room.

Oh no. We have written it so, because that was the charming arrangement planned by them before we left the ship; but something must have happened since then, for it is not they who have flown in, it is Peter and Tinker Bell.

Peter's first words tell all.

"Quick, Tink," he whispered, "close the window; bar it! That's right. Now you and I must get away by the door; and when Wendy comes she will think her mother has barred her out; and she will have to go back with me."

Now I understand what had hitherto puzzled me, why when Peter had exterminated the pirates he did not return to the island and leave Tink to escort the children to the mainland. This trick had been in his head all the time.

Instead of feeling that he was behaving badly he danced with glee; then he peeped into the day-nursery to see who was playing. He whispered to Tink, "It's Wendy's mother! She is a pretty lady, but not so pretty as my mother. Her mouth is full of thimbles, but not so full as my mother's was."

Of course he knew nothing whatever about his mother; but he sometimes bragged about her.

He did not know the tune, which was "Home, Sweet Home," but he knew it was saying, "Come back, Wendy, Wendy, Wendy"; and he cried exultantly, "You will never see Wendy again, lady, for the window is barred!"

He peeped in again to see why the music had stopped, and now he saw that Mrs. Darling had laid her head on the box, and that two tears were sitting on her eyes.

"She wants me to unbar the window," thought Peter, "but I won't, not I!"

He peeped again, and the tears were still there, or another two had taken their place.

"She's awfully fond of Wendy," he said to himself. He was angry with her now for not seeing why she could not have Wendy.

The reason was so simple: "I'm fond of her too. We can't both have her, lady."

But the lady would not make the best of it, and he was unhappy. He ceased to look at her, but even then she would not let go of him. He skipped about and made funny faces, but when he stopped it was just as if she were inside him, knocking.

"Oh, all right," he said at last, and gulped. Then he unbarred the window. "Come on, Tink," he cried, with a frightful sneer at the laws of nature; "we don't want any silly mothers;" and he flew away.

Thus Wendy and John and Michael found the window open for them after all, which of course was more than they deserved. They alighted on the floor, quite unashamed of themselves, and the youngest one had already forgotten his home.

"John," he said, looking around him doubtfully, "I think I have been here before."

"Of course you have, you silly. There is your old bed."

"So it is," Michael said, but not with much conviction.

"I say," cried John, "the kennel!" and he dashed across to look into it.

"Perhaps Nana is inside it," Wendy said.

But John whistled. "Hullo," he said, "there's a man inside it."

"It's father!" exclaimed Wendy.

"Let me see father," Michael begged eagerly, and he took a good look. "He is not so big as the pirate I killed," he said with such frank disappointment that I am glad Mr. Darling was asleep; it would have been sad if those had been the first words he heard his little Michael say.

Wendy and John had been taken aback somewhat at finding their father in the kennel.

"Surely," said John, like one who had lost faith in his memory, "he used not to sleep in the kennel?"

"John," Wendy said falteringly, "perhaps we don't remember the old life as well as we thought we did."

A chill fell upon them; and serve them right.

"It is very careless of mother," said that young scoundrel John, "not to be here when we come back."

It was then that Mrs. Darling began playing again.

"It's mother!" cried Wendy, peeping.

"So it is!" said John.

"Then are you not really our mother, Wendy?" asked Michael, who was surely sleepy.

"Oh dear!" exclaimed Wendy, with her first real twinge of remorse [for having gone], "it was quite time we came back."

"Let us creep in," John suggested, "and put our hands over her eyes."

But Wendy, who saw that they must break the joyous news more gently, had a better plan.

"Let us all slip into our beds, and be there when she comes in, just as if we had never been away."

And so when Mrs. Darling went back to the night-nursery to see if her husband was asleep, all the beds were occupied. The children waited for her cry of joy, but it did not come. She saw them, but she did not believe they were there. You see, she saw them in their beds so often in her dreams that she thought this was just the dream hanging around her still.

She sat down in the chair by the fire, where in the old days she had nursed them.

They could not understand this, and a cold fear fell upon all the three of them.

"Mother!" Wendy cried.

"That's Wendy," she said, but still she was sure it was the dream.

"Mother!"

"That's John," she said.

"Mother!" cried Michael. He knew her now.

"That's Michael," she said, and she stretched out her arms for the three little selfish children they would never envelop again. Yes, they did, they went round Wendy and John and Michael, who had slipped out of bed and run to her.

"George, George!" she cried when she could speak; and Mr. Darling woke to share her bliss, and Nana came rushing in. There could not have been a lovelier sight; but there was none to see it except a little boy who was staring in at the window. He had had ecstasies innumerable that other children can never know; but he was looking through the window at the one joy from which he must be for ever barred.

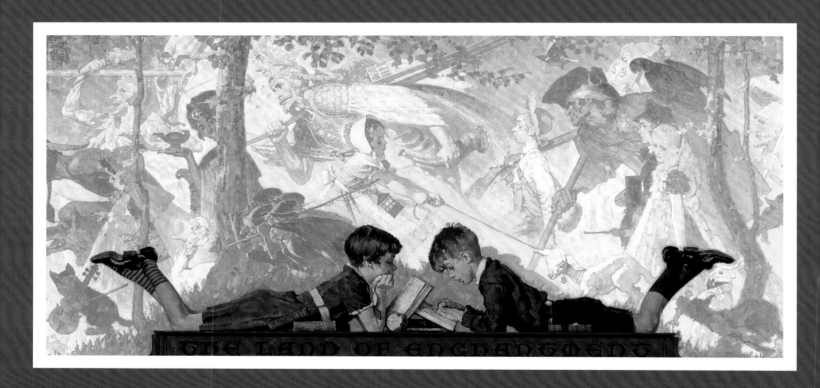

IN THE GARDEN

from *The Secret Garden*

FRANCES HODGSON BURNETT

IN EACH CENTURY since the beginning of the world wonderful things have been discovered. In the last century more amazing things were found out than in any century before. In this new century hundreds of things still more astounding will be brought to light. At first people refuse to believe that a strange new thing can be done, then they begin to hope it can be done, then they see it can be done—then it is done and all the world wonders why it was not done centuries ago. One of the new things people began to find out in the last century was that thoughts—just mere thoughts—are as powerful as electric batteries—as good for one as sunlight is, or as bad for one as poison. To let a sad thought or a bad one get into your mind is as dangerous as letting a scarlet fever germ get into your body. If you let it stay there after it has got in you may never get over it as long as you live.

So long as Mistress Mary's mind was full of disagreeable thoughts about her dislikes and sour opinions of people and her determination not to be pleased by or interested in anything, she was a yellow-faced, sickly, bored and wretched child. Circumstances, however, were very kind to her, though she was not at all aware of it. They began to push her about for her own good. When her mind gradually filled itself with robins, and moorland cottages crowded with children, with queer crabbed old gardeners and common little Yorkshire housemaids, with springtime and with secret gardens coming alive day by day, and also with a moor boy and his "creatures," there was no room left for the disagreeable thoughts which affected her liver and her digestion and made her yellow and tired.

So long as Colin shut himself up in his room and thought only of his fears and weakness and his detestation of people who looked at him and reflected hourly on humps and early death, he was a hysterical half-crazy little hypochondriac who knew nothing of the sunshine and the spring and also did not know that he could get well and could stand upon his feet if he tried to do it. When new beautiful thoughts began to push out the old hideous ones, life began to come back to him, his blood ran healthily through his veins and strength poured into him like a flood. His scientific experiment was quite practical and simple and there was nothing weird about it at all. Much more surprising things can happen to any one who, when a disagreeable or discouraged thought comes into his mind, just has the sense to remember in time and push it out by putting in an agreeable determinedly courageous one. Two things cannot be in one place.

"Where you tend a rose, my lad,

A thistle cannot grow."

While the secret garden was coming alive and two children were coming alive with it, there was a man wandering about certain far-away beautiful places in the Norwegian fiords and the valleys and mountains of Switzerland and he was a man who for ten years had kept his mind filled with dark and heart-broken thinking. He had not been courageous; he had never tried to put any other thoughts in the place of the dark ones. He had

wandered by blue lakes and thought them; he had lain on mountain-sides with sheets of deep blue gentians blooming all about him and flower breaths filling all the air and he had thought them. A terrible sorrow had fallen upon him when he had been happy and he had let his soul fill itself with blackness and had refused obstinately to allow any rift of light to pierce through. He had forgotten and deserted his home and his duties. When he traveled about, darkness so brooded over him that the sight of him was a wrong done to other people because it was as if he poisoned the air about him with gloom. Most strangers thought he must be either half mad or a man with some hidden crime on his soul. He was a tall man with a drawn face and crooked shoulders and the name he always entered on hotel registers was "Archibald Craven, Misselthwaite Manor, Yorkshire, England."

He had traveled far and wide since the day he saw Mistress Mary in his study and told her she might have her "bit of earth." He had been in the most beautiful places in Europe, though he had remained nowhere more than a few days. He had chosen the quietest and remotest spots. He had been on the tops of mountains whose heads were in the clouds and had looked down on other mountains when the sun rose and touched them with such light as made it seem as if the world were just being born.

But the light had never seemed to touch himself until one day when he realized that for the first time in ten years a strange thing had happened. He was in a wonderful valley in the Austrian Tyrol and he had been walking alone through such beauty as might have lifted any man's soul out of shadow. He had walked a long way and it had not lifted his. But at last he had felt tired and had thrown himself down to rest on a carpet of moss by a stream. It was a clear little stream which ran quite merrily along on its narrow way through the luscious damp greenness. Sometimes it made a sound rather like very low laughter as it bubbled over and round stones. He saw birds come and dip their heads to drink in it and then flick their wings and fly away. It seemed like a thing alive and yet its tiny voice made the stillness seem deeper. The valley was very, very still.

As he sat gazing into the clear running of the water, Archibald Craven gradually felt his mind and body both grow quiet, as quiet as the valley itself. He wondered if he were going to sleep, but he was not. He sat and gazed at the sunlit water and his eyes began to see things growing at its edge. There was one lovely mass of blue forget-me-nots growing so close to the stream that its leaves were wet and at these he found himself looking as he remembered he had looked at such things years ago. He was actually thinking tenderly how lovely it was and what wonders of blue its hundreds of little blossoms were. He did not know that just that simple thought was slowly filling his mind—filling and filling it until other things were softly pushed aside. It was as if a sweet clear spring had begun to rise in a stagnant pool and had risen and risen until at last it swept the dark water away. But of course he did not think of this himself. He only knew that the valley seemed to grow quieter and quieter as he sat and stared at the bright delicate blueness. He did not know how long he sat there or what was happening to him, but at last he moved as if he were awakening and he got up slowly and stood on the moss carpet, drawing a long, deep, soft breath and wondering at himself. Something seemed to have been unbound and released in him, very quietly.

"What is it?" he said, almost in a whisper, and he passed his hand over his forehead. "I almost feel as if—I were alive!"

I do not know enough about the wonderfulness of undiscovered things to be able to explain how this had happened to him. Neither does any one else yet. He did not understand at all himself—but he remembered this strange hour months afterward when he was at Misselthwaite again and he found out quite by accident that on this very day Colin had cried out as he went into the secret garden:

"I am going to live forever and ever and ever!"

The singular calmness remained with him the rest of the evening and he slept a new reposeful sleep; but it was not with him very long. He did not know that it could be kept. By the next night he had opened the doors wide to his dark thoughts and they had come

trooping and rushing back. He left the valley and went on his wandering way again. But, strange as it seemed to him, there were minutes—sometimes half-hours—when, without his knowing why, the black burden seemed to lift itself again and he knew he was a living man and not a dead one. Slowly—slowly—for no reason that he knew of—he was "coming alive" with the garden.

As the golden summer changed into the deep golden autumn he went to the Lake of Como. There he found the loveliness of a dream. He spent his days upon the crystal blueness of the lake or he walked back into the soft thick verdure of the hills and tramped until he was tired so that he might sleep. But by this time he had begun to sleep better, he knew, and his dreams had ceased to be a terror to him.

"Perhaps," he thought, "my body is growing stronger."

It was growing stronger but—because of the rare peaceful hours when his thoughts were changed—his soul was slowly growing stronger, too. He began to think of Misselthwaite and wonder if he should not go home. Now and then he wondered vaguely about his boy and asked himself what he should feel when he went and stood by the carved four-posted bed again and looked down at the sharply chiseled ivory-white face while it slept and the black lashes rimmed so startlingly the close-shut eyes. He shrank from it.

One marvel of a day he had walked so far that when he returned the moon was high and full and all the world was purple shadow and silver. The stillness of lake and shore and wood was so wonderful that he did not go into the villa he lived in. He walked down to a little bowered terrace at the water's edge and sat upon a seat and breathed in all the heavenly scents of the night. He felt the strange calmness stealing over him and it grew deeper and deeper until he fell asleep.

He did not know when he fell asleep and when he began to dream; his dream was so real that he did not feel as if he were dreaming. He remembered afterward how intensely wide awake and alert he had thought he was. He thought that as he sat and breathed in the scent of the late roses and listened to the lapping of the water at his feet he heard a voice calling. It was sweet and clear and happy and far away. It seemed very far, but he heard it as distinctly as if it had been at his very side.

"Archie! Archie! Archie!" it said, and then again, sweeter and clearer than before, "Archie! Archie!"

He thought he sprang to his feet not even startled. It was such a real voice and it seemed so natural that he should hear it.

"Lilias! Lilias!" he answered. "Lilias! where are you?"

"In the garden," it came back like a sound from a golden flute. "In the garden!"

And then the dream ended. But he did not awaken. He slept soundly and sweetly all through the lovely night. When he did awake at last it was brilliant morning and a servant was standing staring at him. He was an Italian servant and was accustomed, as all the servants of the villa were, to accepting without question any strange thing his foreign master might do. No one ever knew when he would go out or come in or where he would choose to sleep or if he would roam about the garden or lie in the boat on the lake all night. The man held a salver with some letters on it and he waited quietly until Mr. Craven took them. When he had gone away Mr. Craven sat a few moments holding them in his hand and looking at the lake. His strange calm was still upon him and something more—a lightness as if the cruel thing which had been done had not happened as he thought—as if something had changed. He was remembering the dream—the real— real dream.

"In the garden!" he said, wondering at himself. "In the garden! But the door is locked and the key is buried deep."

When he glanced at the letters a few minutes later he saw that the one lying at the top of the rest was an English letter and came from Yorkshire. It was directed in a plain woman's hand but it was not a hand he knew. He opened it, scarcely thinking of the writer, but the first words attracted his attention at once.

"*Dear Sir:*

I am Susan Sowerby that made bold to speak to you once on the moor. It was about Miss Mary I spoke. I will make bold to speak again. Please, sir, I would come home if I was you. I think you would be glad to come and—if you will excuse me, sir—I think your lady would ask you to come if she was here.

Your obedient servant,
Susan Sowerby."

Mr. Craven read the letter twice before he put it back in its envelope. He kept thinking about the dream.

"I will go back to Misselthwaite," he said. "Yes, I'll go at once."

And he went through the garden to the villa and ordered Pitcher to prepare for his return to England.

In a few days he was in Yorkshire again, and on his long railroad journey he found himself thinking of his boy as he had never thought in all the ten years past. During those years he had only wished to forget him. Now, though he did not intend to think about him, memories of him constantly drifted into his mind. He remembered the black days when he had raved like a madman because the child was alive and the mother was dead. He had refused to see it, and when he had gone to look at it at last it had been such a weak wretched thing that everyone had been sure it would die in a few days. But to the surprise of those who took care of it the days passed and it lived and then everyone believed it would be a deformed and crippled creature.

He had not meant to be a bad father, but he had not felt like a father at all. He had supplied doctors and nurses and luxuries, but he had shrunk from the mere thought of the boy and had buried himself in his own misery. The first time after a year's absence he returned to Misselthwaite and the small miserable looking thing languidly and indifferently lifted to his face the great gray eyes with black lashes round them, so like and yet so horribly unlike the happy eyes he had adored, he could not bear the sight of them and turned away pale as death. After that he scarcely ever saw him except when he was asleep, and all he knew of him was that he was a confirmed invalid, with a vicious, hysterical, half-insane temper. He could only be kept from furies dangerous to himself by being given his own way in every detail.

All this was not an uplifting thing to recall, but as the train whirled him through mountain passes and golden plains the man who was "coming alive" began to think in a new way and he thought long and steadily and deeply.

"Perhaps I have been all wrong for ten years," he said to himself. "Ten years is a long time. It may be too late to do anything—quite too late. What have I been thinking of!"

Of course this was the wrong Magic—to begin by saying "too late." Even Colin could have told him that. But he knew nothing of Magic—either black or white. This he had yet to learn. He wondered if Susan Sowerby had taken courage and written to him only because the motherly creature had realized that the boy was much worse—was fatally ill. If he had not been under the spell of the curious calmness which had taken possession of him he would have been more wretched than ever. But the calm had brought a sort of courage and hope with it. Instead of giving way to thoughts of the worst he actually found he was trying to believe in better things.

"Could it be possible that she sees that I may be able to do him good and control him?" he thought. "I will go and see her on my way to Misselthwaite."

But when on his way across the moor he stopped the carriage at the cottage, seven or eight children who were playing about gathered in a group and bobbing seven or eight friendly and polite curtsies told him that their mother had gone to the other side of the moor early in the morning to help a woman who had a new baby. "Our Dickon," they volunteered, was over at the Manor working in one of the gardens where he went several days each week.

Mr. Craven looked over the collection of sturdy little bodies and round red-cheeked faces, each one grinning in its own particular way, and he awoke to the fact that they were a healthy likable lot. He smiled at their friendly grins and took a golden sovereign from his pocket and gave it to "our 'Lizabeth Ellen" who was the oldest.

"If you divide that into eight parts there will be half a crown for each of you," he said.

Then amid grins and chuckles and bobbing of curtsies he drove away, leaving ecstasy and nudging elbows and little jumps of joy behind.

The drive across the wonderfulness of the moor was a soothing thing. Why did it seem to give him a sense of homecoming which he had been sure he could never feel again—that sense of the beauty of land and sky and purple bloom of distance and a warming of the heart at drawing, nearer to the great old house which had held those of his blood for six hundred years? How he had driven away from it the last time, shuddering to think of its closed rooms and the boy lying in the four-posted bed with the brocaded hangings. Was it possible that perhaps he might find him changed a little for the better and that he might overcome his shrinking from him? How real that dream had been—how wonderful and clear the voice which called back to him, "In the garden—In the garden!"

"I will try to find the key," he said. "I will try to open the door. I must—though I don't know why."

When he arrived at the Manor the servants who received him with the usual ceremony noticed that he looked better and that he did not go to the remote rooms where he usually lived attended by Pitcher. He went into the library and sent for Mrs. Medlock. She came to him somewhat excited and curious and flustered.

"How is Master Colin, Medlock?" he inquired. "Well, sir," Mrs. Medlock answered, "he's—he's different, in a manner of speaking."

"Worse?" he suggested.

Mrs. Medlock really was flushed.

"Well, you see, sir," she tried to explain, "neither Dr. Craven, nor the nurse, nor me can exactly make him out."

"Why is that?"

"To tell the truth, sir, Master Colin might be better and he might be changing for the worse. His appetite, sir, is past understanding—and his ways—"

"Has he become more—more peculiar?" her master, asked, knitting his brows anxiously.

"That's it, sir. He's growing very peculiar—when you compare him with what he used to be. He used to eat nothing and then suddenly he began to eat something enormous—and then he stopped again all at once and the meals were sent back just as they used to be. You never knew, sir, perhaps, that out of doors he never would let himself be taken. The things we've gone through to get him to go out in his chair would leave a body trembling like a leaf. He'd throw himself into such a state that Dr. Craven said he couldn't be responsible for forcing him. Well, sir, just without warning—not long after one of his worst tantrums he suddenly insisted on being taken out every day by Miss Mary and Susan Sowerby's boy Dickon that could push his chair. He took a fancy to both Miss Mary and Dickon, and Dickon brought his tame animals, and, if you'll credit it, sir, out of doors he will stay from morning until night."

"How does he look?" was the next question.

"If he took his food natural, sir, you'd think he was putting on flesh—but we're afraid it may be a sort of bloat. He laughs sometimes in a queer way when he's alone with Miss Mary. He never used to laugh at all. Dr. Craven is coming to see you at once, if you'll allow him. He never was as puzzled in his life."

"Where is Master Colin now?" Mr. Craven asked.

"In the garden, sir. He's always in the garden—though not a human creature is allowed to go near for fear they'll look at him."

Mr. Craven scarcely heard her last words.

"In the garden," he said, and after he had sent Mrs. Medlock away he stood and repeated it again and again. "In the garden!"

He had to make an effort to bring himself back to the place he was standing in and when he felt he was on earth again he turned and went out of the room. He took his way, as Mary had done, through the door in the shrubbery and among the laurels and the fountain beds. The fountain was playing now and was encircled by beds of brilliant autumn flowers. He crossed the lawn and turned into the Long Walk by the ivied walls. He did not walk quickly, but slowly, and his eyes were on the path. He felt as if he were being drawn back to the place he had so long forsaken, and he did not know why. As he drew near to it his step became still more slow. He knew where the door was even though the ivy hung thick over it—but he did not know exactly where it lay—that buried key.

So he stopped and stood still, looking about him, and almost the moment after he had paused he started and listened—asking himself if he were walking in a dream.

The ivy hung thick over the door, the key was buried under the shrubs, no human being had passed that portal for ten lonely years—and yet inside the garden there were sounds. They were the sounds of running scuffling feet seeming to chase round and round under the trees, they were strange sounds of lowered suppressed voices—exclamations and smothered joyous cries. It seemed actually like the laughter of young things, the uncontrollable laughter of children who were trying not to be heard but who in a moment or so—as their excitement mounted—would burst forth. What in heaven's name was he dreaming of—what in heaven's name did he hear? Was he losing his reason and thinking he heard things which were not for human ears? Was it that the far clear voice had meant?

And then the moment came, the uncontrollable moment when the sounds forgot to hush themselves. The feet ran faster and faster—they were nearing the garden door—there was quick strong young breathing and a wild outbreak of laughing shows which could not be contained—and the door in the wall was flung wide open, the sheet of ivy swinging back, and a boy burst through it at full speed and, without seeing the outsider, dashed almost into his arms.

Mr. Craven had extended them just in time to save him from falling as a result of his unseeing dash against him, and when he held him away to look at him in amazement at his being there he truly gasped for breath.

He was a tall boy and a handsome one. He was glowing with life and his running had sent splendid color leaping to his face. He threw the thick hair back from his forehead and lifted a pair of strange gray eyes—eyes full of boyish laughter and rimmed with black lashes like a fringe. It was the eyes which made Mr. Craven gasp for breath. "Who—What? Who!" he stammered.

This was not what Colin had expected—this was not what he had planned. He had never thought of such a meeting. And yet to come dashing out—winning a race—

perhaps it was even better. He drew himself up to his very tallest. Mary, who had been running with him and had dashed through the door too, believed that he managed to make himself look taller than he had ever looked before.

"Father," he said, "I'm Colin. You can't believe it. I scarcely can myself. I'm Colin."

Like Mrs. Medlock, he did not understand what his father meant when he said hurriedly:

"In the garden! In the garden!"

"Yes," hurried on Colin. "It was the garden that did it—and Mary and Dickon and the creatures—and the Magic. No one knows. We kept it to tell you when you came. I'm well, I can beat Mary in a race. I'm going to be an athlete."

He said it all so like a healthy boy—his face flushed, his words tumbling over each other in his eagerness—that Mr. Craven's soul shook with unbelieving joy.

Colin put out his hand and laid it on his father's arm.

"Aren't you glad, Father?" he ended. "Aren't you glad? I'm going to live forever and ever and ever!"

Mr. Craven put his hands on both the boy's shoulders and held him still. He knew he dared not even try to speak for a moment.

"Take me into the garden, my boy," he said at last. "And tell me all about it."

And so they led him in.

The place was a wilderness of autumn gold and purple and violet blue and flaming scarlet and on every side were sheaves of late lilies standing together—lilies which were white or white and ruby. He remembered well when the first of them had been planted that just at this season of the year their late glories should reveal themselves. Late roses climbed and hung and clustered and the sunshine deepening the hue of the yellowing trees made one feel that one, stood in an embowered temple of gold. The newcomer stood silent just as the children had done when they came into its grayness. He looked round and round.

"I thought it would be dead," he said.

"Mary thought so at first," said Colin. "But it came alive."

Then they sat down under their tree—all but Colin, who wanted to stand while he told the story.

It was the strangest thing he had ever heard, Archibald Craven thought, as it was poured forth in headlong boy fashion. Mystery and Magic and wild creatures, the weird midnight meeting—the coming of the spring—the passion of insulted pride which had dragged the young Rajah to his feet to defy old Ben Weatherstaff to his face. The odd companionship, the play acting, the great secret so carefully kept. The listener laughed until tears came into his eyes and sometimes tears came into his eyes when he was not laughing. The Athlete, the Lecturer, the Scientific Discoverer was a laughable, lovable, healthy young human thing.

"Now," he said at the end of the story, "it need not be a secret any more. I dare say it will frighten them nearly into fits when they see me—but I am never going to get into the chair again. I shall walk back with you, Father—to the house."

Ben Weatherstaff's duties rarely took him away from the gardens, but on this occasion he made an excuse to carry some vegetables to the kitchen and being invited into the servants' hall by Mrs. Medlock to drink a glass of beer he was on the spot—as he had hoped to be—when the most dramatic event Misselthwaite Manor had seen during the present generation actually took place. One of the windows looking upon the courtyard gave also a glimpse of the lawn. Mrs. Medlock, knowing Ben had come from the gardens, hoped that he might have caught sight of his master and even by chance of his meeting with Master Colin.

"Did you see either of them, Weatherstaff?" she asked.

Ben took his beer-mug from his mouth and wiped his lips with the back of his hand.

"Aye, that I did," he answered with a shrewdly significant air.

"Both of them?" suggested Mrs. Medlock.

"Both of 'em," returned Ben Weatherstaff. "Thank ye kindly, ma'am, I could sup up another mug of it."

"Together?" said Mrs. Medlock, hastily overfilling his beer-mug in her excitement.

"Together, ma'am," and Ben gulped down half of his new mug at one gulp.

"Where was Master Colin? How did he look? What did they say to each other?"

"I didna' hear that," said Ben, "along o' only bein' on th' stepladder lookin, over th' wall. But I'll tell thee this. There's been things goin' on outside as you house people knows nowt about. An' what tha'll find out tha'll find out soon."

And it was not two minutes before he swallowed the last of his beer and waved his mug solemnly toward the window which took in through the shrubbery a piece of the lawn.

"Look there," he said, "if tha's curious. Look what's comin' across th' grass."

When Mrs. Medlock looked she threw up her hands and gave a little shriek and every man and woman servant within hearing bolted across the servants' hall and stood looking through the window with their eyes almost starting out of their heads.

Across the lawn came the Master of Misselthwaite and he looked as many of them had never seen him. And by his, side with his head up in the air and his eyes full of laughter walked as strongly and steadily as any boy in Yorkshire—

Master Colin!

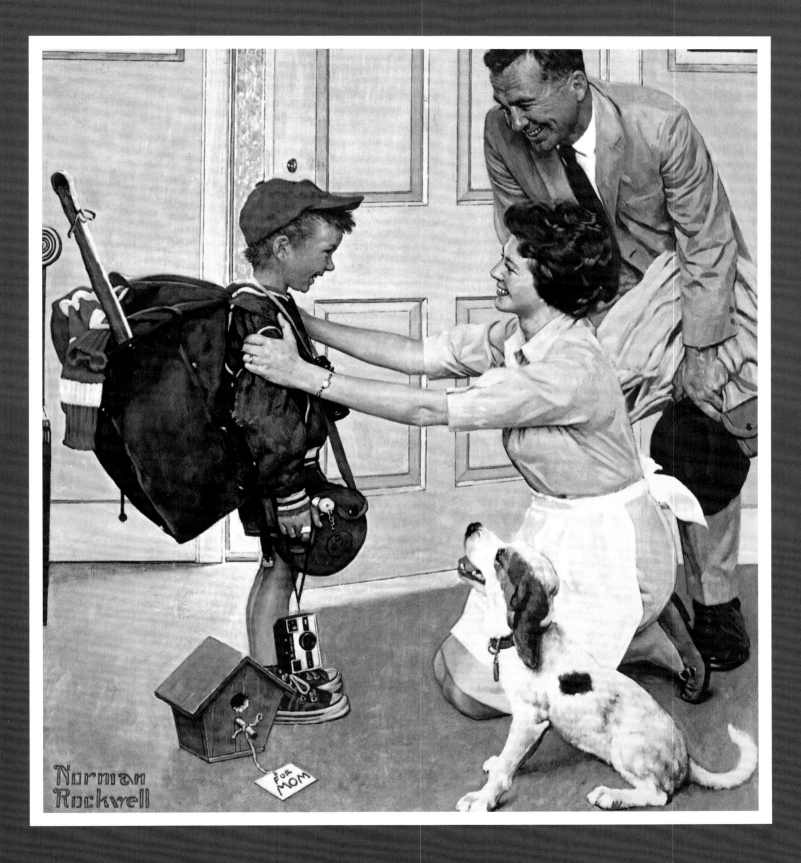

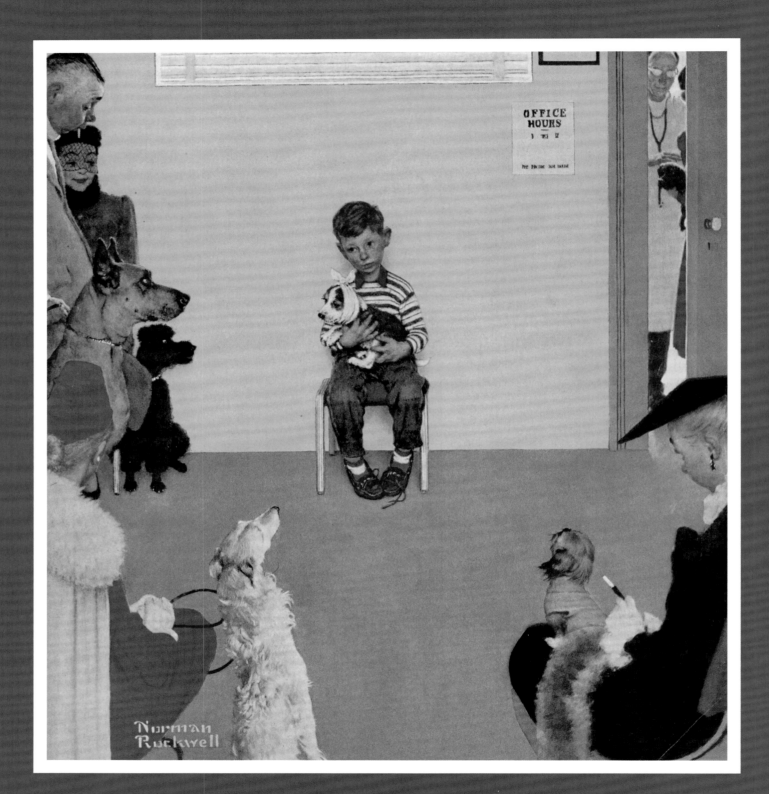

PUDDLEBY

HUGH LOFTING

ONCE UPON A TIME, many years ago when
our grandfathers were little children—there was a
doctor; and his name was Dolittle—John Dolittle,
M.D. "M.D." means that he was a proper doctor
and knew a whole lot.

He lived in a little town called Puddleby-on-the-Marsh. All the folks, young and old, knew him well by sight. And whenever he walked down the street in his high hat everyone would say, "There goes the Doctor!—He's a clever man." And the dogs and the children would all run up and follow behind him; and even the crows that lived in the church-tower would caw and nod their heads.

The house he lived in, on the edge of the town, was quite small; but his garden was very large and had a wide lawn and stone seats and weeping-willows hanging over. His sister, Sarah Dolittle, was housekeeper for him; but the Doctor looked after the garden himself.

He was very fond of animals and kept many kinds of pets. Besides the goldfish in the pond at the bottom of his garden, he had rabbits in the pantry, white mice in his piano, a squirrel in the linen closet and a hedgehog in the cellar. He had a cow with a calf too, and an old lame horse—twenty-five years of age—and chickens, and pigeons, and two lambs, and many other animals. But his favorite pets were Dab-Dab the duck, Jip the dog, Gub-Gub the baby pig, Polynesia the parrot, and the owl Too-Too.

His sister used to grumble about all these animals and said they made the house untidy. And one day when an old lady with rheumatism came to see the Doctor, she sat on the hedgehog who was sleeping on the sofa and never came to see him any more, but drove every Saturday all the way to Oxenthorpe, another town ten miles off, to see a different doctor.

Then his sister, Sarah Dolittle, came to him and said, "John, how can you expect sick people to come and see you when you keep all these animals in the house? It's a fine doctor would have his parlor full of hedgehogs and mice! That's the fourth personage these animals have driven away. Squire Jenkins and the Parson say they wouldn't come near your house again—no matter how sick they are. We are getting poorer every day. If you go on like this, none of the best people will have you for a doctor."

"But I like the animals better than the 'best people'," said the Doctor.

"You are ridiculous," said his sister, and walked out of the room.

So, as time went on, the Doctor got more and more animals; and the people who came to see him got less and less. Till at last he had no one left—except the Cat's-meat-Man, who didn't mind any kind of animals. But the Cat's-meat-Man wasn't very rich and he only got sick once a year—at Christmas-time, when he used to give the Doctor sixpence for a bottle of medicine.

Sixpence a year wasn't enough to live on—even in those days, long ago; and if the Doctor hadn't had some money saved up in his money-box, no one knows what would have happened.

And he kept on getting still more pets; and of course it cost a lot to feed them. And the money he had saved up grew littler and littler.

Then he sold his piano, and let the mice live in a bureau-drawer. But the money he got for that too began to go, so he sold the brown suit he wore on Sundays and went on becoming poorer and poorer.

And now, when he walked down the street in his high hat, people would say to one another, "There goes John Dolittle, M.D.! There was a time when he was the best known doctor in the West Country—Look at him now—He hasn't any money and his stockings are full of holes!"

But the dogs and the cats and the children still ran up and followed him through the town—the same as they had done when he was rich.

"ANIMAL LANGUAGE"

It happened one day that the Doctor was sitting in his kitchen talking with the Cat's-meat-Man who had come to see him with a stomach-ache.

"Why don't you give up being a people's doctor, and be an animal-doctor?" asked the Cat's-meat-Man.

The parrot, Polynesia, was sitting in the window looking out at the rain and singing a sailor-song to herself. She stopped singing and started to listen.

"You see, Doctor," the Cat's-meat-Man went on, "you know all about animals—much more than what these here vets do. That book you wrote—about cats, why, it's wonderful! I can't read or write myself—or maybe I'd write some books. But my wife, Theodosia, she's a scholar, she is. And she read your book to me. Well, it's wonderful—that's all can be said—wonderful. You might have been a cat yourself. You know the way they think. And listen: You can make a lot of money doctoring animals. Do you know that? You see, I'd send all the old women who had sick cats or dogs to you. And if they didn't get sick fast enough, I could put something in the meat I sell 'em to make 'em sick, see?"

"Oh, no," said the Doctor quickly. "You mustn't do that. That wouldn't be right."

"Oh, I didn't mean real sick," answered the Cat's-meat-Man. "Just a little something to make them droopy-like was what I had reference to. But as you say, maybe it ain't quite fair on the animals. But they'll get sick anyway, because the old women always give 'em too much to eat. And look, all the farmers 'round about who had lame horses and weak lambs—they'd come. Be an animal-doctor."

When the Cat's-meat-Man had gone the parrot flew off the window on to the Doctor's table and said, "That man's got sense. That's what you ought to do. Be an animal-doctor. Give the silly people up—if they haven't brains enough to see you're the best doctor in the world. Take care of animals instead—THEY'll soon find it out. Be an animal-doctor."

"Oh, there are plenty of animal-doctors," said John Dolittle, putting the flower-pots outside on the window-sill to get the rain.

"Yes, there *are* plenty," said Polynesia. "But none of them are any good at all. Now listen, Doctor, and I'll tell you something. Did you know that animals can talk?"

"I knew that parrots can talk," said the Doctor.

"Oh, we parrots can talk in two languages—people's language and bird-language," said Polynesia proudly. "If I say, 'Polly wants a cracker,' you understand me. But hear this: Ka-ka oi-ee, fee-fee?"

"Good Gracious!" cried the Doctor. "What does that mean?"

"That means, 'Is the porridge hot yet?'—in bird-language."

"My! You don't say so!" said the Doctor. "You never talked that way to me before."

"What would have been the good?" said Polynesia, dusting some cracker-crumbs off her left wing. "You wouldn't have understood me if I had."

"Tell me some more," said the Doctor, all excited; and he rushed over to the dresser-drawer and came back with the butcher's book and a pencil. "Now don't go too fast—and I'll write it down. This is interesting—very interesting—something quite new. Give me the Birds' A.B.C. first—slowly now."

So that was the way the Doctor came to know that animals had a language of their own and could talk to one another. And all that afternoon, while it was raining, Polynesia sat on the kitchen table giving him bird words to put down in the book.

At tea-time, when the dog, Jip, came in, the parrot said to the Doctor, "See, *he's* talking to you."

"Looks to me as though he were scratching his ear," said the Doctor.

"But animals don't always speak with their mouths," said the parrot in a high voice, raising her eyebrows. "They talk with their ears, with their feet, with their tails—with everything. Sometimes they don't WANT to make a noise. Do you see now the way he's twitching up one side of his nose?"

"What's that mean?" asked the Doctor.

"That means, 'Can't you see that it has stopped raining?'" Polynesia answered. "He is asking you a question. Dogs nearly always use their noses for asking questions."

After a while, with the parrot's help, the Doctor got to learn the language of the animals so well that he could talk to them himself and understand everything they said. Then he gave up being a people's doctor altogether.

As soon as the Cat's-meat-Man had told every one that John Dolittle was going to become an animal-doctor, old ladies began to bring him their pet pugs and poodles who had eaten too much cake; and farmers came many miles to show him sick cows and sheep.

One day a plow-horse was brought to him; and the poor thing was terribly glad to find a man who could talk in horse-language.

"You know, Doctor," said the horse, "that vet over the hill knows nothing at all. He has been treating me six weeks now—for spavins. What I need is *spectacles*. I am going blind in one eye. There's no reason why horses shouldn't wear glasses, the same as people. But that stupid man over the hill never even looked at my eyes. He kept on giving me big pills. I tried to tell him; but he couldn't understand a word of horse-language. What I need is spectacles."

"Of course—of course," said the Doctor. "I'll get you some at once."

"I would like a pair like yours," said the horse—"only green. They'll keep the sun out of my eyes while I'm plowing the Fifty-Acre Field."

"Certainly," said the Doctor. "Green ones you shall have."

"You know, the trouble is, Sir," said the plow-horse as the Doctor opened the front door to let him out—"the trouble is that *anybody* thinks he can doctor animals—just because the animals don't complain. As a matter of fact it takes a much cleverer man to be a really good animal-doctor than it does to be a good people's doctor. My farmer's boy thinks he knows all about horses. I wish you could see him—his face is so fat he looks as though he had no eyes—and he has got as much brain as a potato-bug. He tried to put a mustard-plaster on me last week."

"Where did he put it?" asked the Doctor.

"Oh, he didn't put it anywhere—on me," said the horse. "He only tried to. I kicked him into the duck-pond."

"Well, well!" said the Doctor.

"I'm a pretty quiet creature as a rule," said the horse—"very patient with people—don't make much fuss. But it was bad enough to have that vet giving me the wrong medicine. And when that red-faced booby started to monkey with me, I just couldn't bear it any more."

"Did you hurt the boy much?" asked the Doctor.

"Oh, no," said the horse. "I kicked him in the right place. The vet's looking after him now. When will my glasses be ready?"

"I'll have them for you next week," said the Doctor. "Come in again Tuesday—Good morning!"

Then John Dolittle got a fine, big pair of green spectacles; and the plow-horse stopped going blind in one eye and could see as well as ever.

And soon it became a common sight to see farm-animals wearing glasses in the country round Puddleby; and a blind horse was a thing unknown.

And so it was with all the other animals that were brought to him. As soon as they found that he could talk their language, they told him where the pain was and how they felt, and of course it was easy for him to cure them.

Now all these animals went back and told their brothers and friends that there was a doctor in the little house with the big garden who really *was* a doctor. And whenever any creatures got sick—not only horses and cows and dogs—but all the little things of the fields, like harvest-mice and water-voles, badgers and bats, they came at once to his house on the edge of the town, so that his big garden was nearly always crowded with animals trying to get in to see him.

There were so many that came that he had to have special doors made for the different kinds. He wrote "HORSES" over the front door, "COWS" over the side door, and "SHEEP" on the kitchen door. Each kind of animal had a separate door—even the mice had a tiny tunnel made for them into the cellar, where they waited patiently in rows for the Doctor to come round to them.

And so, in a few years' time, every living thing for miles and miles got to know about John Dolittle, M.D. And the birds who flew to other countries in the winter told the animals in foreign lands of the wonderful doctor of Puddleby-on-the-Marsh, who could understand their talk and help them in their troubles. In this way he became famous among the animals—all over the world— better known even than he had been among the folks of the West Country. And he was happy and liked his life very much.

One afternoon when the Doctor was busy writing in a book, Polynesia sat in the window—as she nearly always did—looking out at the leaves blowing about in the garden. Presently she laughed aloud.

"What is it, Polynesia?" asked the Doctor, looking up from his book.

"I was just thinking," said the parrot; and she went on looking at the leaves.

"What were you thinking?"

"I was thinking about people," said Polynesia. "People make me sick. They think they're so wonderful. The world has been going on now for thousands of years, hasn't it?

And the only thing in animal-language that *people* have learned to understand is that when a dog wags his tail he means 'I'm glad!'—It's funny, isn't it? You are the very first man to talk like us. Oh, sometimes people annoy me dreadfully—such airs they put on—talking about 'the dumb animals.' *Dumb!*—Huh! Why I knew a macaw once who could say 'Good morning!' in seven different ways without once opening his mouth. He could talk every language—and Greek. An old professor with a gray beard bought him. But he didn't stay. He said the old man didn't talk Greek right, and he couldn't stand listening to him teach the language wrong. I often wonder what's become of him. That bird knew more geography than people will ever know.—PEOPLE, Golly! I suppose if people ever learn to fly—like any common hedge-sparrow—we shall never hear the end of it!"

"You're a wise old bird," said the Doctor. "How old are you really? I know that parrots and elephants sometimes live to be very, very old."

"I can never be quite sure of my age," said Polynesia. "It's either a hundred and eighty-three or a hundred and eighty-two. But I know that when I first came here from Africa, King Charles was still hiding in the oak-tree—because I saw him. He looked scared to death."

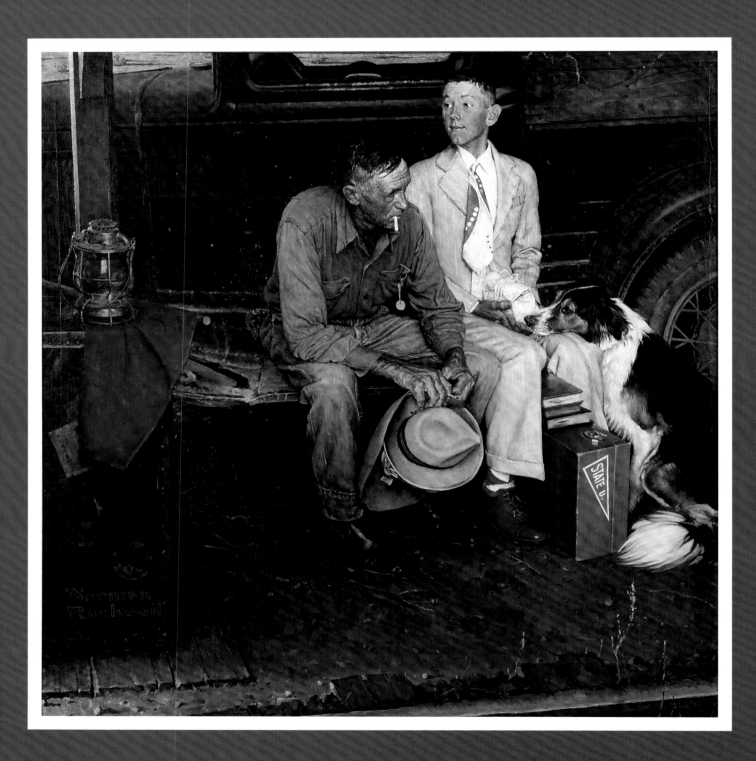

SPLIT CHERRY TREE

JESSE STUART

"I DON'T MIND staying after school," I says to Professor Herbert, "but I'd rather you'd whip me with a switch and let me go home early. Pa will whip me anyway for getting home two hours late."

"You are too big to whip," says Professor Herbert, "and I have to punish you for climbing up in that cherry tree. You boys knew better than that! The other five boys have paid their dollar each. You have been the only one who has not helped pay for the tree. Can't you borrow a dollar?"

"I can't," I says. "I'll have to take the punishment. I wish it would be quicker punishment. I wouldn't mind."

Professor Herbert stood and looked at me. He was a big man. He wore a grey suit of clothes. The suit matched his grey hair.

"You don't know my father," I says to Professor Herbert. "He might be called a little old-fashioned. He makes us mind him until we're twenty-one years old. He believes: 'If you spare the rod you spoil the child.' I'll never be able to make him understand about the cherry tree. I'm the first of my people to go to high school."

"You must take the punishment," says Professor Herbert. "You must stay two hours after school today and two hours after school tomorrow. I am allowing you twenty-five cents an hour. That is good money for a high-school student. You can sweep the schoolhouse floor, wash the blackboards, and clean windows. I'll pay the dollar for you."

I couldn't ask Professor Herbert to loan me a dollar. He never offered to loan it to me. I had to stay and help the janitor and work out my fine at a quarter an hour.

I thought as I swept the floor, "What will Pa do to me? What lie can I tell him when I go home? Why did we ever climb that cherry tree and break it down for anyway? Why did we run crazy over the hills away from the crowd? Why did we do all of this? Six of us climbed up in a little cherry tree after one little lizard! Why did the tree split and fall with us? It should have been a stronger tree! Why did Eif Crabtree just happen to be below us plowing and catch us in his cherry tree? Why wasn't he a better man than to charge us six dollars for the tree?"

It was six o'clock when I left the schoolhouse. I had six miles to walk home. It would be after seven when I got home. I had all my work to do when I got home. It took Pa and I both to do the work. Seven cows to milk. Nineteen head of cattle to feed, four mules, twenty-five hogs, firewood and stovewood to cut, and water to draw from the well. He would be doing it when I got home. He would be mad and wondering what was keeping me!

I hurried home. I would run under the dark, leafless trees. I would walk fast uphill. I would run down the hill.

The ground was freezing. I had to hurry. I had to run. I reached the long ridge that led to our cow pasture. I ran along this ridge. The wind dried the sweat on my face. I ran across the pasture to the house.

I threw down my books in the chipyard. I ran to the barn to spread fodder on the ground for the cattle. I didn't take time to change my clean school clothes for my old work clothes. I ran out to the barn. I saw Pa spreading fodder on the ground to the cattle. That was my job. I ran up to the fence. I says, "Leave that for me, Pa. I'll do it. I'm just a little late."

"I see you are," says Pa. He turned and looked at me. His eyes danced fire. "What in th' world has kept you so? Why ain't you been here to help me with this work? Make a gentleman out'n one boy in th' family and this is what you get! Send you to high school and you get too onery fer th' buzzards to smell!"

I never said anything. I didn't want to tell why I was late from school. Pa stopped scattering the bundles of fodder. He looked at me. He says, "Why are you gettin' in here this time o' night? You tell me or I'll take a hickory withe to you right here on th' spot!"

I says, "I had to stay after school." I couldn't lie to Pa. He'd go to school and find out why I had to stay. If I lied to him it would be too bad for me.

"Why did you haf to stay atter school?" says Pa.

I says, "Our biology class went on a field trip today. Six of us boys broke down a cherry tree. We had to give a dollar apiece to pay for the tree. I didn't have the dollar. Professor Herbert is making me work out my dollar. He gives me twenty-five cents an hour. I had to stay in this afternoon. I'll have to stay in tomorrow afternoon!"

"Are you telling me th' truth?" says Pa.

"I'm telling you the truth," I says. "Go and see for yourself."

"That's just what I'll do in th' mornin'," says Pa. "Jist whose cherry tree did you break down?"

"Eif Crabtree's cherry tree!"

"What was you doin' clear out in Eif Crabtree's place?" says Pa. "He lives four miles from th' county high school. Don't they teach you no books at that high school? Do they jist let you get out and gad over th' hillsides? If that's all they do I'll keep you at home, Dave. I've got work here fer you to do!"

"Pa," I says, "spring is just getting here. We take a subject in school where we have to have bugs, snakes, flowers, lizards, frogs, and plants. It is biology. It was a pretly day today. We went out to find a few of these. Six of us boys saw a lizard at the same time sunning on a cherry tree. We all went up the tree to get it. We broke the tree down. It split at the forks. Eif Crabtree was plowing down below us. He ran up the hill and got our names. The other boys gave their dollar apiece. I didn't have mine. Professor Herbert put mine in for me. I have to work it out at school."

"Poor man's son, huh," says Pa. "I'll attend to that myself in th' mornin'. I'll take keer o' 'im. He ain't from this county nohow. I'll go down there in th' mornin' and see 'im. Lettin' you leave your books and galavant all over th' hills. What kind of a school is it nohow! Didn't do that, my son, when I's a little shaver in school. All fared alike too."

"Pa, please don't go down there," I says, "just let me have fifty cents and pay the rest of my fine! I don't want you to go down there! I don't want you to start anything with Professor Herbert!"

"Ashamed of your old Pap are you, Dave," says Pa, "atter th' way I've worked to raise you! Tryin' to send you to school so you can make a better livin' than I've made.

"I'll straighten this thing out myself! I'll take keer o' Professor Herbert myself! He ain't got no right to keep you in and let the other boys off jist because they've got th' money! I'm a poor man. A bullet will go in a professor same as it will any man. It will go in a rich man same as it will a poor man. Now you get into this work before I take one o' these withes and cut the shirt off'n your back!"

I thought once I'd run through the woods above the barn just as hard as I could go. I thought I'd leave high school and home forever! Pa could not catch me! I'd get away! I couldn't go back to school with him. He'd have a gun and maybe he'd shoot Professor Herbert. It was hard to tell what he would do. I could tell Pa that school

had changed in the hills from the way it was when he was a boy, but he wouldn't understand. I could tell him we studied frogs, birds, snakes, lizards, flowers, insects. But Pa wouldn't understand. If I did run away from home it wouldn't matter to Pa. He would see Professor Herbert anyway. He would think that high school and Professor Herbert had run me away from home. There was no need to run away. I'd just have to stay, finish foddering the cattle, and go to school with Pa the next morning.

I would take a bundle of fodder, remove the hickory witheband from around it, and scatter it on rocks, clumps of green briers, and brush so the cattle wouldn't tramp it under their feet. I would lean it up against the oak trees and the rocks in the pasture just above our pigpen on the hill. The fodder was cold and frosty where it had set out in the stacks. I would carry bundles of the fodder from the stack until I had spread out a bundle for each steer. Pa went to the barn to feed the mules and throw corn in the pen to the hogs.

The moon shone bright in the cold March sky. I finished my work by moonlight. Professor Herbert really didn't know how much work I had to do at home. If he had known he would not have kept me after school. He would have loaned me a dollar to have paid my part on the cherry tree. He had never lived in the hills. He didn't know the way the hill boys had to work so that they could go to school. Now he was teaching in a county high school where all the boys who attended were from hill farms.

After I'd finished doing my work I went to the house and ate my supper. Pa and Mom had eaten. My supper was getting cold. I heard Pa and Mom talking in the front room. Pa was telling Mom about me staying in after school.

"I had to do all th' milkin' tonight, chop th' wood myself. It's too hard on me atter I've turned ground all day. I'm goin' to take a day off tomorrow and see if I can't remedy things a little. I'll go down to that high school tomorrow. I won't be a very good scholar fer Professor Herbert nohow. He won't keep me in atter school. I'll take a different kind of lesson down there and make 'im acquainted with it."

"Now, Luster," says Mom, "you jist stay away from there. Don't cause a lot o' trouble. You can be jailed fer a trick like that. You'll get th' Law atter you. You'll jist go down there and show off and plague your own boy Dave to death in front o' all th' scholars!"

"Plague or no plague," says Pa, "he don't take into consideration what all I haf to do here, does he? I'll show 'im it ain't right to keep one boy in and let the rest go scot-free. My boy is good as th' rest, ain't he? A bullet will make a hole in a schoolteacher same as it will anybody else. He can't do me that way and get by with it. I'll plug 'im first. I aim to go down there bright and early in the mornin' and get all this straight! I aim to see about bug larnin' and this runnin' all over God's creation huntin' snakes, lizards, and frogs. Ransackin' th' country and goin' through cherry orchards and breakin' th' trees down atter lizards! Old Eif Crabtree ought to a-poured th' hot lead to 'em instead o' chargin' six dollars fer th' tree! He ought to a-got old Herbert th' first one!"

I ate my supper. I slipped upstairs and lit the lamp. I tried to forget the whole thing. I studied plane geometry. Then I studied my biology lesson. I could hardly study for thinking about Pa. "He'll go to school with me in the morning. He'll take a gun for Professor Herbert! What will Professor Herbert think of me! I'll tell him when Pa leaves that I couldn't help it. But Pa might shoot him. I hate to go with Pa. Maybe he'll cool off about it tonight and not go in the morning."

Pa got up at four o'clock. He built a fire in the stove. Then he built a fire in the fireplace. He got Mom up to get breakfast. Then he got me up to help feed and milk. By the time we had our work done at the barn, Mom had breakfast ready for us. We ate our breakfast. Daylight came and we could see the bare oak trees covered white with frost. The hills were white with frost. A cold wind was blowing. The sky was clear. The sun would soon come out and melt the frost. The afternoon would be warm with sunshine and the frozen ground with thaw. There would be mud on the hills again. Muddy water would then run down the little ditches on the hills.

"Now, Dave," says Pa, "let's get ready fer school. I aim to go with you this mornin' and look into bug larnin', frog larnin', lizard and snake larnin', and breakin' down cherry trees! I don't like no sicha foolish way o' larnin' myself!"

Pa hadn't forgot. I'd have to take him to school with me. He would take me to school with him. We were going early. I was glad we were going early. If Pa pulled a gun on Professor Herbert there wouldn't be so many of my classmates there to see him.

I knew that Pa wouldn't be at home in the high school. He wore overalls, big boots, a blue shirt and a sheepskin coat and a slouched black hat gone to seed at the top. He put his gun in its holster. We started trudging toward the high school across the hill.

It was early when we got to the county high school. Professor Herbert had just got there. I just thought as we walked up the steps into the schoolhouse, "Maybe Pa will find out Professor Herbert is a good man. He just doesn't know him. Just like I felt toward the Lambert boys across the hill. I didn't like them until I'd seen them and talked to them. After I went to school with them and talked to them, I liked them and we were friends. It's a lot in knowing the other fellow."

"You're th' Professor here, ain't you?" says Pa.

"Yes," says Professor Herbert, "and you are Dave's father."

"Yes," says Pa, pulling out his gun and laying it on the seat in Professor Herbert's office. Professor Herbert's eyes got big behind his black-rimmed glasses when he saw Pa's gun. Color came into his pale cheeks.

"Jist a few things about this school I want to know," says Pa. "I'm tryin' to make a scholar out'n Dave. He's the only one out'n eleven youngins I've sent to high school. Here he comes in late and leaves me all th' work to do! He said you's all out bug huntin' yesterday and broke a cherry tree down. He had to stay two hours atter school yesterday and work out money to pay on that cherry tree! Is that right?"

"Wwwwy," says Professor Herbert, "I guess it is."

He looked at Pa's gun.

"Well," says Pa, "this ain't no high school. It's a bug school, a lizard school, a snake school! It ain't no school nohow!"

"Why did you bring that gun?" says Professor Herbert to Pa.

"You see that little hole," says Pa as he picked up the long blue forty-four and put his finger on the end of the barrel, "a bullet can come out'n that hole that will kill a schoolteacher same as it will any other man. It will kill a rich man same as a poor man. It will kill a man. But atter I come in and saw you, I know'd I wouldn't need it. This maul o' mine could do you up in a few minutes."

Pa stood there, big, hard, brown-skinned, and mighty beside of Professor Herbert. I didn't know Pa was so much bigger and harder. I'd never seen Pa in a schoolhouse before. I'd seen Professor Herbert. He'd always looked big before to me. He didn't look big standing beside of Pa.

"I was only doing my duty," says Professor Herbert, "Mr. Sexton, and following the course of study the state provided us with."

"Course o' study," says Pa, "what study, bug study? Varmint study? Takin' youngins to th' woods and their poor old Ma's and Pa's at home a-slavin' to keep 'em in school and give 'em a education! You know that's dangerous, too, puttin' a lot o' boys and girls out together like that!"

Students were coming into the schoolhouse now.

Professor Herbert says, "Close the door, Dave, so others won't hear."

I walked over and closed the door. I was shaking like a leaf in the wind. I thought Pa was going to hit Professor Herbert every minute. He was doing all the talking. His face was getting red. The red color was coming through the brown, weather-beaten skin on Pa's face.

"I was right with these students," says Professor Herbert. "I know what they got into and what they didn't. I didn't send one of the other teachers with them on this field trip. I went myself. Yes, I took the boys and girls together. Why not?"

"It jist don't look good to me," says Pa, "a-takin' all this swarm of youngins out to pillage th' whole deestrict. Breakin' down cherry trees. Keepin' boys in atter school."

"What else could I have done with Dave, Mr. Sexton?" says Professor Herbert. "The boys didn't have any business all climbing that cherry tree after one lizard. One boy could have gone up in the tree and got it. The farmer charged us six dollars. It was a little steep, I think, but we had it to pay. Must I make five boys pay and let your boy off? He said he didn't have the dollar and couldn't get it. So I put it in for him. I'm letting him work it out. He's not working for me. He's working for the school!"

"I jist don't know what you could a-done with 'im," says Pa, "only a-larruped im with a withe! That's what he needed!"

"He's too big to whip," says Professor Herbert, pointing at me. "He's a man in size."

"He's not too big fer me to whip," says Pa. "They ain't too big until they're over twenty-one! It jist didn't look fair to me! Work one and let th' rest out because they got th' money. I don't see what bugs has got to do with a high school! It don't look good to me nohow!"

Pa picked up his gun and put it back in its holster. The red color left Professor Herbert's face. He talked more to Pa. Pa softened a little. It looked funny to see Pa in the high-school building. It was the first time he'd ever been there.

"We were not only hunting snakes, toads, flowers, butterflies, lizards," says Professor Herbert, "but, Mr. Sexton, I was hunting dry timothy grass to put in an incubator and raise some protozoa."

"I don't know what that is," says Pa. "Th' incubator is th' new-fangled way o' cheatin' th' hens and raisin' chickens. I ain't so sure about th' breed o' chickens you mentioned."

"You've heard of germs, Mr. Sexton, haven't you?" says Professor Herbert.

"Jist call me Luster, if you don't mind," says Pa, very casual like.

"All right, Luster, you've heard of germs, haven't you?"

"Yes," says Pa, "but I don't believe in germs. I'm sixty-five years old and I ain't seen one yet!"

"You can't see them with your naked eye," says Professor Herbert. "Just keep that gun in the holster and stay with me in the high school today. I have a few things want to show you. That scum on your teeth has germs in it."

"What," says Pa, "you mean to tell me I've got germs on my teeth!"

"Yes," says Professor Herbert. "The same kind as we might be able to find in a living black snake if we dissect it!"

"I don't mean to dispute your word," says Pa, "but I don't believe it. I don't believe I have germs on my teeth!"

"Stay with me today and I'll show you. I want to take you through the school anyway! School has changed a lot in the hills since you went to school. I don't guess we had high schools in this county when you went to school!"

"No," says Pa, "jist readin', writin', and cipherin'. We didn't have all this bug larnin', frog larnin', and findin' germs on your teeth and in the middle o' black snakes! Th' world's changin'."

"It is," says Professor Herbert, "and we hope all for the better. Boys like your own there are going to help change it. He's your boy. He knows all of what I've told you. You stay with me today."

"I'll shore stay with you," says Pa. "I want to see th' germs off'n my teeth. I jist want to see a germ. I've never seen one in my life. 'Seein' is believin',' Pap allus told me."

Pa walks out of the office with Professor Herbert. I just hoped Professor Herbert didn't have Pa arrested for pulling his gun. Pa's gun has always been a friend to him when he goes to settle disputes.

The bell rang. School took up. I saw the students when they marched in the schoolhouse look at Pa. They would grin and punch each other. Pa just stood and watched them pass in at the schoolhouse door. Two long lines marched in the house. The boys and girls were clean and well dressed. Pa stood over in the schoolyard under a leafless elm, in his sheepskin coat, his big boots laced in front with buckskin, and his heavy socks stuck above his boot tops. Pa's overalls legs were baggy and wrinkled between his coat and boot tops. His blue work shirt showed at the collar. His big black hat showed his gray-streaked black hair. His face was hard and weather-tanned to the color of a ripe fodder blade. His hands were big and gnarled like the roots of the elm tree he stood beside.

When I went to my first class I saw Pa and Professor Herbert going around over the schoolhouse. I was in my geometry class when Pa and Professor Herbert came in the room. We were explaining our propositions on the blackboard. Professor Herbert and Pa just quietly came in and sat down for awhile. I heard Fred Wutts whisper to Glenn Armstrong, "Who is that old man? Lord, he's a rough-looking scamp." Glenn whispered back, "I think he's Dave's Pap." The students in geometry looked at Pa. They must have wondered what he was doing in school. Before the class was over, Pa and Professor Herbert got up and went out. I saw them together down on the playground. Professor Herbert was explaining to Pa. I could see the prints of Pa's gun under his coat when he'd walk around.

At noon in the high-school cafeteria Pa and Professor Herbert sat together at the little table where Professor Herbert always ate by himself. They ate together. The students watched the way Pa ate. He ate with his knife instead of his fork. A lot of the students felt sorry for me after they found out he was my father. They didn't have to feel sorry for me. I wasn't ashamed of Pa after I found out he wasn't going to shoot Professor Herbert. I was glad they had made friends. I wasn't ashamed of Pa. I wouldn't be as long as he behaved. He would find out about the high school as I had found out about the Lambert boys across the hill.

In the afternoon when we went to biology Pa was in the class. He was sitting on one of the high stools beside the microscope. We went ahead with our work just as if Pa wasn't in the class. I saw Pa take his knife and scrape tartar from one of his teeth. Professor Herbert put it on the lens and adjusted the microscope for Pa. He adjusted it and worked awhile. Then he says: "Now Luster, look! Put your eye right down to the light. Squint the other eye!"

Pa put his head down and did as Professor Herbert said. "I see 'im," says Pa. "Who'd a ever thought that? Right on a body's teeth! Right in a body's mouth. You're right certain they ain't no fake to this, Professor Herbert?"

"No, Luster," says Professor Herbert. "It's there. That's the germ. Germs live in a world we cannot see with the naked eye. We must use the microscope. There are millions of them in our bodies. Some are harmful. Others are helpful."

Pa holds his face down and looks through the microscope. We stop and watch Pa. He sits upon the tall stool. His knees are against the table. His legs are long. His coat slips up behind when he bends over. The handle of his gun shows. Professor Herbert pulls his coat down quickly.

"Oh, yes," says Pa. He gets up and pulls his coat down. Pa's face gets a little red. He knows about his gun and he knows he doesn't have any use for it in high school.

"We have a big black snake over here we caught yesterday," says Professor Herbert. "We'll chloroform him and dissect him and show you he has germs in his body, too."

"Don't do it," says Pa. "I believe you. I jist don't want to see you kill the black snake. I never kill one. They are good mousers and a lot o' help to us on the farm. I like black snakes. I jist hate to see people kill 'em. I don't allow 'em killed on my place."

The students look at Pa. They seem to like him better after he said that. Pa with a gun in his pocket but a tender heart beneath his ribs for snakes, but not for man! Pa won't whip a mule at home. He won't whip his cattle.

"Man can defend hisself," says Pa, "but cattle and mules can't. We have the drop on 'em. Ain't nothin' to a man that'll beat a good pullin' mule. He ain't got th' right kind o' a heart!"

Professor Herbert took Pa through the laboratory. He showed him the different kinds of work we were doing. He showed him our equipment. They stood and talked while we worked. Then they walked out together. They talked louder when they got out in the hall.

When our biology class was over I walked out of the room. It was our last class for the day. I would have to take my broom and sweep two hours to finish paying for the split cherry tree. I just wondered if Pa would want me to stay. He was standing in the hallway watching the students march out. He looked lost among us. He looked like a leaf turned brown on the tree among the treetop filled with growing leaves.

I got my broom and started to sweep. Professor Herbert walked up and says, "I'm going to let you do that some other time. You can go home with your father. He is waiting out there."

I laid my broom down, got my books, and went down the steps.

Pa says, "Ain't you got two hours o' sweepin' yet to do?"

I says, "Professor Herbert said I could do it some other time. He said for me to go home with you."

"No," says Pa. "You are goin' to do as he says. He's a good man. School has changed from my day and time. I'm a dead leaf, Dave. I'm behind. I don't belong here. If he'll let me I'll get a broom and we'll both sweep one hour. That pays your debt. I'll hep you pay it. I'll ast 'im and see if he won't let me hep you."

"I'm going to cancel the debt," says Professor Herbert. "I just wanted you to understand, Luster."

"I understand," says Pa, "and since I understand he must pay his debt fer th' tree and I'm goin' to hep 'im."

"Don't do that," says Professor Herbert. "It's all on me."

"We don't do things like that," says Pa, "we're just and honest people. We don't want somethin' fer nothin'. Professor Herbert, you're wrong now and I'm right. You'll haf to listen to me. I've larned a lot from you. My boy must go on. Th' world has left me. It changed while I've raised my family and plowed th' hills. I'm a just and honest man. I don' skip debts. I ain't larned 'em to do that. I ain't got much larnin' myself but I do know right from wrong atter I see through a thing."

Professor Herbert went home. Pa and I stayed and swept one hour. It looked funny to see Pa use a broom. He never used one at home. Mom used the broom. Pa used the plow. Pa did hard work. Pa says, "I can't sweep. Durned if I can. Look at th' streaks o' dirt I leave on th' floor! Seems like no work a-tall fer me. Brooms is too light 'r somethin'. I'll jist do th' best I can, Dave. I've been wrong about th' school."

I says, "Did you know Professor Herbert can get a warrant out for you for bringing your pistol to school and showing it in his office! They can railroad you for that!"

"That's all made right," says Pa. "I've made that right. Professor Herbert ain't goin' to take it to court. He likes me. I like 'im. We jist had to get together. He had the remedies. He showed me. You must go on to school. I am as strong a man as ever come out'n th' hills fer my years and th' hard work I've done. But I'm behind, Dave.

I'm a little man. Your hands will be softer than mine. Your clothes will be better. You'll allus look cleaner than your old Pap. Jist remember, Dave, to pay your debts and be honest. Jist be kind to animals and don't bother th' snakes. That's all I got agin th' school. Puttin' black snakes to sleep and cuttin' 'em open."

It was late when we got home. Stars were in the sky. The moon was up. The ground was frozen. Pa took his time going home. I couldn't run like I did the night before. It was ten o'clock before we got the work finished, our suppers eaten. Pa sat before the fire and told Mom he was going to take her and show her a germ sometime. Mom hadn't seen one either. Pa told her about the high school and the fine man Professor Herbert was. He told Mom about the strange school across the hill and how different it was from the school in their day and time.

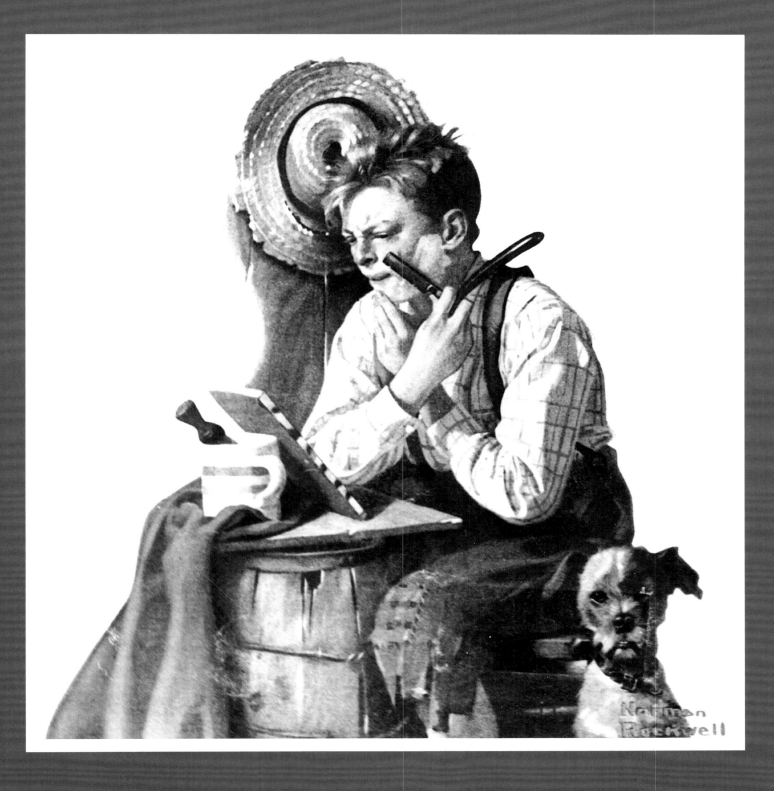

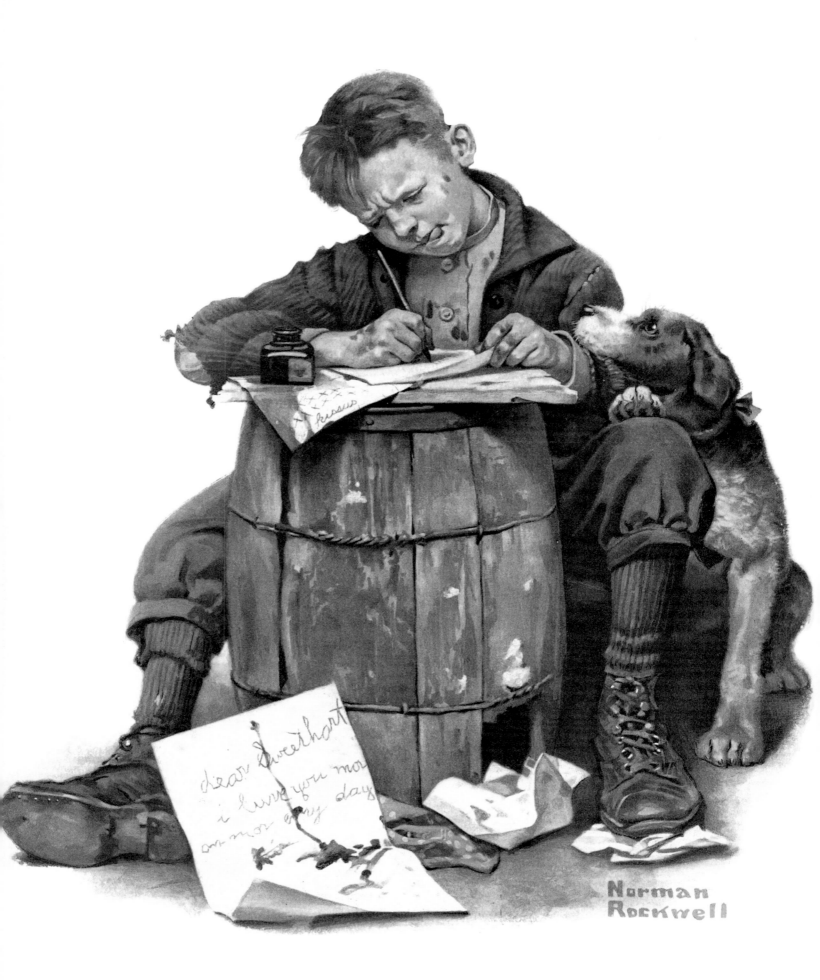

Part Six

Letters
from Dad

*

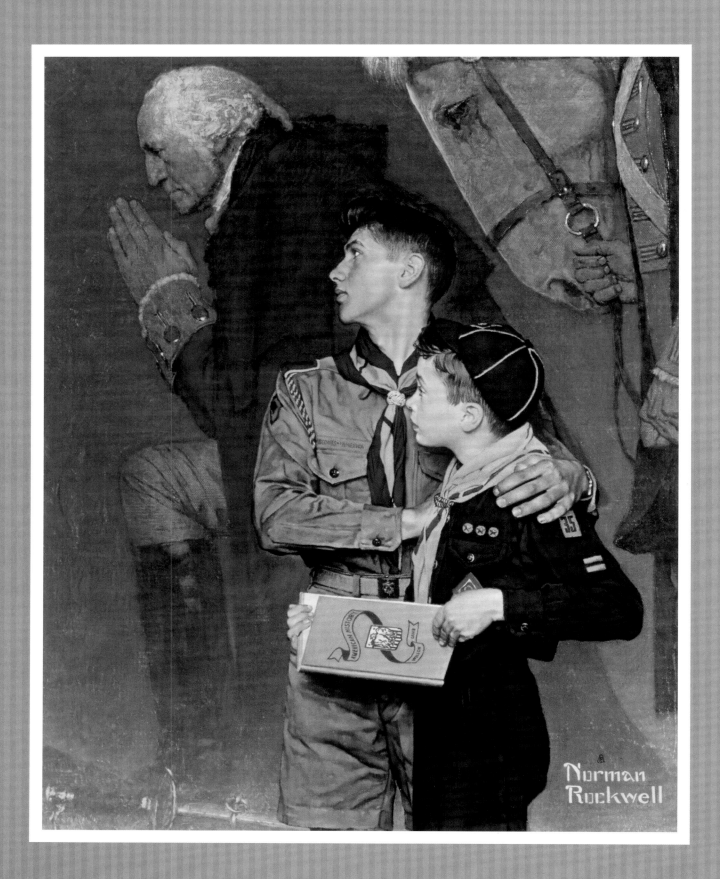

WILLIAM HENRY SEWARD *to*
WILLIAM HENRY SEWARD, JR.

My dear Boy

I am very much obliged to you for your letter which gives me much interesting information. I will try to procure in New York a filter which will purify the water of the new pump.

I have been at many places in Pennsylvania where I wished that you were strong enough to be with me. When you grow strong enough I shall want you to travel with me. I saw on the banks of the Schuylkill, Valley Forge, the place where General Washington had his camp during one of the most severe winters which occurred during the American Revolution. His camp extended four miles long with two entrenchments in front and high mountains on the one side and a deep creek on the other. From the mountain in rear he could see with his spy glass the British army in Philadelphia seventy miles off. He was almost destitute of ammunition to protect himself. The Congress was not able to supply him with money, the army was in deplorable want of bread and meat clothes and shoes. They suffered exceedingly. The poor horses and dogs died of hunger and diarrhea and death extended to the men, a dozen were buried in a day and in one place, scarcely beneath the frost in the surface of the ground. The farmer now often turns up the bones of the lost men when plowing his fields. Mrs. Washington was a good woman, she spent the winter in the camp and she served and consoled the sick and dying. It was by such sacrifice that Liberty was obtained for the American people. How good and virtuous and just ought we to be and how thankful to God that we have blessings secured by the virtue and sufferings of our ancestors. I hope you will get Peter Parley's history of the Revolution and ask Ma to read to you the account of the Revolution and then I hope you will resolve to be a good man like General Washington that all people may love and bless you.

I saw canal boats on railroad cars in Pennsylvania loaded with freight, and what is very strange is that as the boats are too long for the curves of the Rail Roads, they build the boats into three pieces, and when they get on the mountains they put them together with hooks and let them down into the Canal and float them to Lake Erie. Yet they do not take in a drop of water. Can you guess how this is done?

Your affectionate father

William H. Seward.

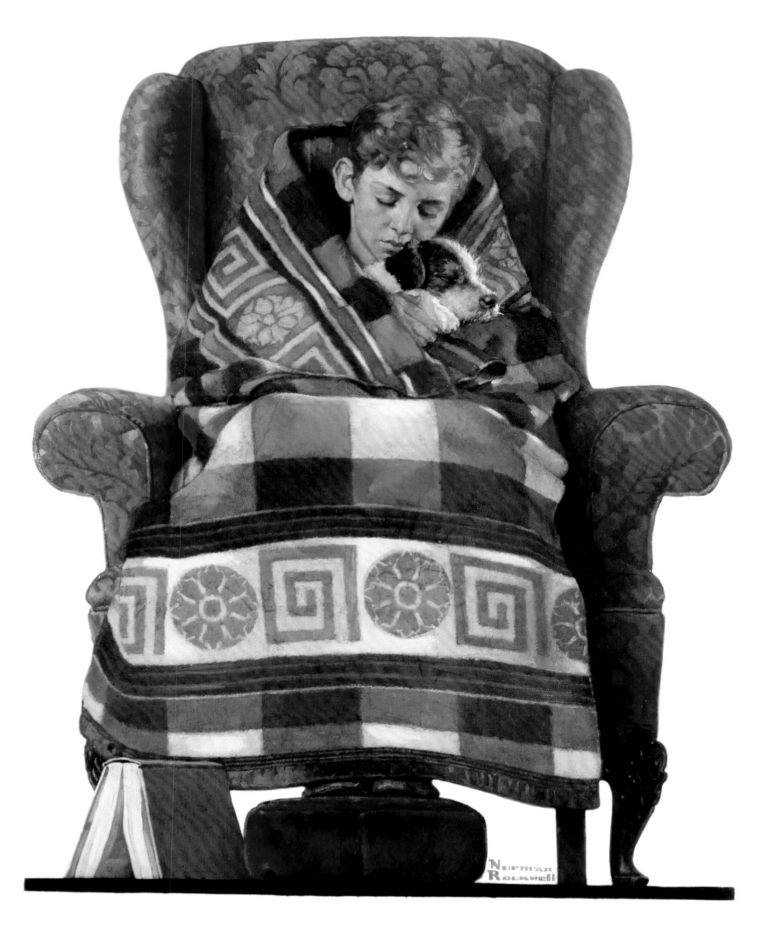

FREDERICK LAW OLMSTEAD

to

HENRY PERKINS OLMSTEAD

13th May, 1875

Dear Henry:

The cats keep coming into the yard, six of them every day, and Quiz drives them out. If I should send Quiz to you to drive the cows away from your rhubarb he would not be here to drive the cats out of the yard. If six cats should keep coming into the yard every day and not go out, in a week there would be 42 of them and in a month 180 and before you came back next November 1260. Then if there should be 1260 cats in the yard before next November half of them at least would have kittens and if half of them should have 6 kittens apiece, there would be more than 5000 cats and kittens in the yard. There would not be any place for Rosanna to spread the clothes unless she drove them all off the grass plot, and if she did they would have to crowd at the end of the yard nearest the house, and if they did that they would make a great pile as high as the top of my windows. A pile of 5000 cats and kittens, some of them black ones, in front of my window would make my office so dark I should not be able to write in it. Besides that those underneath, particularly the kittens, would be hurt by those standing on top of them and I expect they would make such a great squalling all the time that I should not be able to sleep, and if I was not able to sleep, I should not be able to work, and if I did not work I should not have any money, and if I had not any money, I could not send any to Plymouth to pay your fare back on the Fall River boat, and I could not pay my fare to go to Plymouth and so you and I would not ever see each other any more. No, Sir. I can't spare Quiz and you have to watch for the cows and drive them off yourself or you will raise no rhubarb.

Your affectionate father.

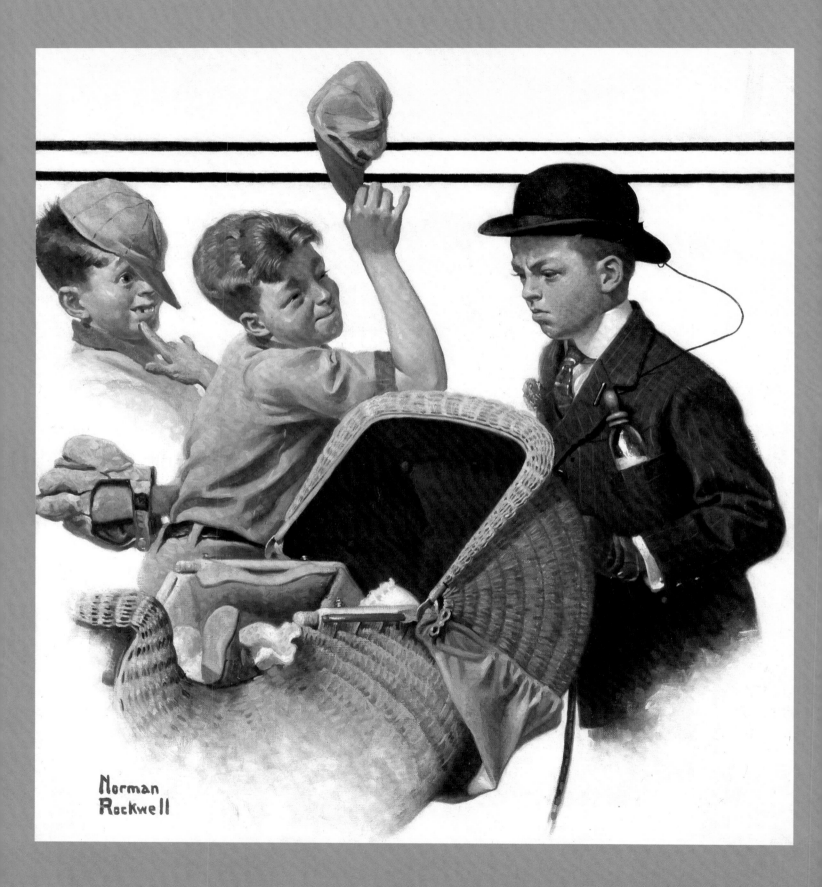

SIDNEY LANIER

to

CHARLES D. LANIER

August 15, 1880
WEST CHESTER, PA.

My dear Charley:

A young man came to our house yesterday morning who claims that he is a brother of yours and Sidney's and Harry's, and that he is entitled to all the rights and privileges appertaining unto that honorable connection. You will be surprised to learn that both your mother and I are disposed to allow his pretensions, from the fact that he looks a great deal like Sidney,—and from several other circumstances which I need not detail. Indeed your mother has already gone so far as to take him on her breast and nurse him exactly as she did you three young scamps somewhere between twelve and seven years ago. I write therefore to ask you whether and Sidney and Harry are willing to accept our opinion of this young person's genuine kinship to you, or whether you will require him to employ a number of lawyers, like the Tichborne Claimant in England, to assert his rights in due form before the courts of the United States. If the latter, you had best give him early notice of your intention; for the fact is he has taken such a hold upon our affections here, by the quietness and modesty of his demeanor and by the beauty of his person, that if we were summoned into Court as witnesses in the case of

ROBERT SAMPSON LANIER JR.

(so called), Plaintiff Action on a Bond (of brotherhood),

Versus

CHARLES DAY LANIER

Sidney   "   Jr.   Defendants

and

Henry   "

we would be obliged to testify that we feel almost as sure—if not quite—that he is your brother as that you are our son.

As I have said, he is a most exemplary young man. He never stays out late at night; neither chews, smokes, nor uses snuff; abstains from all intoxicating liquors, and does not touch even tea or coffee; however much preserves and fruit-cake there may be on the supper-table, he never asks for any; he does no kind of work on the Sabbath; he honors his father and mother, particularly his mother; he plays not games of hazard, not even marbles for winnance; and I am positively certain that in the whole course of his life he has never uttered a single angry or ungentlemanly word. I am bound to admit that he has his shortcomings: he *isn't* as particular about his clothes as I would like to see him; he has a way of trying to get both fists in his mouth which certainly does look odd in company; and he wants his breakfast in the morning at four o'clock—an hour at which it is very inconvenient, with our household arrangements, to furnish it to him. But we hope that perhaps he will amend in these particulars, as time rolls on, and that he will become as perfect a gentleman as his three brothers. In fact we attribute these little faults of his to the fact that he appears to have been in a Far Country—like the Tichborne Claimant—, and the manners and customs of peoples are so different that we really don't know whether it may not be considered a sign of good breeding *There* to cram one's fists into one's mouth, and perhaps the very highest circles of the nobility and gentry in that Region take their breakfasts before daylight.

Earnestly hoping that this lovely little (for I omitted to mention that he is small of stature) brother Rob may find a good warm place in your three hearts without being obliged to resort to extreme measures, and with a hundred embraces for you, me dear big Charley,

I am
Your &c &c &c

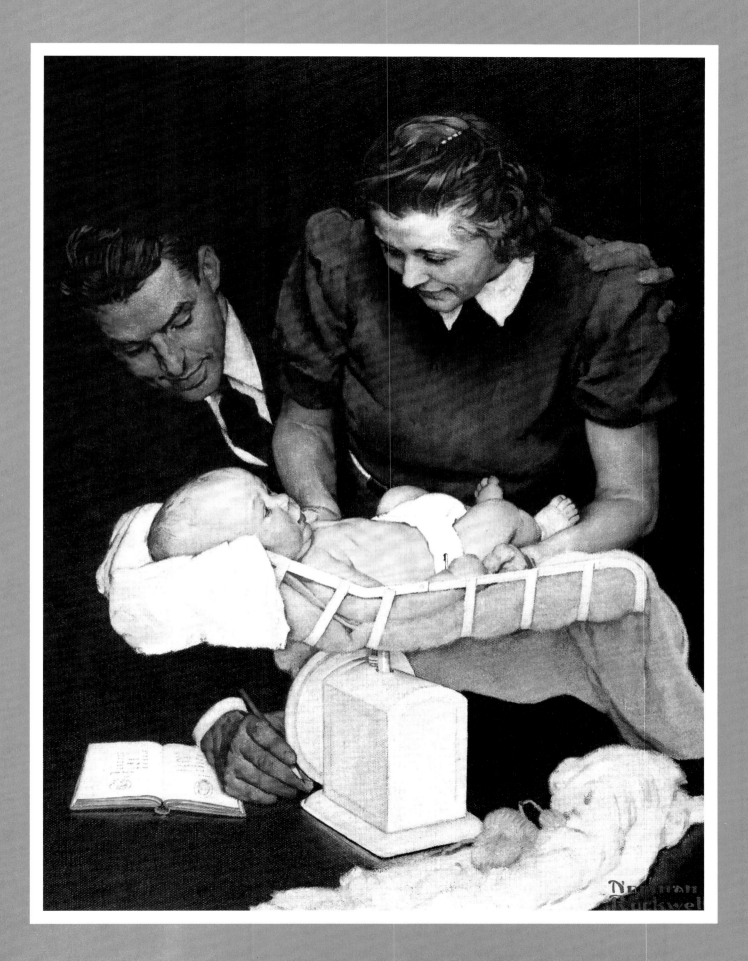

ALEXANDER GRAHAM BELL

to

ELSIE AND MARIAN (DAISY) BELL

⸺∘∞∘⸺

EDGARTOWN, MARTHA'S VINEYARD

Sunday, November 13th, 1887

My dear Elsie and Daisy

I wish you could be here with me in Martha's Vineyard, for I am sure you would enjoy playing on the sandy beach, and watching the great big waves dashing on the shore. I am sure you would enjoy looking for the beautiful shells and pebbles that are thrown on the beach after every storm.

I was walking on the beach this afternoon with Mr. [Hity?] when I saw a funny blacked object on the shore. It looked like a book with a long tail!!

What do you think it was? It was the dead body of a fish—and it was the funniest fish I ever saw! It was flat like a book. Its eyes were on the top of its head, and its mouth was in its stomach! But where do you think its teeth were? I opened its mouth—but there were no teeth there. Guess where they were. Did you ever hear of a fish with teeth on its tail?!!!! I never did, but this fish had teeth all over its tail, and all over its back. It was covered with teeth so that you could not touch it without being bitten.

It could bite you by wagging its tail. I cut off the tail and sent it to Elsie by mail today so that you might see it. I hope it will reach you safely.

The mouth of this wonderful fish was very beautiful. Its lips were not soft like yours but quite hard and covered all over with beautiful little ivory pearls. I cut off the lips so that you might see them. I sent them to Daisy by mail.

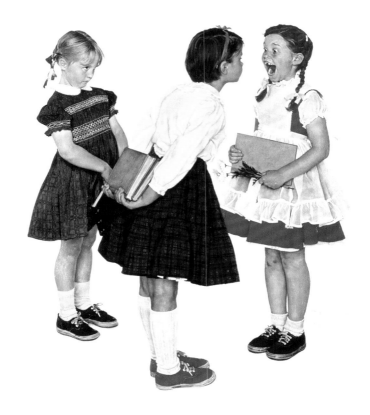

The people here call the fish the "Stingaree" though its proper name is "The stinging ray." The fish I saw was only a baby. Captain Osborne says he has seen one with a tail four feet long covered with teeth an inch long. He says that the teeth have poison on them when the fish is alive, so that it is dangerous to touch them. He knew a man who tried to catch one in the water, but the fish stuck its long tail into his leg and hurt him so much that he was glad to let it go. The leg swelled up and he was unable to walk for months. You need not be afraid of the tail I have sent you, because the fish has been dead for a long time, the teeth are dry and there is now no poison on them. Now my dear little girls I must say good-bye. I hope you are both good and gentle. I hope you are trying to learn as much as you can from Miss Hudson and I hope you try to make Mamma very happy and proud of you both. I expect Grandpapa and Grandmamma Bell tomorrow. Won't you write a nice letter to Grandmamma? I am sure she would be glad to hear from you—and so would I. Good bye for the present.

Your loving father
Alexander Graham Bell

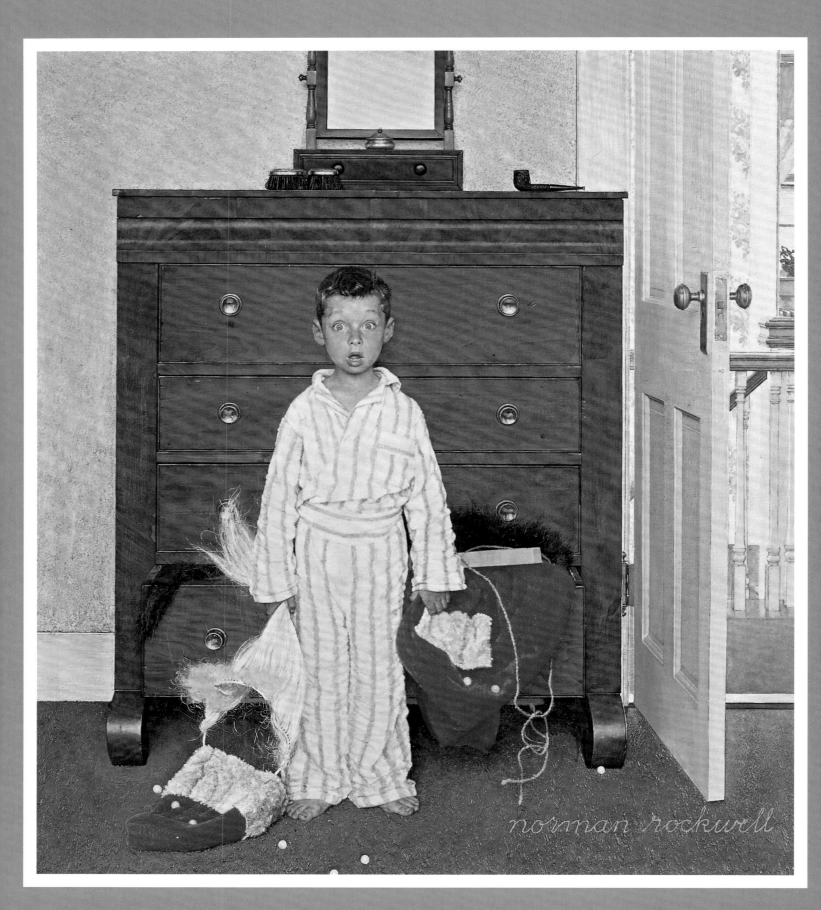

Mark Twain (Samuel Clemens) as Santa Claus

to

Susie Clemens

My dear Susie Clemens:

I have received & read all the letters which you & your little sister have written me by the hand of your mother & your nurses; & I have also read those which you little people have written me with your own hands—for although you did not use any characters that are in grown people's alphabets, you used the characters which *all* children in all lands on earth & in the twinkling stars use; & as all my subjects in the moon are children & use no character but that, you will easily understand that I can read your & your baby sister's jagged & fantastic marks without any trouble at all. But I had trouble with those letters which you dictated through your mother and the nurses, for I am a foreigner & cannot read English writing well. You will find that I made no mistakes about the things which you & the baby ordered in your *own* letters—I went down your chimney at midnight when you were asleep, & delivered them all myself—& kissed both of you, too, because you are good children, well trained, nice mannered, & about the most obedient little people I ever saw. But in the letters which you dictated there were some words which I could not make out, for certain, & one or two small orders which I could not fill because we ran out of stock. Our last lot of kitchen furniture for dolls has just gone to a very poor little child in the North Star, away up in the cold country about the Big Dipper. Your mama can show you that star & you will say: "Little Snow Flake (for that is the child's name) I'm glad you got that furniture, for you need it more than I." That is, you must *write* that, with your own hand, & Snow Flake will write you an answer. If you only spoke it, she wouldn't hear you. Make your letter light & thin, for the distance is great and the postage very heavy.

There was a word or two in your mama's letter which I couldn't be certain of. I took it be "trunk full of doll's clothes"? Is that it? I will call at your kitchen door about nine oclock this morning to inquire. But I must not see anybody, & I must not speak to anybody but you. When the kitchen door-bell rings, George must be blindfolded & sent to open the door. Then he must go back to the dining room or the china closet & take the cook with him. You must tell George he must walk on tip-toe & not speak— otherwise he will die some day. Then you must go up to the nursery & stand on a chair or the nurse's bed, & put your ear to the speaking tube that leads down to the kitchen, & when I whistle through it you must speak in the tube and say, "Welcome, Santa Claus!" Then I will ask whether it was a trunk you ordered or not? If you say it was, I shall ask you what *color* you want the trunk to be. Your mama will help you name a nice color, & then you must tell every single thing in detail which you want the trunk to contain. Then when I say "Good bye & a Merry Christmas to my little Susie Clemens," you must say "Good bye, good old Santa Claus, & I thank you very much—& please tell that little Snow Flake I will look at her star tonight and she must look down here—I will be right in the west bay-window; & every fine night I will look her star & say, "I know somebody up there & *like* her, too." Then you must go down in the library & make George close all the doors that open to the moon and get those things, in a few minutes I will come down from the chimney which belongs to the fire-place that is in the hall—if it is a trunk you want, because I couldn't get such a thing as a trunk down the nursery-chimney, you know.

People may talk if they want, until they hear my footsteps in the hall—then you tell them to keep quiet a little while till I go back up the chimney. Maybe you will not hear my footsteps at all—so you may go now & then & peep through the dining-room doors, & by & by you will see that thing which you want, right under the piano in the drawing room—for I shall put it there. If I should leave any snow in the hall, you must tell George to sweep it into the fireplace, for I haven't time to do such things. George must not use a brook, but a rag—else he will die some day. You must watch George, & not let him run into danger. If my boot should leave a stain on the marble, George must not holy-stone it away. Leave it there always in memory of my visit: & whenever you look at it or show it to anybody you must let it remind you to be a good little girl. Whenever you are naughty, & somebody points to that mark which your good old Santa Claus's boot made on the marble, what will you say, little Sweetheart?

Goodbye for a few minutes, till I come down to the world and ring the kitchen door-bell.

Your loving
SANTA CLAUS
Whom people sometimes call
"THE MAN IN THE MOON."

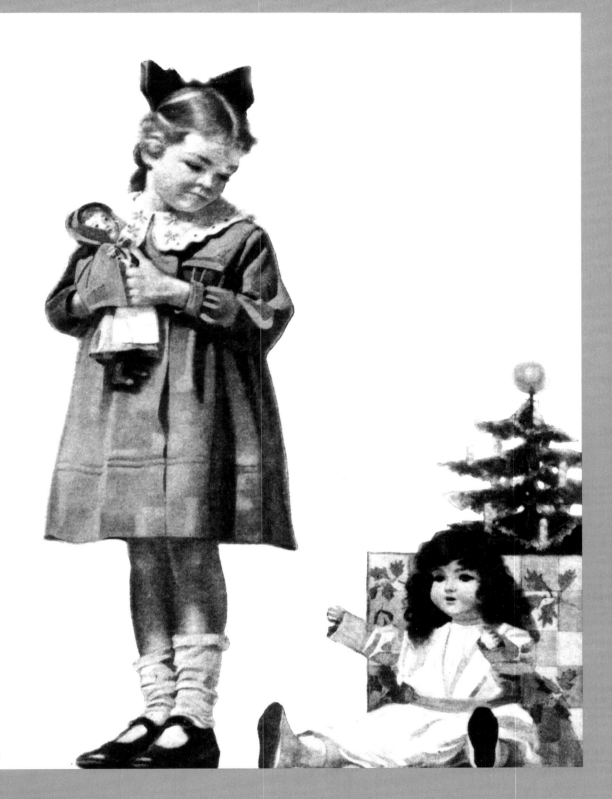

W. E. B. Du Bois

to

Yolande Du Bois

New York, October 29, 1914

Dear Little Daughter:

I have waited for you to get well settled before writing. By this time I hope some of the strangeness has worn off and that my little girl is working hard and regularly.

Of course, everything is new and unusual. You miss the newness and smartness of America. Gradually, however, you are going to sense the beauty of the old world: its calm and eternity and you will grow to love it.

Above all remember, dear, that you have a great opportunity. You are in one of the world's best schools, in one of the world's greatest modern empires. Millions of boys and girls all over this world would give almost anything they possess to be where you are. You are there by no desert or merit of yours, but only by lucky chance.

Deserve it, then. Study, do your work. Be honest, frank and fearless and get some grasp of the real values of life. You will meet, of course, curious little annoyances. People will wonder at your dear brown and the sweet crinkley hair. But that simply is of no importance and will soon be forgotten. Remember that most folk laugh at anything unusual, whether it is beautiful, fine or not. You, however, must not laugh at yourself. You must know that brown is as pretty as white or prettier and crinkley hair as straight even though it is harder to comb. The main thing is the YOU beneath the clothes and the skin—the ability to do, the will to conquer, the determination to understand and know this great, wonderful curious world. Don't shrink from new experiences and custom. Take the cold bath bravely. Enter into the spirit of your big bed-room. Enjoy what is and not pine for what is not. Read some good, heavy, serious books just for discipline: Tale yourself

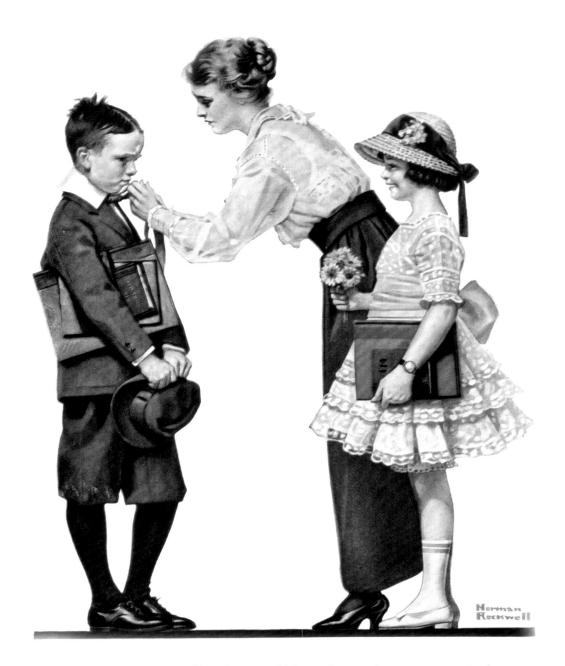

in hand and master yourself. Make yourself do unpleasant things, so as to gain the upper hand of your soul.

Above all remember: your father loves you and believes in you and expects you to be a wonderful woman.

I shall write each week and expect a weekly letter from you.

Lovingly yours,
Papa

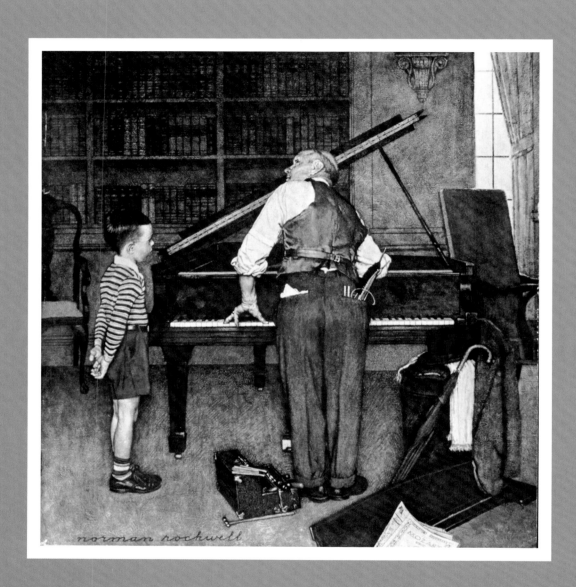

ALBERT EINSTEIN

to

HANS ALBERT EINSTEIN

[Berlin,] 4 November [1915]

My dear Albert,

Yesterday I received your dear letter and was very happy with it. I was already afraid you wouldn't write to me at all any more. You told me when I was in Zurich, that it is awkward for you when I come to Zurich. Therefore I think it is better if we get together in a different place, where nobody will interfere with our comfort. I will in any case urge that each year we spend a whole month together, so that you see that you have a father who is fond of you and who loves you. You can also learn many good and beautiful things from me, something another cannot as easily offer you. What I have achieved through such a lot of strenuous work shall not only be there for strangers but especially for my own boys. These days I have completed one of the most beautiful works of my life, when you are bigger, I will tell you about it.

I am very pleased that you find joy with the piano. This and carpentry are in my opinion for your age the best pursuits, better even than school. Because those are things which fit a young person such as you very well. Mainly play the things on the piano which please you, even if the teacher does not assign those. That is the way to learn the most, that when you are doing something with such enjoyment that you don't notice that the time passes. I am sometimes so wrapped up in my work that I forget about the noon meal. Also play ringtoss with Tete. That teaches you agility. Also go to my friend Zangger sometimes. He is a dear man.

Be with Tete kissed by your

Papa.

Regards to Mama.

N. C. Wyeth

to

Nat and Caroline Wyeth

---coxoo---

October 19, 1943

Dear Nat and Caroline,

The memories of last week with you all are not dimmed as each event stands lens-clear. The beautiful and powerful little figure of Newell dominates it all however. His personality, for one so very young, is truly astonishing to me; the clarity of it remains in my memory, as does his blonde face and figure, cameolike—in sharp preciseness and ultimate delicacy. I like to think mostly of the glow of his hair and face in the cavernous gloom of that cathedrallike woods of "the grotto." I shall never forget him there.

Obviously he is blessed with a quick and attentive spirit. Nourish these traits by every means you can think of. This will comprise his greatest and profoundest education, no matter what imposing institutions he may encounter later on. To keep alive and to intensify his sense of wonderment and his curiosity about simple things—these will become and remain the most potent factors is his life, no matter what he is destined to do.

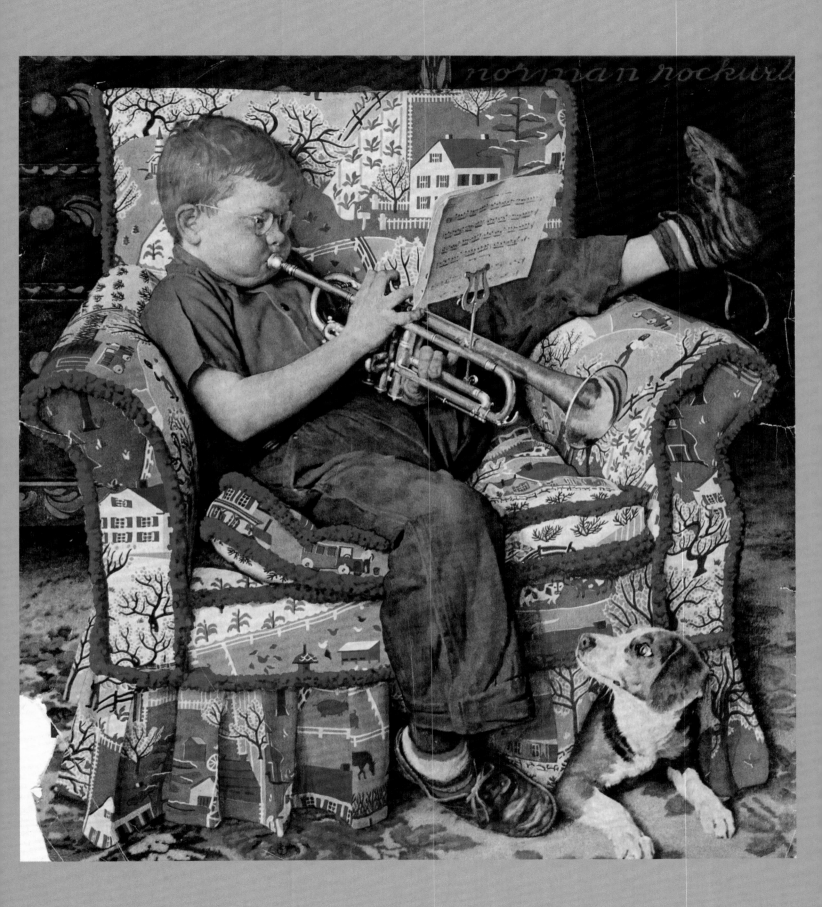

A variety of sources were used in researching the poetry, pastimes, songs, and stories in *Norman Rockwell's Treasure for Fathers*. Among the most helpful were the following:

"A History of Father's Day," The History Channel website, http://www.history.com/topics/fathers-day (accessed November 27, 2012).

"Those Winter Sundays." Copyright © 1966 by Robert Hayden, from *Collected Poems of Robert Hayden*, edited by Frederick Glaysher. Used by permission of Liveright Publishing Corporation.

"My Father's Hats" from *Bright Hunger* by Mark Irwin. Copyright ©2004 by Mark Irwin. All reprinted with the permission of The Permissions Company, Inc. on behalf of BOA Editions, Ltd., www.boaeditions.org.

"Soliloquy in Circles" by Ogden Nash. Copyright © 1948 by Ogden Nash. Reprinted by permission of Curtis Brown, Ltd.

"Oh! Write Me a Song of My Father," written and composed by C. Henry, courtesy Duke University Libraries.

"Take Me Out to the Ball Game," written by Jack Norworth and composed by Albert von Tilzer, courtesy Lester S. Levy Collection of Sheet Music, Sheridan Libraries, Johns Hopkins University.

"Commonly Used Baseball Terms and Phrases," Major League Baseball website, http://mlb.mlb.com/mlb/official_info/baseball_basics/lingo.jsp (accessed November 27, 2012).

"Scoring a Baseball Game," Major League Baseball website, http://mlb.mlb.com/mlb/official_info/baseball_basics/keeping_score.jsp (accessed November 27, 2012).

Hand shadows shown in "Making Hand Shadows" from *Hand Shadows to Be Thrown Upon the Wall* by Henry Bursill.

"Stargazing with Binoculars" courtesy Alan M. MacRobert/*Sky & Telescope Magazine*.

"Song to Be Sung by the Father of Infant Female Children" by Ogden Nash. Copyright © 1933 by Ogden Nash. Reprinted by permission of Curtis Brown, Ltd.

"Daddy's Home, See You Tomorrow" by Ogden Nash. Copyright © 1956 by Ogden Nash. Reprinted by permission of Curtis Brown, Ltd.

"The Writer" from *The Mind-Reader* by Richard Wilbur. Copyright © 1971, and renewed 1999 by Richard Wilbur. Reprinted by permission of Houghton Mifflin Harcourt Publishing Company. All rights reserved.

"Fishing Secrets" from "Make Fishing Elementary and Fun," Indiana Department of Natural Resources website, www.in.gov/dnr/fishwild/3600.htm (accessed November 27, 2012).

"My Father" from *The Cat and the Cuckoo* by Ted Hughes. Copyright © 1987, 2001 by the Estate of Ted Hughes. Reprinted by permission of Roaring Brook Press.

"The Golden Touch" by Nathaniel Hawthorne.

"Playing Pilgrims" from *Little Women* by Louisa May Alcott.

"A Grand Transformation Scene" from *Vice Versa or A Lesson to Fathers*, by F. Anstey.

"The Captain's Papers" from *Treasure Island* by Robert Louis Stevenson.

PHOTO CREDITS AND ACKNOWLEDGMENTS

The publisher wishes to thank The Norman Rockwell
Family Agency, Inc. for permission of use for images in
the book. Unless otherwise noted, all images are courtesy
of The Norman Rockwell Family Entities.

The publisher would also like to thank The Norman
Rockwell Museum for their help in obtaining the images
for publication. The following lists the particular museum
collection from which each image was obtained.

Norman Rockwell Museum Collection: 4, 6, 7, 19, 25, 41,
60, 62, 73, 77, 106, 109, 204

Norman Rockwell Museum Digital Collection: cover, title
page, 8, 12, 14, 16, 21, 23, 26, 28, 29, 31, 32, 34, 37, 39, 42,
47, 48, 52, 56, 58, 61, 63, 66, 68, 71, 75, 79, 80, 82, 85, 86,
88, 90, 92, 94, 98, 100, 103, 105, 111, 113, 114, 115, 116,
118, 127, 128, 135, 136, 139, 142, 151, 152, 157, 158, 160,
181, 182, 188, 197, 198, 202, 207, 209, 210, 213, 219, 223